Praise for

Mattie, Milo, and Me

"I love *Mattie, Milo, and Me*. It had me laughing out loud—yet it's so touching that it had me in tears, too. This book is brilliant. Anne's joys and struggles are relatable. I learned a lot. I highly recommend *Mattie, Milo, and Me*."

—NATALIE ARONOW, Doctor of Veterinary Medicine

"*Mattie, Milo, and Me* is a beautifully written testament to the journey of dog ownership. This memoir takes you on an emotional ride. You'll laugh, cry, and want to hug a dog by the end. A must read!"

—GARY AND ALLIE VIDER, owners of Metro Pets NYC

"A touching story that made me smile with joy, yet the heartbreak around loss touched my heart as well. The joy, the comfort that Anne experienced with Mattie and then with Milo filled the pages. The joy of loving and the pain of losing them was heartfelt. The mutual love that the Abel family experienced with each other was real, honest, and unconditional, even as Anne dealt with her mother's inability to express the human connection of a mother's love. This story shows us how love and sorrow are so intertwined."

—SISTER KATHY MCSHANE, Sisters of Saint Joseph

"Not every book a person reads is worth time and energy. *Mattie, Milo, and Me* is a rare combination: an absorbing, well-told tale that also leaves the reader changed in an unexpected and positive way. This is not just a book about an aggressive and abandoned rescue dog and the woman who courageously rescued him. This is also a book about love and hope; despair and depression. It is an entertaining and absorbing story on one level, and on another level, a deep dive into love and loss; hope and redemption; and what gives life meaning."

—JEANNE GEMMILL GRIFFIN, PHD

"*Mattie, Milo, and Me* is a tender story with opposite emotional strings. One is love denied by emotionally abusive parents; the other is love received from a very caring husband and beloved sons. Through steadfast determination and a loving heart, the writer's lifelong quest to be a good mother is realized in both the human and animal realms. Most of all it spins a loving tale of how dogs bring true joy, healing, and comfort to us. Mattie, Milo, and Anne were true gifts to each other."

—SISTER MARIAN BEHRLE, Sisters of Saint Joseph

Mattie, Milo, and Me

Mattie, Milo, and Me

A Memoir

Anne Abel

SHE WRITES PRESS

Published 2024
Printed in the United States of America
Print ISBN: 978-1-64742-622-4
E-ISBN: 978-1-64742-623-1
Library of Congress Control Number: 2023915782

For information, address:
She Writes Press
1569 Solano Ave #546
Berkeley, CA 94707

Interior design by Stacey Aaronson

She Writes Press is a division of SparkPoint Studio, LLC.

Names and identifying characteristics have been changed to protect the privacy of certain individuals.

For Andy

One

I pulled open the heavy, arched, wooden door and saw a jacket-less, package-less UPS man staring at me.

"I'm sorry, ma'am. I just hit your dog," he said as soon as the door had swung open.

I had just returned home and let Mattie, our wheaten terrier, out the back door. I hadn't taken off my jacket yet or even heard anyone coming up our long, winding driveway when the front doorbell rang.

"But she's okay, isn't she?" I asked.

At that moment, in response to the UPS man's declaration, I had no alternative but to be uncharacteristically hopeful. I was unwilling, unable even, to imagine anything else.

"I killed her. She's wrapped in my jacket by my truck."

He said this as if he were reciting the coordinates of his last delivery.

I stood there staring at the jacket-less, package-less UPS man. I tried to feel reassured by his calm voice. But his words assaulted me, as if red. Red, bloody, red. My knees collapsed, and I fell into a heap.

"No!" I shrieked, lying flat on my stomach, my arms and legs flailing, my face burrowing into the rug beneath me. "No, no, no!" I shrieked again, feeling the already tear-soaked wool rug scratching my cheeks.

"I'm sorry, ma'am," I heard the UPS man say. He had stepped inside and stood next to me. "I wish I could stay here with you, but I have to go to my truck and wait with the dog for the police."

The police? Why were the police coming? Why did the UPS man have to stand by his truck? I tried to picture Mattie being squashed by a UPS truck, but the only vision I could summon was a blur. Even the blur was more than my mind could handle. I could not bring myself to stand up and follow him down the driveway to Mattie, even though I knew it was the right thing to do. To stand by her. It felt wrong to abandon her and have her be watched over by the UPS man—the UPS man who had killed her. I was not strong enough to see her as she was now. I couldn't bear to see this dog I loved so much, this dog who five minutes earlier had jumped for joy when I walked in the door, now bloody and maimed. Now dead. I could not force myself up physically. I could not will myself to see my dog dead.

I lifted my tear-stung face and looked at the UPS man.

"It's okay if you don't wait with me," I said. "I'll be fine."

Fine? Had I actually just told this man who killed my dog that I would be fine? My mouth had uttered the word "fine" as the voice in my head said to the UPS driver, *What does it matter what you do? What does anything matter now? You just destroyed not only my dog, but also me. I don't want to live another moment, knowing what happened to my sweet, defenseless Mattie.*

We stared at each other. Me on the ground, craning my neck upward; him standing with his feet inches from my face, looking down from high above. Then he stepped backward until he reached the door.

"Okay," he said, still facing me. "You know where I am if you need me."

He pushed open the storm door and walked out.

I balled my fists, crisscrossed my arms beneath my chest, and dropped my lolling head onto the damp rug. I could barely get through my day even when things were outwardly okay. I suffer with depression. How would I ever be able to cope with Mattie's senseless, painful death? My head exploded with images. Mattie trotting out the back door minutes earlier. Mattie immobile beneath the wheel of the UPS truck. Mattie curled up beside me in bed. The images came faster and faster until my mind went black. I was frozen in time and space. My mind went back and forth between a fast-forward reel of Mattie's seven years as our dog and a vast, cold nothingness.

After the UPS driver went back to wait for the police, I eventually managed to hoist myself up off the floor and go into the kitchen. The first things I noticed as I walked in were Mattie's metal bowls. The water bowl was almost full. I wailed as I picked up the bowl and emptied it into the sink behind me. Next, I picked up the empty food bowl and stacked it into the water bowl, with an absurd sense of purpose.

There was no stopping me. I took a few steps and picked up a half-chewed stuffed unicorn. The one toy Mattie had brought with her from the breeder. Now I was running through the hall, the den, up the stairs, through the bedrooms, picking up Mattie's toys. I didn't stop until my arms could hold no more partially chewed stuffed animals and rubber tug toys.

I could not bear seeing anything of Mattie's lying around the house, as if at any moment she might scurry over to pick it up. I ran back down the stairs, into the garage, and dropped everything in my arms into the nearest trash can. It landed with an unimpressive, anticlimactic thud. It was the day after trash day. I scrutinized the familiar toys covering the grimy bottom of the plastic bin. This is what Mattie's life with us had amounted to: death beneath the wheel of a UPS truck and an armful of partially chewed toys at the bottom of an empty plastic trash can.

I stumbled from the garage into the kitchen, then into the dining room. There I crumbled to my knees on the rug and, dropping to my stomach, I crawled between two chairs until I was nestled, face down, beneath the dining room table.

I mashed my forehead into the rug and sobbed. The images and thoughts of Mattie that had filled my mind earlier were replaced with wrenching gasps convulsing through my body. Mercifully, my grief took control and shut me down mentally and physically, as if inducing me into a lifesaving coma in the silent house. I was aware of nothing. Not even myself.

After an indeterminate amount of time, I heard someone walk across the kitchen and pick up the phone.

"I know, sir," I heard the UPS man say. "I know we're busy, but I can't just leave her here. I can't leave her here alone. Don't worry. I'll get my packages delivered today, I promise. I'll do what I have to do. I'll work until what I have to do is done. I'll call you when I'm leaving the house."

It was ten days before Christmas, 2001. Even in my distraught state, I could appreciate the frustration of the UPS supervisor but also, more importantly, the driver's sudden kindness and concern for me despite the demands being put upon him.

Moments after I heard the driver hang up the phone, I felt him slither up beside me under the table. I faced away from him, but I knew he was lying next to me. I could feel his warm breath on the back of my neck. I didn't feel comforted by his presence or even his closeness. But I also didn't feel uncomfortable or annoyed to have this stranger, this man who had killed my dog, sidling up beside me beneath the bar of my dining room trestle table. My dog had been killed. It didn't seem real. I did not want to think about anything other than getting through the minutes until Andy, my husband, arrived. He was due home soon.

"I never had a dog," the UPS man said to the back of my head. "But I have cats, and I know just how you feel."

His voice was calm and gentle, not mechanical as it had been when he told me he'd killed Mattie. I didn't turn to look at him. I quivered, my body as brittle as my mind. It seemed as if any movement would shatter me, leaving me as dust.

"Last year my cat was hit by a car," he said sadly. "So you can believe me when I say I know how you feel."

I didn't want to hear about his cat. I didn't care about his cat. I wasn't a cat person. I wasn't even a dog person. I just happened to fall in love with one in my never-ending struggle to be a good mother.

Two

The first word spoken by my middle son, Joseph, was "dog." His first complete sentence was, "I want a dog." I would not be surprised if he was already dreaming of having a dog when he came into this world. Unfortunately for Joseph, even though my primary goal in life was to be a good mother, I absolutely positively did not want a dog. I had no interest in dogs. Certainly no interest in the work that would come with owning a dog.

My plan was to placate Joseph with dog alternatives. When he was three, I mail-ordered him a frog. Actually, I ordered a tadpole. A few weeks later, on a damp, cold morning in March, the mailman left a note that said we had a package waiting at the post office. I strapped Joseph into his car seat, and we headed over to retrieve it. I handed to the man behind the counter the green slip of paper that had been left in my mailbox. In return, he handed me a small box with an orange sticker that read, TADPOLE INSIDE. KEEP AT ROOM TEMPERATURE.

"You understand, ma'am," the postal worker said, "we couldn't leave this in your mailbox. It's far too cold."

"No, indeed," I said.

"Can I see? Can I see?" Joseph said, jumping up and down.

"Would you like me to open the box for you?" the postal worker said.

"Yes, yes!" Joseph answered before I could open my mouth. "I want to see it."

"So do I," said the postal worker, who cut the tape with a box cutter before handing the package across the counter to Joseph, who reached his hands up as high as he could.

Joseph clutched the box to his chest with one hand and pulled out a Styrofoam cup with the other. I pulled back the mesh covering the top of the cup.

The tadpole, who had been submerged in water for his trip to his new home, jumped up above the water line, probably startled by the burst of daylight.

"Oh, look, Joseph," I said. "He's so excited to meet you that he's jumping for joy."

"That's a mighty fine tadpole," said the postal worker, who had joined us in the lobby for the unveiling. "He's a lucky tadpole, too, to be going home with you."

In his red corduroy OshKosh B'gosh winter jacket, Joseph beamed.

As we headed home, the tadpole safely back in his Styrofoam cup, Joseph said, "Let's call him JJ, for Jonny and Joseph."

"That's nice of you, Joseph, to include your brother in your frog's name," I said.

The tadpole became JJ, and then he became a frog. A translucent, genetically engineered frog. We kept JJ in a Lucite tank and made him the centerpiece of our kitchen table. As JJ grew, we moved him into bigger and bigger tanks until, finally, the pet store owner told us that frogs grow in proportion to the size of their tanks.

Friends of Joseph's also got tadpoles that changed into genetically engineered frogs. Most of them lasted a few months, at best. Not JJ. A year went by, two years, then three. JJ continued to thrive. As our time with JJ went on, every morning when I walked into the kitchen and turned on the light, JJ jumped as if woken from his night's sleep. And every time, I would shudder as I imagined the morning I would walk in and find JJ inert, crushing my son's faith in our ability to nurture this pet forever. But month after month, year after year, JJ continued to jump every morning when I came into the kitchen.

Despite JJ's seemingly eternal presence, Joseph's determination to get a dog persisted. Every time he asked, "Can we get a dog?" I lured him to the pet store with the promise of a smaller, less demanding creature. Our pet menagerie grew to include gerbils, hamsters, fish, and more fish.

Toward the end of third grade, when he was eight, he asked if he could adopt the five newts that had lived in his science class since the beginning of the school year. In my four decades on this earth, I had never given any thought to newts. I knew only one thing about them. That they were small. Tiny. That was all I needed to know to give Joseph a full-hearted, enthusiastic yes about adopting the newts. Not just one newt, or two newts, but five! Sometimes it felt so easy to be a good mother. On the last day of school, Joseph stood on the curb at pickup, waiting for me, a beaming smile on his face and holding a six-inch rectangular aquarium snugly against his belly.

"Mommy, aren't they cute?" he said as soon as he had secured his seat belt in the back passenger seat, the newt-filled aquarium on his lap.

I leaned back and peered into the glass tank. It took some seconds for my eyes to be able to focus enough to distinguish the tiny, blackish-green creatures from the mossy black pebbles upon which they were perched.

"Joseph, I've never seen such cute insects," I said, feigning enthusiasm while simultaneously picturing the Terminix Pest Control technician who came to our house at the beginning of every month to spray for insects and rodents. Non-caged insects and rodents.

"Mommy," Joseph said, interrupting my Terminix reverie. "Newts aren't insects. They're amphibians."

"That's so interesting," I said, still focused on the newts. "I didn't know that newts are amphibians. I'm always learning things from you."

It was true. I was continually amazed at the things I learned from my boys. I had never heard of Beowulf until Jonathan had come home recently describing the clay models his teacher had sculpted to depict scenes of the epic poem. I learned about deciduous forests when Joseph wistfully told me, "Jonny said I shouldn't be sad that he is going to middle school. He said my staying in lower school without him is like the trees in a deciduous forest losing their leaves and letting the sun reach the plants and trees below, and that I will rise and become a tall tree too."

Sitting with Joseph, both of us staring at the still life that was the five newts huddled together in a corner of the small aquarium, I was once again relieved that I was able to be a good mother and fulfill Joseph's desire to nurture without getting the dreaded dog.

"Mommy," Joseph said, taking his eyes off the newts for the first time since he'd gotten into the car and looking at me. "Could we go to Petco on the way home and get things for the newts? I used to feel bad that they had to stay alone in the science room when everyone went home. Now that they're my newts, I want to create a perfect universe for them."

I stared at him, awestruck. Awestruck by his compassion and empathy. By his ability to imagine the newts lonely at night in the empty classroom. And by his ability to imagine a perfect universe for them and his desire to create it.

"Joseph, that's such a lovely, kind idea. These are five very lucky newts," I said and turned the key in the ignition. "Yes, let's go to Petco."

As I followed Joseph up and down the aisles at Petco, watching him drop big rocks and small rocks, water features, a plastic pond, and varieties of food into the shopping cart, I found myself thinking how fortunate these newts were. Once they were settled into their perfect universe, they were free to be who and what they wanted to be. They wouldn't have to learn right from wrong. They wouldn't have to learn to do things they didn't want to do. They wouldn't have to someday venture out into the big, unknown world all by themselves. These five lucky newts would be together in their perfect universe for . . . well, I didn't know how long newts lived, but for at least their life span, whatever it was, the fivesome would be content together and very well cared for.

Except for JJ—who had staked out his territory in our kitchen—the newts, like the rest of Joseph's pets, lived in his room. He loved them and cared for them. And, amazingly, like JJ, they all exceeded their life expectancies. Three of the five newts, who, I had learned, can live twenty years, lived for twenty-two.

Joseph loved his newts as much as the other creatures populating his bedroom. But still, he dreamed of getting a dog. In the months leading up to his tenth birthday, he began lobbying me again, now joining forces with his older brother, twelve-year-old Jonathan.

"Dogs are a lot of work," I said.

"That's okay, we don't mind taking care of a dog," they said in unison.

"You know," I said, "when I leave the house at five thirty in the morning to go swimming, I see people bundled up walking their dogs on the cold, dark sidewalks. I can see their breath, it's so cold."

"That's okay. We don't mind the cold."

Over and over we went, back and forth. No one was willing to give in.

Finally, two weeks before Joseph's tenth birthday, I saw an article in the paper about African hedgehogs. "The perfect pet," the headline proclaimed. That was what we needed, the perfect pet. I showed the article to Joseph.

"Okay," he said dejectedly. "If we can't get a dog, I'd like an African hedgehog."

I was so excited. I had avoided the dog for ten years. I just needed to placate Joseph for eight more years until he left for college. I was more than halfway there. I called the pet shop mentioned in the newspaper to get directions.

"You need to know," the store manager said, "African hedgehogs are basically porcupines. You must wear rubber gloves when you handle them."

My heart dropped. We didn't need a prickly animal who would require us to wear gloves if we wanted to touch him. I pictured Joseph trying to bond with a porcupine. I realized I could no longer deny it. I could no longer put off the inevitable. We had enough creatures in tanks and cages.

It was time for the dog.

Three

I don't like to shop. When we relocated from Boston to Philadelphia, I looked at three houses in one day and bought one of them that evening. While raising my boys, Jonathan, Joseph, and Josh, I would go to Gap twice a year and buy seven sets of sweatpants and sweatshirts or shorts and T-shirts—one for each day of the week—for each of them. I do pretty much the same thing for my own clothes. I'm not a comparison shopper. When I need an appliance, I walk into the store, buy the one the salesperson recommends, and hope for the best.

Merely hoping for the best was not going to cut it with a dog. For the first time in my life, I needed to be an informed consumer. I went to Borders and bought *Every Dog*, a 536-page book describing over 450 breeds. We took turns paging through the book and looking at the different breeds. Suddenly, I was interested in the dogs my kids' friends owned. Joseph wanted a big dog. Though I didn't even want a dog, I thought small would surely be better than big. I had often heard people with older children say, "Small children, small problems. Big children, big problems." I wasn't convinced this applied to children, but I was unwavering that it applied to dogs.

One Monday, just a few weeks into our search, Jonathan came home from a soccer teammate's house gushing about his wheaten terrier. I looked up this breed in my book. It was a medium, hypoallergenic breed. A breed, it seemed from the description, that did everything but empty the dishwasher. *This* was our dog.

I called the mother of Jonathan's teammate and got the name of the breeder.

"We're having a litter in May," the breeder said when I called. "I'll put you on the list."

The boys were happy. I was ecstatic. I had been a good mother and found the right dog for our family, and it had cost me nothing. After all, it was only January. May was so far away that it felt like it would never arrive. A lifetime away. As I passed through my dog-free house, I was even able to convince myself that the possibility of a cushion-chewing, rug-peeing, yapping dog would never become a reality. Life was good.

Three days later, the breeder called me back.

"We have a ten-month-old dog, Mattie, we had planned to use as a show dog," she said. "But her neck is too short, and we're putting her up for adoption. If you're interested, you and your family could come over on Sunday. We can meet all of you, and you can meet Mattie. If everything works out, you could take her home right away."

My heart fell with a thud. What could I say? It never occurred to me to buy myself some time by saying we would prefer to wait for a puppy in May. It never occurred to me that I could keep this conversation a secret from the kids. I knew my kids would want to get Mattie now rather than wait. So I said the only thing I could think to say: "That would be great."

Friday after school, we went to Petco. We went through the aisles buying bowls and beds and toys and food. Listening to the boys excitedly debate which bed, which toy, which bowl would be best for Mattie, I wondered if adoptive parents go shopping like this when they find out they have been matched with a child. I wish I could say that my boys' happiness lifted my spirits and made me even a little bit happy about Mattie, but it didn't. The truth was irrevocable. I. Did. Not. Want. A. Dog. Still, as much as I did not want a dog, I wanted many more times than that to be a good mother.

That Sunday morning, as Andy and the boys got ready for our fifty-minute drive to the breeder's, I took one sad, slow walk through my house. It would never look the same.

If Andy and the boys talked during our ride, I didn't hear them. I was mired in an amorphous sense of dread. It wasn't just the dog that was pulling me down. My baseline sense of hopelessness and despair was digging in even deeper within me. I could feel my depression pulling me down.

The breeder and her husband welcomed us into their split-level house and ushered us into their family room. They began asking the boys about their schools and hobbies, pets and sports. It seemed pretty clear that they were assessing them to see if they would be good with Mattie. I wasn't surprised when after not too long my boys had put them at ease.

"Why don't you go into the kitchen," the woman said, pointing across the hall. "I'll go downstairs and send Mattie up to meet you."

I followed the boys into the kitchen. I stood in the middle of the bright, airy room, waiting. I wasn't anticipating anything. I wasn't dreading anything. My mind had gone numb. Suddenly, a white blur burst through the door and landed at my feet. Without thinking, I dropped to the ground and wrapped my arms around Mattie. I felt my heart open.

I sat back while Mattie scurried excitedly around the circle, from Andy to Josh to Jonathan and Joseph. Her tail was high and wagging. Then she came back to me and plopped herself in my lap. Oh my God, I was in love. What was not to love about this happy, endearing, medium-sized ball of white fluff? Her unbridled happiness and unmitigated affection were contagious. Very, very contagious. My own happiness about Mattie was magnified that much more when I looked up and saw my gleeful boys.

The breeder put a leash on Mattie. Then Andy and the breeder's husband carried a metal crate from the house and put it in the trunk of our station wagon. The breeder lifted Mattie into the crate. Before she shut it, she pulled out a partially chewed stuffed unicorn from her pocket.

"This is Mattie's special toy," she said to the boys, and she put it next to Mattie.

They all nodded in knowing agreement. Each of them had had a special stuffed animal too. They still did, even if the older two kept them farther away, on their bureaus. But not out of sight.

We said our goodbyes and began the ride home. We had not gone a full block when I heard Mattie whimpering.

"Mommy," I heard six-year-old Josh say, "Mattie's crying because she misses her mommy."

I turned to look back at them. All three of my boys had tears dripping down their cheeks.

When we got home, the phone was ringing as I unlocked the door. It was my mother.

"What's new?" she asked.

"We just got back from the breeder. We have the dog," I told her.

"So?" my mother asked. She knew I had agreed to a dog only because I was trying to be a good mother.

"She's great. When the breeder opened the kitchen door, Mattie galloped into the middle of the room and I melted to the floor to hug her as if she were my long-lost dog." I was swooning. "She seemed so sweet and affectionate. I just fell in love."

"And the boys? I don't imagine they're interested in *sweet*."

"Oh, they're as excited as I am," I said, so relieved and surprised that the dog thing was turning out well that I'd forgotten to stay vigilant for my mother's ridicule. I'd forgotten to listen and speak like a lawyer. My mother is a master at finding the bad in any good. "The breeder put Mattie in her crate in the back of our station wagon, and when we pulled out of the driveway, she began whimpering. At the end of the street Josh said, 'I think she misses her mommy,' and when I turned to look at him, all three boys were crying."

My mother said nothing. She reminded us often that she was from Maine, where people know how to talk slowly and wait out their opponents. When my mother wasn't giving me the silent treatment, she would call on Sundays. As abusive as she was to me, I could not cut her out of my life. Or my father. I couldn't help it. They were at the core of my being. I loved them. I couldn't stop hoping that at some point they would finally be kind or nice to me.

I'm not from Maine. I needed to fill in the silence.

"I think this is going to work."

"And then Josh will go to college and the dog will die," my mother said.

I did the arithmetic. She was right. There was a good chance Mattie might die when Josh left for college. My mother never missed an opportunity to squash any happiness I might find. From Mattie's first night with us and every night thereafter, when I got into bed with her nuzzled against my feet, I heard my mother's words. And I was reminded anew that Mattie's days with us were finite, numbered.

For years my mother gleefully told the story over and over that it had been her present to Josh for his bar mitzvah that the UPS man was delivering when he killed Mattie.

Four

As I lay under the dining room table with the UPS man, I was completely and wholly absorbed in my own grief. I did not begrudge the UPS man's effort to console me with the story of his cat. Oddly, I was not even angry with him for destroying my dog or for destroying me.

I heard the kitchen door slam shut.

"Anne? Anne?" I heard Andy calling.

"We're in the dining room," the UPS man called out from under the table when it became clear I wasn't going to speak. Before I knew it, Andy had climbed under the table, too, and now I had the UPS man lying beside me on my left and my husband on my right.

I lifted my head from the tear-drenched wool rug to wipe my face dry with the sleeve of my jacket. As I did, I saw two policemen standing shoulder to shoulder in the hallway, looking down at us under the table.

"I think things are pretty much under control here," one said, shaking his head and turning toward the other. "In any case, she seems taken care of."

His colleague nodded, and together they turned and walked out the door.

I put my head back down on the scratchy rug and resumed my crying. Nobody said anything. Nobody moved.

I suffer with severe depression. The only thing that helps elevate my mood is physical activity. I work out vigorously an hour every day, ratcheting my heart rate up. Some days, when I finish, I feel better for a few hours. Other days, it's only for a few minutes. But any amount of time is better than nothing. I take what I can get. For me, it's all about action and movement. Staying still tends to mire me even more. Staying still is not something I do often.

After some unknown amount of time lying between Andy and the UPS man beneath the dining room table, I felt the need to get up. I wiggled my way out from under the table and, with tears streaming down my face, I hurried upstairs to my desk. As I dropped into my desk chair, I was already fingering through my Rolodex, looking for the phone number of Mattie's breeder. I tapped in the number.

"Hello, my name is Anne Abel," I said when a man answered the phone. "Seven years ago, we adopted a dog from you. Mattie?"

"Oh, yes. We were going to use her as a show dog, but she didn't work out," he said, surprising me with his memory.

"Last month, Mattie was hit by a car," I said, grounded enough in reality to at least realize I couldn't tell him that it had been less than an hour since Mattie had been killed. "We're looking for another dog."

As I spoke, I could hear the UPS truck start up outside my window.

"I'm sorry. We no longer breed dogs."

My shoulders slumped. "Do you know anyone who does?"

He gave me the information for someone who was having a litter in May. I called and got on the list. But I knew there was no way I'd be able to wait that long—it was December. It was tragic enough that sweet Mattie had been killed. Sad for her, sad for everyone in our family. As I took down the information of the breeder who was having a litter in May, I was thinking mostly about myself. As a freelance writer, most of my days were spent home at my desk, with Mattie curled up in a ball in a dog bed beside me. Every time I took a break from my computer screen and looked down at Mattie sleeping peacefully, my heart lifted, and I felt buoyed. I could not imagine a better companion. Every couple of hours I rustled her awake and gently patted her behind the ears or rubbed her belly. Then I led her downstairs and let her outside for a few minutes. When she came back in, I gave her a treat, and we went upstairs together for another work session for me and a nap for Mattie.

The first day after we got Mattie, after everyone had left for school and work, Mattie came with me to my desk and immediately fell asleep in her new dog bed. I worked and I watched her. I worked and I watched her. She did not fidget. She did not open her eyes and look around. She just breathed in and breathed out, breathed in and breathed out. I picked up the phone and called Andy at work.

"Andy, all she does is lie in her bed sleeping," I said. "Do you think something's wrong with her?"

Andy laughed. "What do you want her to do? Read a book?"

I got his point. From then on, it was enough, more than enough, for both Mattie and me to be together while I worked and she slept. With Mattie beside me, I never felt isolated or alone. So, when she was killed, in addition to feeling distraught and despondent, I was also terrified of being home alone. Terrified that my depression would be exacerbated whenever I glanced at the spot where Mattie used to be. I needed another dog to fill the space left by Mattie, not only emotionally but also physically. I was fully aware that replacing her in my heart would be difficult, if not impossible. But I was hopeful that having another dog around would be at least somewhat distracting and help make Mattie's physical absence less glaring and painful.

One phone call after another, from one breeder to the next, I kept pushing onward. And one after another disappointed me. Some were no longer breeding. Some seemed irritated at me for getting a puppy as a Christmas present, a present they said I would surely return when the holidays were over.

I was tapping in another phone number when Andy appeared in the doorway, startling me. In retrospect, it is clear I was experiencing trauma. My instinct to survive had pulled me from beneath the dining room table and sent me upstairs to my desk to do what I needed to do to move forward and keep myself from falling into the abyss that was widening and deepening before me. Now, as I looked up at Andy, I felt my all-consuming focus to find a dog to replace Mattie crumble.

"It's almost time to pick up Joseph and Josh," he said, shaking his head in sadness.

I looked at the clock. He was right. I looked back at him, panic now replacing grief.

"Oh, Andy, what are we going to tell them?" I asked.

Up until that moment I'd been drowning in my own grief and hadn't absorbed the pain that would reverberate through the rest of the family. It was the first time I had thought about anyone else in the family. I hadn't focused on anyone besides Mattie and me.

"We'll go together to get the boys," Andy said. "We'll figure it out."

Neither Andy nor I spoke during the ten-minute ride to school. It was still early when we got there. We parked in the lower parking lot, where I always met the boys, and waited. It wasn't long before one kid, then another and another, began to descend on the parking lot, scan the cars, and hustle across when each one saw their ride, happy that they would not have to wait.

Andy and I had gotten out of the car and stood in the middle of the parking lot, looking up toward the school. A few kids recognized us and gave us a wave or a hello. I smiled back wanly. Finally, we saw Joseph and Josh coming toward us, together. When they saw Andy, smiles spread across their faces, and they came running.

"What are you doing here?" Joseph said excitedly as soon as they had reached us.

I was looking at the boys, not at Andy. In that moment, between when Joseph finished asking his question and before either one of us answered, I knew from the change in the expressions on my boys' faces that they knew something was horribly wrong.

"Mattie was killed by a UPS truck in the driveway," I said, putting my arms around both of them and beginning to sob all over again.

"No!" Joseph shrieked. "No!"

He dropped his book bag and clutched me to him with both arms.

"No, no," he said again, nestling his head into the shoulder of my jacket, his voice muffled.

The four of us stood in the middle of the parking lot, engaged in a sad, mourning, desperate version of a family hug. At one point I lifted my eyes and caught the gaze of the mother of one of Joseph's friends. She smiled at me sadly.

The parking lot was empty by the time we were finally able to let go of one another and get in the car. Except for my sobs and the sniffling of Joseph and Josh, the ride home from school was as quiet as the ride to school.

When we got home, we sat together at the kitchen table, just looking at each other's teary faces. After some amount of time, Joseph pushed himself up from his chair.

"I need to start my homework," he said, shaking his head and wiping his eyes.

"Me too," Josh said as he stood up and hoisted his book bag onto his shoulder.

Andy and I watched the boys leave the kitchen.

"I can't just sit here," I said to Andy who sat across the table from me. "I'm going to go work out."

Although I had already ridden my exercise bike in the morning, I put on my workout clothes and did it again. It was the closest thing I had to a tranquilizer. I sat down on the seat of the stationary bike, clapped the headphones onto my head, and began blasting the golden oldies Andy had downloaded for me. My legs were more tired than usual because I had already worked out. I concentrated on the energetic beat, let it enter my head and travel to my legs, willing them to pedal forward. I shut off my brain to everything except the beat of the music and the countdown of my workout. One minute at a time, I coached myself from sixty minutes to zero.

When my workout was over, I dropped my head onto the console. My heart pounded. Sweat dripped down my arms, down my torso. My tank top was soaked. I took a deep breath, lifted my head, and jumped off the bike. Harnessing my post-workout energy spike, I grabbed a sweatshirt and ran back to my desk, back to the phone. I continued my search for another dog.

As I sat in my chair, I suddenly remembered Jane, the wife of one of Andy's colleagues. She had five dogs. One was a bichon frise, a small lapdog that doesn't shed. Jane didn't answer the phone. I left her a teary voice mail. Then, not bothering to shower, not bothering to eat dinner, I got into bed, hoping to fall asleep and put an end to this horrible day.

Five

I had trouble falling asleep that night. The image of a birthday card I had once received from my mother came to mind. TO OUR WONDERFUL DAUGHTER, was emblazoned on the front, in gold, above a bouquet of pastel flowers. Inside, on the right page, in the same Hallmark font: ANOTHER YEAR OF THE ONE-AND-ONLY YOU. On the left was my mother's black-scripted, personalized birthday message: "Dear Anne, I was only 22 when you were born. I didn't want to have you because I had other things I wanted to do. But here you are. Love, Mom."

She sent me the card three weeks after my forty-fourth birthday. Even though it had been five years earlier, the words still stung. My mother had waged guerrilla warfare on me for my whole life. She rarely missed an opportunity to attack me. When she wasn't attacking, she was withholding. As a result, I had battled depression for decades. I talked to a therapist weekly and tried over twenty antidepressants. For the most part, I managed to keep myself upright. But despite my best efforts, each time she struck I was devastated.

When the birthday card arrived, I had dropped it on the hall table and gone upstairs and thrown myself face down on my bed. I don't know how long I'd been face down on the bed when Joseph, then twelve years old, came into my room, Mattie beside him, wagging her tail.

"Mommy, are you okay?" I sat up on the bed and shook my head just enough to acknowledge his question.

"Is it Grandma?" He had been with me when I opened the card.

I nodded. My mother's mean spirit was nothing new. We'd been through this before.

"Are you going to Jonny's game?" Jonathan was fourteen years old at the time. Joseph and I had been planning to walk over to Jonathan's soccer game later in the afternoon.

"I'm not going anywhere," I said in a monotone. Joseph stood in the doorway but didn't say anything. When I turned away and stared ahead at the window, he left, closing the bedroom door softly behind him.

I focused on a bare, skeletal branch stretching across the windowpanes in front of me. I was tired. So tired of everything, tired of hating my mother.

I felt myself breathe in and breathe out. I pictured Joseph going to the soccer game without me. Throwing my legs over the edge of the bed, I moved toward the closet, dropped my sweats, and pulled on a pair of jeans and a sweater. Staring in front of me at the mirror, I blotted my eyes and nose with face powder and stepped back to see how I looked. My jaw was hanging, and my eyelids, puffed from tears, were halfway shut. I was still at the mirror when Joseph returned.

"Mommy, I think we have to put Whiskers to sleep." His voice quivered. "When he tries to walk, I can see he's suffering."

Whiskers was Joseph's four-year-old gerbil. Three months earlier Whiskers had undergone surgery to remove a tumor on his right front paw. Now the tumor had reappeared. The vet told us that the only treatment option was amputation. But she advised against it because it would make his quality of life dismal.

I looked at Joseph slouching in front of me and then back at the clock. It was ten minutes before six on a Friday. I grabbed the phone and called the vet to ask them to wait. I didn't want to prolong the ordeal until Monday. I grabbed my coat, Joseph got Whiskers, and we rushed for the car.

Generally a haphazard driver, I concentrated on navigating the traffic's rush-hour knots. Beside me, in the passenger seat, Joseph was whimpering.

"Joseph, Whiskers has had a long and very good life. You loved him and took very good care of him."

Joseph closed his eyes, nodded, and swallowed a sob. "I know, Mommy. But it's still sad. I'm going to miss him."

"It is sad; it's very sad. But he won't know what's happening. He won't feel anything, Joseph. He'll be sleepy, that's all. We're all going to miss him."

Even though I rarely saw Whiskers, whose home was a cage on Joseph's bureau, at that moment I really did think I would miss the little rodent.

There were only two cars in the parking lot outside the veterinarian. With a sympathetic smile, a woman in cranberry-pink scrubs greeted us from behind her counter.

"Have a seat. We'll be with you in just a few minutes."

Joseph and I sat down in the empty waiting room. Joseph hunched forward and hugged Whiskers's tank to his chest. I put my arm around him and massaged his shoulder. My hands and feet were cold, my shoulders tight, and I thought about the gold-scripted words, TO OUR DAUGHTER. The receptionist came to usher us to the examining room, and I pulled back, hesitating. But when Joseph jumped up, I followed instinctively.

The vet scooped Whiskers out of his tank and cupped him in her hands. Whiskers was trembling. Rubbing the back of his head with her index finger and cooing down at him, the vet fingered his right paw and manipulated the tumor. Her manner was calm and her gentleness lulling. I hoped she'd look up at us and have another option. But she didn't.

"You're right, Joseph. Whiskers's tumor is growing rapidly now. It's getting awkward for him to move with it." The vet was a petite woman, around thirty, and still stroking Whiskers's head. She had stooped down a notch to be at eye level with Joseph.

"He's had a very good and very long life. He won't feel any pain. His life will be good until the very end, and he'll be very happy in heaven."

Joseph nodded. His body was locked with his eyes focused on Whiskers, who was clasped in the vet's hands. The vet smiled at me sadly and left, taking Whiskers with her. When the door closed behind her, Joseph spun around and threw himself into me, burrowing his head in the bosom of my down jacket. We held onto each other and cried. I could have sobbed there with him forever. It was Joseph who first moved away. He wiped his eyes on the sleeves of his jacket until I found a box of Kleenex behind the examining table. After many Kleenex and as many deep breaths, we decided we were composed enough to make it through the waiting room.

We raced to the car, slammed the doors, looked at each other, and cried. I leaned toward Joseph, put one arm on his shoulders, and stroked his hair with the other. The vet and the receptionist walked by, smiled sadly at us, and got into their cars. I keep a box of Kleenex on the car floor, and Joseph and I passed it back and forth.

The traffic on the street and sidewalk had quieted, but neither of us said anything about going home. We cocooned in our car, camouflaged by the dark. Joseph and I held hands, with me squeezing his and him squeezing mine. With each clench, I took a deep breath, closed my eyes, and tried not to picture my mother's black-scripted birthday message, "I didn't want to have you."

"Do you want to go get another gerbil, Joseph?" I asked after a while. There was a pet store ten minutes away and I wondered if a new gerbil might lessen Joseph's grief.

"Mommy, no," he answered. "I can't just replace Whiskers with another gerbil." I smiled at him, moved by the depth of his feelings.

The house was dark when we pulled into the garage. I turned off the ignition, but neither of us moved to get out of the car, and our crying began again. The garage lights flicked off.

"Mommy, are you crying about Grandma?" Joseph asked in a soft, unwavering voice.

"Yes, Joseph. I'm crying about Whiskers and Grandma and . . . Joseph, I'm crying about everything."

He reached across the front seat and put his hand in mine. "Mommy, we're your family now, and we love you."

His words deepened my sobs, and tightening the wrap of my hand around his, I closed my eyes.

"Let's go inside," I said, opening the car door, finally.

Mattie bounded into the kitchen to greet us.

"Mattie, it is so good to see you," Joseph said, falling to his knees and cuddling her.

After focusing on the palm-sized gerbil, I had to readjust to Mattie's size and responsive, boisterous demeanor. Watching Mattie gallop after Joseph toward the mud room, I shuddered as I extrapolated Joseph's sadness for Whiskers into the sadness and loss he'd be feeling for Mattie someday.

At dinner, Andy talked a little about Whiskers and Joseph's love for animals. Other than that, the rest of us had been quiet. Toward the end of the meal, when Mattie responded to a call from

Joseph by running in from the hall wagging her tail, we all reached out to pat her. Harnessing energy garnered from watching Mattie's display of carefree love and the boys' resulting glee, I hoisted myself from my chair and trudged upstairs and into the bathroom to wash up.

The bathroom was cold, and as I looked into the mirror above the sink, I wondered if my face's pallid tint was due to the bathroom's avocado-green tiles. I picked up my toothbrush. One more hurdle and this horrible day with my mother's belated birthday card and Whiskers's death would be over. I dotted the toothbrush with toothpaste and raised it to my bared teeth.

"Mommy, I already know by heart two blessings for my bar mitzvah. Do you want to hear them?" Joseph asked, posing himself at the bathroom door. The saturated richness of his olive skin and dark, wavy hair transcended the glare of the unforgiving fluorescent light emanating from the closet behind him. I compared this perky boy, holding his blue bar mitzvah workbook rolled up in one hand, with the boy who two or three hours earlier at the vet's had thrust his shaking body into my arms. His lips turned up in a tentative smile, and he shifted his weight from leg to leg. I couldn't bring back Whiskers, but I could listen to his blessings.

"Uh-huh," I gargled, wondering how he had propelled himself into his room after dinner on a Friday night—a Friday night of a traumatic day no less—to study for a bar mitzvah that at nine months in the future was a lifetime away.

Pulling back his shoulders and lifting up his head, Joseph positioned himself on the bathroom threshold. "*Baruch ata Adonai*," he began, looking me in the eyes. A smile spread across the face of this son who just a few hours earlier had been my fellow mourner. I lowered the toothbrush from my mouth, swallowed the toothpaste, and leaned on the sink, conserving all my consciousness for absorbing him. His voice was so sweet. I didn't feel the grit of the toothpaste lining my teeth or notice the nauseous reflection of the bathroom's green tiles.

I had never before heard these melodies anywhere but in the comfort of the synagogue. It seemed that a column of light reaching toward the ceiling had wrapped around Joseph. The glaring image of my mother in the foreground of my mind squeezed to the background and faded to a ghost.

The mass of futility that had been suffocating me began to shrink. I imagined Joseph the morning of his bar mitzvah, and I spanned his transformation from the newborn bag of reflexes I had carried home from the hospital to the son who had come to my bathroom and sung poetry on that sad Friday night three weeks after my birthday. A memory that, with each advancing year, still brings me joy.

Six

Waking up the morning after Mattie was killed by the UPS truck, I forgot for a moment what had happened. Instinctively, I looked at the foot of the bed for her. It was empty. No Mattie awake and staring at me expectantly, waiting for me to rise. No Mattie excited for the day to begin. I felt my insides seize up and my entire body clench. I stumbled out of bed and mechanically dressed, thankful that my muscle memory knew what to do without any direction from me. As I walked down the stairs, I could not block my mind from noticing that the white ball of fluffy, happy energy that had been Mattie was not bouncing down the stairs in front of me. I felt my legs beginning to lock midway down, ready to bend at the knees so I could sit down and cry. But I willed them onward with the same mental force I use to propel myself from one minute to the next when I work out. One step, then another. One step, then another.

Joseph and Josh were already at the kitchen table, eating their Honey Nut Cheerios. They looked up at me. I looked at them and shook my head sadly. Only twenty-four hours earlier, Mattie had bounded ahead of me into the kitchen. Only twenty-four hours earlier, in this very spot, Joseph and Josh had smiled and said in unison, "Mattie, good morning. It's so good to see you." Twenty-four hours earlier, forty-eight hours earlier. Days earlier, weeks earlier, months earlier. Years earlier. We had never *not* noticed Mattie's buoyancy. We had never *not* paid attention to her happy energy.

"Mattie, good morning, it's so good to see you," Joseph would say.

"Yes, Mattie. It's so exciting, another day," Josh would say.

"What's on your schedule today?" Jonathan would say, until he left for college.

Mattie would go from one boy to the next, accepting a pat or a rub behind the ears from each one before running to the door, ready to be let out.

Today, I had come into the kitchen alone, unannounced. I went over to each boy and bent down and gave each one a prolonged hug. No one spoke. There was nothing to say. We did not know how to put the wrenching pain and sadness we were feeling into words. There was nothing, nothing at all that would mitigate, even a little, what had happened. Mattie hadn't had a tumor like Whiskers. She hadn't been suffering. She hadn't been a bother or a nuisance. She hadn't been any work. There was not one thing about her that we could use to rationalize that she, we, the world, were in any way better now that she was dead.

Our silent, sad breakfast was followed by a silent, sad ride to school. I watched the boys get out of the car and hoist their book bags onto their backs. I was always surprised whenever I found one of these book bags somewhere in the house and tried to lift it or even kick it out of my way. They were so heavy, too heavy for me to move. Yet the boys hauled them around as if they were filled with feathers. But not today. The boys lifted their bags as if they were lifting the weight of all the world's sorrows onto their backs. I sat in the car and watched them shuffle away out of sight.

When I got home, I found Andy on the phone in the kitchen.

"Oh, here she is right now," he said as I unzipped my jacket.

I looked at him.

"It's Jane," he said.

Jane was the wife of Andy's colleague whom I had called the previous night and left a message. I took the phone from Andy.

"I'm sorry about Mattie," she said.

I didn't know Jane well. Once a year, we made small talk at the Wharton School Finance Department's September cocktail party. Mostly I heard about Jane from Andy, who worked closely with her husband, Rich, on department affairs.

"Oh, thank you," I said mechanically. "I'm having so much trouble speaking with breeders. So many of them get angry at me, assuming I'm getting a puppy for Christmas and that I'll be returning it in January."

"That doesn't really surprise me," Jane said. "Breeders, for some reason, are a quirky bunch. I think maybe they bond with the puppies and it's hard for them to give them up for adoption."

"I know you have a bichon. Do you think there's a chance your breeder has any available?"

"I know she's having a litter in the spring. But it sounds like you don't want to wait until then."

"No," I said, shaking my head. "I know another dog isn't going to make me—I mean us—miss Mattie less. But I feel like I need a distraction. For some reason, I just feel like I have to have a dog right away. Right now." As I spoke, I felt tears spilling out of my eyes and dripping down my cheeks. Oh, how I wanted my Mattie back. I wanted her here, now. I wanted her safe. I wanted her happy.

"Would you take a rescue?" Jane asked.

"I'll take anything," I heard myself say.

I didn't know anything about rescues. I didn't really know anything about dogs. All I knew was that I needed help, more help than ever, to stay afloat. I needed a lifeline. And the only lifeline I could think of reaching for was a dog.

"I volunteer at Main Line Animal Rescue," Jane replied. "I'll have Bill Smith, the man who runs it, give you a call."

"Could I have *his* number?" I asked immediately.

I knew it would be nerve-racking waiting for this Bill Smith person to call me. I was sure he was busy. It could be hours, even days, before he'd get around to calling me back. I wanted to have *some* control. I would feel better knowing I had called him and left a message. And another message and another and another one after that. I would call again and again until I got him. Calling would give me something to do. It would make me feel as if I were moving forward at least a little. Whenever Andy or the boys were reluctant to "bother" someone about something they thought needed attention, I'd say, "The squeaky wheel gets the oil. Pick up the phone and call."

I wrote Bill Smith's phone number on a yellow sticky and said goodbye to Jane. I looked at the kitchen clock. It was eight forty-five. I decided I should have the decency to wait until nine before I began to harass this man. I stepped away from the phone and hung up my jacket in the mudroom. The phone rang.

"Hello?" I said.

"Hi, this is Bill Smith. Is Anne there?"

"Yes," I said, my heart pounding with relief. I might have even been smiling.

"I'm sorry about your loss."

"Thank you. We're very upset. I don't expect another dog to replace Mattie. But we'll definitely be getting another dog sooner or later, so it might as well be sooner, so he or she can offer some distraction," I said, trying not to sound like a desperate woman teetering on the edge of the abyss.

"That makes a lot of sense," Bill said, agreeably. "I hear that from people a lot."

It was amazing to think that others had gone through this. It felt like such a singular agony. I was relieved to hear that I was not alone.

"I'd like a small lapdog that doesn't shed," I said. I didn't see any reason not to get right to the point.

"Oh, we have lots of dogs. But let me tell you about Milo," Bill said, jumping in before I could continue with more details about the kind of dog I wanted.

I took a pad of yellow lined paper and a pen from the drawer, sat down at the kitchen table, and wrote M-I-L-O in blue ink at the top of the page.

"Milo is a Doris Day dog," Bill said in a matter-of-fact voice, as if he had named a breed of dog.

"What's a Doris Day dog?" I asked, truly perplexed.

"You know, the kind of dog you see in the old Doris Day movies. A Disney dog. Furry and lovable looking. Truly a beautiful, one-of-a-kind dog. I think he's part wheaten terrier, just like Mattie."

Wheaten terrier was what I wanted to hear.

"Why did the family give him up?" I said, asking the obvious first question.

"The mother went back to work, and they didn't have time to take care of him."

"Is Milo a lapdog?" I asked.

"Well, when I went to pick him up from the family, he was lying on the couch with his head in the kid's lap," Bill said, faltering. He sounded like an unprepared middle-school student blustering his way through a vocabulary quiz. I put down my pen and rested my head on the kitchen table. A dog whose head fit on a lap wasn't my definition of a lapdog.

"He's really a wonderful animal," Bill said. "You could come see him today. If you don't like him, there are plenty of others. I even have a bichon."

This was my kind of man. A man who did things *now*. Even though his definitions were a bit off, and he sounded a little like a salesman who believes that the sale doesn't begin until the customer says no. *But wait*, I thought, *he isn't forcing me to do anything. He's merely suggesting that I take a look at Milo. Give Milo a chance. If I don't like Milo, he has other dogs.* We agreed to meet at the horse farm that housed Main Line Animal Rescue at four o'clock, after we'd picked the kids up from school.

Andy was upstairs working. I hung up the phone and went to tell him the plan.

Then I said, "Andy, I think we should call Dr. Stewart and ask if we are setting a bad example for the kids by replacing Mattie so fast."

"You're right," Andy said. "Dr. Stewart has been your therapist for a long time. I think it's a good idea to talk to her about this."

I dropped into the chair near his desk and reached for the phone.

When Dr. Stewart answered, I told her quickly about Mattie and my plan to get a new dog as soon as possible. Then I took a deep breath and said, "Am I setting a bad example for the kids? Will it make them think that they are replaceable? That lives are replaceable? To me? To people in general?" I paused, tears dripping down my face. "But, Dr. Stewart, I need a distraction. I don't know how I'll go on alone all day in this quiet, still house. The void of Mattie, the sadness of what happened to her, is pulling me down, deeper and deeper."

My sobs increased as I spoke. I handed the phone to Andy, trusting the two of them to weigh the pros and cons and to decide what was right, or at least what was best between my plummeting mental health and the possible negative effects on the boys if we replaced Mattie quickly.

I did not think it was possible to trust anyone more than I trusted both Dr. Stewart and Andy. I believed that Dr. Stewart understood me better than I understood myself. I was confident that she would judiciously weigh how much I needed the distraction of another dog to keep Mattie's death from pushing me into thc abyss of depression against how detrimental such a quick substitute could be to my kids' emotional well-being.

Andy and I had been married for twenty-three years. If he did not always understand me with the depth of a professional, that did not stop him from always supporting me as I navigated my toxic relationship with my parents and my ongoing emotional suffering. He did not have the psychological tools to help me recover from the emotional abuse of my parents, past and present, but he continually offered himself as a decoy, sometimes a shield, between them and me. When we all got together, he acted as the professor and tapped into their keen interest in all things economic and financial. When he would return from driving the boys to Hebrew school on Sunday mornings and find me wailing and writhing on the kitchen floor after a phone call with my mother, he would drop down beside me and hug me until my gulping sobs subsided and my breathing returned, almost, to normal.

Other than the well-being of me and our children, the only things Andy cared about were his research, his teaching, and his responsibilities as a member of his department at Wharton. He had few material needs. He didn't care about clothes or cars or gadgets. He liked to spend his alone time writing economics papers. After dinner each night, he cleaned up the kitchen, spent time with the boys, and watched television with me. When I went to bed, he went into his study to work until two or three in the morning.

I was the one who was vigilant about what was going on inside each child and helped them navigate their ways. I signed them up for soccer, Little League, and Saturday morning basketball. Andy went to the games. Andy coached the games. He drove hours with the boys, carting them to endless team sports across the state.

Andy gave me full rein to do what I thought best for our family. When I decided it was time to get Joseph a dog, Andy didn't balk. But he was not interested in selecting or finding the dog. Whatever I decided was fine with him. And when that dog was killed by a UPS truck, Andy was fine with my need to replace her ASAP.

So the day after Mattie was killed, when I became overwhelmed with grief and called my therapist to see if she thought it was okay to replace Mattie so quickly, I had no qualms about putting Andy on the phone and leaving the discussion to the two of them.

After a few minutes, Andy hung up the phone and looked at me.

"Dr. Stewart thinks that the boys are old enough and secure enough to understand the situation," he said. "She said we should use this as a teachable moment with them and that the best way to offset any worries they might have about being replaceable is to discuss it with them. We can explain that Mattie made us love dogs. Getting another dog is a way of honoring Mattie, a testament to how much we loved her and will continue to love her."

I nodded in agreement.

"Dr. Stewart thinks the most important thing is to help you," Andy continued. "She agrees that the distraction involved in getting a new dog might help you from getting pulled down even more by Mattie's being killed. We can explain to the boys that, given your depression and the added sadness you feel about losing Mattie, getting a dog now is the best thing to do."

I let out a deep sigh of relief.

At two o'clock that day, we picked up our eldest son, Jonathan, at the airport. He had just finished his first semester at Harvard. Andy had called Jonathan the previous night to tell him what had happened. From the first day we dropped him off at Harvard, I was counting down the weeks until his return. But after Mattie was killed, my brain became so immersed in dark sorrow that I stopped trying to make myself feel better. Life sucked. It truly sucked. I didn't want to waste energy trying to convince myself otherwise. I wasn't up to the effort required to help myself look forward to anything, including Jonathan's coming home.

Andy and I got out of the car when we saw him coming out of the terminal toward us with his backpack and roller suitcase. The three of us embraced. Then Jonathan put his arms around me and gave me a solo hug. I was surprised to feel the heaviness in my heart, soul, and mind lift, at least a bit. I had dreaded Jonathan's leaving for college since he was three days old and we brought him home from the hospital. I had really missed him.

"I'm so sorry, Mom," he said. "Mattie really was a special dog."

We got into the car and went to pick up Joseph and Josh. After that, we were headed to Main Line Animal Rescue.

"Mom," Jonathan said from the back seat, "I don't think I ever told you this. But the day I got the letter from Harvard saying I had been accepted, no one was home. I picked up the phone to call Daddy at work, but I got his voice mail and I didn't want to waste great news like that in a message. When I hung up the phone, I looked down and saw Mattie sitting beside me, looking up at me, wagging her tail. I wanted to say my great news out loud; I wanted to tell *someone* what had happened. I said, 'Mattie, something very good has just happened to Jonny. Jonny got into Harvard.' And I sat down on the floor and gave her a hug."

"Jonny, that's such a nice story," I said, turning around to look at him. "I wouldn't be surprised if somehow Mattie sensed how happy you were."

It was comforting to hear this story about Mattie. I couldn't help but think about funerals and eulogies. About how when someone dies, people share uplifting stories with the family and with each other about the person who died. It makes it feel as if the person is present, at least in our minds. For a moment or two or three, we forget our abject sorrow.

Jonathan's story about Mattie's enthusiasm when he told her he'd been accepted to Harvard reminded me of my mother's response. As the memory rolled through my mind, my body began shaking.

We had called her on speakerphone.

"Grandma, I got in! I just found out I got into Harvard," Jonathan said, looking at me and beaming.

For a few moments, my mother didn't say anything. Jonathan looked at me, quizzically. I shrugged and shook my head.

"That's because you're a middle-class boy whose parents can pay the tuition," my mother said, as if she were stating the obvious. "The good thing is that now that you'll be in Boston, you'll be able to come to my Hanukkah parties," she said, sounding pleased. "It's busy here at work today. I've got to go."

There was a click. The connection went dead.

"I'm so sorry, Jonathan," I said as he hung up the phone.

"I know, I know," he said with a commiserating smile. "It's okay."

"It's not okay. What she said isn't true, and she should never have said it. She's a mean, angry woman. She should have congratulated you and congratulated you and congratulated you. Harvard picked you. It's quite an accomplishment, and you should feel very proud of yourself. You set yourself a daunting goal. You knew the odds were against you. But you didn't let that stop you from trying. I am so proud of you for that and for so many things."

"I know," Jonathan said, picking up his backpack. "It doesn't matter what Grandma thinks. You've told me that a million times and I know you're right. I'm gonna go upstairs and start my homework."

"First let me give you a hug," I said, moving toward him. I wrapped my arms around him and pulled him close, backpack and all. "Jonny, I love you so much and I'm so proud of you. I'm always proud of you. I'm proud of you for so many reasons, but mostly I'm proud of you for being you."

"Thanks, Mommy. I know. I'm okay," he said, pulling away. "Actually, I'm more than okay. I'm great." He broke into a smile that filled his entire face. "I got into fuckin' Harvard. Can you believe it?"

"I absolutely can," I said.

My mother's maliciousness never ceased to catch me off guard and send me plummeting toward the pit of despair. I was grateful Jonathan really was okay. My mother's attack had not hurt *him*. This was one more testament that I had been able to create a mentally healthy human being. A boy who was secure enough not to allow his grandmother's hostility to ruin his happy moment. I felt hopeful that my determination to create an environment of unconditional love was working.

Seven

Jonathan, Andy, and I arrived at school as the kids were beginning to stream out of the building. We pulled into the lower parking lot to wait for Joseph and Josh. It was the last day before winter break, and the exuberance of the kids running down the hill to their rides was palpable. Sadly, unlike their classmates, Joseph and Josh lumbered down toward the parking lot. Jonathan got out of the car and walked up to greet them. They gave each other loose hugs. Then, when Joseph looked at the car and saw Andy and me, a look of terror swept across his face. He knew Jonathan was coming home and was not surprised that he had come to pick up him and Josh. I realized that upon seeing Andy and me with him, Joseph instinctively braced for the worst.

"Did you think we had come with more bad news?" I asked Joseph as he got into the car.

"Yeah, I did," he said, shaking his head in relief.

As the boys clicked their seat belts, I turned toward them in the back seat.

"You probably heard me calling people last night, looking for another dog," I said.

Joseph and Josh nodded.

"Well, this morning I spoke with a man at an animal rescue not too far from here. He has a dog he thinks we will like. If not, he says he has lots of others," I said, looking first at Josh and then

Joseph for a reaction. We had already spoken to Jonathan about our plan on the ride from the airport.

They were both silent.

"You both know how much I loved Mattie," I said.

They nodded yes in unison.

"I really hadn't wanted a dog, but Joseph wanted one so badly that I agreed. And then, the moment I saw Mattie in the breeder's kitchen, I fell in love with her. I know that getting another dog isn't going to make me miss her less. But I really think I need a distraction. I'm home alone most of the day. Not having her following me or nestled at my feet like she used to do will be really hard for me."

I paused. I hoped someone would say something, but no one did.

"If I didn't love Mattie so much, I would not be so eager to get another dog. I don't want you to feel that my rush to get another dog detracts at all from Mattie in any way. It's a testament to what a wonderful creature she was. But if you're uncomfortable moving so fast to get another dog, we can wait."

"Mommy," Joseph said, "if it were just me, I would wait to get another dog. I'm really sad about Mattie. We had her for almost seven years, since I was ten. I don't know if I'm ready for another dog. But I can see how hard it will be for you to be home alone and why a distraction might be good for you. If you think it will make your day any better to have a new dog, it's okay with me to get one. I'm just not sure I'm ready to love another dog."

"I understand, Joseph," I said, smiling sadly. "And I appreciate your understanding my situation."

I looked at Josh.

"It's okay, Mommy," he said. "I agree with Joseph. I really loved Mattie, and I don't think I'm ready to love another dog. But if you think it will help you to get one now, it's okay."

I smiled. "You guys are really wonderful. I really appreciate your trying to understand how I feel. I've been thinking about us getting a rescue dog. A dog who doesn't have a home. There was nothing at all good about Mattie being killed. But if we get a rescue dog, at least one creature will be better off now than he or she was a few days ago."

The forty-minute ride to Main Line Animal Rescue was quiet. I stared ahead at nothing, lost in a reverie about Mattie. Before we got her, if I had dared to fantasize about or even contemplate my ideal dog, I would not have been able to imagine one as perfect for our family. Mattie was like a stuffed animal who gave and took love. But that does not do justice to her zest and to her seemingly innate ability to make each one of us stop and smile and hug her every time we came in the door.

As soon as she heard the door open, she would pop up from her bed in the kitchen and trot over, tail high and wagging. She didn't jump on us, but instead ran circles around us, unable to contain her glee.

The most magical thing Mattie did for our family was teach us her favorite game, Family Hug. None of us can remember quite how she taught us this game. We only know that shortly after she arrived, if anyone called "family hug," Mattie came running. Then whoever was interested in playing the game would put their arms around one another while Mattie jumped and danced among us. She was happiest when all five of us played. We would come together in our large center hallway, where there was room for all of us to form a tight circle.

"Family hug!" one or all of us would call out.

Mattie would run around us, in one direction and then the other, stopping to jump for joy next to one of us, then the next, then the next. It reminded me of the children's game Duck, Duck,

Goose. Except no one had to be "it." There was no winner or loser. When we were done, Mattie went to her bed and curled into a ball and fell asleep.

It was a lot easier, and more fun, too, to give Mattie the exercise she needed with Family Hug rather than with walks. Shortly after we got Mattie, we had an electric fence installed around the perimeter of our yard. Mattie quickly learned not to go near it and to stay close to the house. Sometimes I'd find her sitting by the back door, waiting to be let out. Other times I would preemptively let her out. If I was upstairs, I would call to the boys, "Will someone please let Mattie out?" Invariably I would hear the boys squabbling: "I let her out last time." "No, I did." "No, I did." A quick reminder about the promise they had made before we got Mattie, that they would take responsibility for the dog walks, was always enough to nudge one of them to open the door and let Mattie out, leaving the others with the responsibility of letting her in.

At night as I lay in bed with Mattie snuggled beside me, I drifted off to sleep marveling that getting a dog, something I had dreaded for years, had turned out to be so wonderful.

The car hurdled a speed bump, startling me out of my daydream about Mattie. I turned to look at the three boys in the back seat. Ordinarily, Jonathan's arrival would have sparked excitement and banter. But today, twenty-six hours after Mattie had been killed, was no ordinary day, and they all gave me sad smiles.

At four o'clock on the dot, we drove through the horse farm gate to meet Bill Smith and Milo and any other four-legged creature he thought might be appropriate for us. Bill was waiting for us down the hill from the parking area, at the edge of a vast green meadow. Lying down beside him at the end of a leash was a large, regal dog. His range of shiny golden highlights would cause any salon colorist to swoon. He was as still as a statue. He held high his square head with its pointy, floppy ears and short, blunt beard. His front paws were bent and positioned straight ahead of him. He could have been a living, breathing sphinx. We waved to Bill and drove toward the Main Line Animal Rescue office to park the car. Before Andy had turned off the ignition, as soon as the car was stopped, the boys and I jumped from our seats and were running toward Milo and Bill.

Even though I had never met Bill, when we reached him and Milo, I didn't stop to introduce myself or show any recognition that there was anyone there but Milo. I, along with Jonathan, Joseph, and Josh, fell to the ground and began rubbing and patting and pawing and hugging and kissing Milo. I moved around to sit face-to-face with him. When I did, Milo focused his gaze and locked his eyes into mine. I felt my soul lifting. Despite my grief, my heart opened, and a bond stretched between us. And Milo? Other than the ones controlling his eyes, he didn't move a muscle.

"Let's call him Mellow Milo," Josh said, in the midst of the excitement.

Andy arrived and stood beside Bill, talking. And smiling. For the first time since Mattie had been killed, we were *all* smiling. At forty-five pounds, Milo was twenty pounds underweight. His hair was as long as his legs and touched the ground when he finally stood up.

"You said you have a bichon?" I said to Bill after some time. Good sense had momentarily taken hold of me, and I felt we should at least *look* at what I had originally wanted.

"Absolutely. I'll take you up to the waiting room. I'll put Milo back in his cage, and I'll introduce you to Scooter," he said, leading us up the hill and opening the door to a room just big enough to hold a couch and an armchair.

We didn't say anything. We just waited. And sure enough, a

few minutes later, Bill appeared in the doorway with a white fluff-ball in his arms.

"This is Scooter," he said, dropping the dog onto the floor.

Instinctively, we all pressed back to keep out of harm's way as poor Scooter began ricocheting back and forth among the four walls of the room. We watched, our mouths open, waiting for the white blitz to end or even slow down. But he didn't. Until, finally, Josh, the Abel of fewest words and fewest demands, said, "Take Scooter back. We want Milo."

And that was it. We all nodded in relief and agreement as Bill flagged Scooter down, scooped him up, and left the room.

A minute later, Bill was back. "Tomorrow morning, I'll have Milo bathed and clipped, and you can pick him up any time after lunch."

"Can't we take him now?" I asked.

Meeting Milo in the meadow, I had felt an instant bond with him. It reminded me of the wonderful feeling I had experienced when I first met Mattie. It was the first time I had felt any relief from the agony of Mattie's death. I didn't want to let go of that feeling. I wanted to take him home right away.

"No," said Josh, starting to cry. "We can't take Milo so soon. It wouldn't be fair to Mattie. We have to wait at least a week."

We all looked at each other. He did have a point. Even if I had felt *I* needed the immediate distraction of a new dog to stay afloat, I would never put my adult emotional needs above my thirteen-year-old son's. How could we not honor Josh's heartfelt request?

I looked at Bill. His mouth agape, his eyes popping, he seemed to have been caught off guard by Josh's desire to respect Mattie's memory. Clearly, Bill was as eager to place Milo as I was to take Milo. But after a moment, he nodded his head.

"Fine. We can hold him here until you're ready, Josh. That's no problem. In the meantime, would you like to walk through the kennel? You might see something else you like. If you have friends looking for dogs, you can tell them about what you see here. Many New York City dogs lost their homes after the World Trade Center attacks three months ago. We have dogs from New York arriving here every week hoping to find new homes."

We followed Bill, single file, through the waiting room door, through a small office and into the kennel. The long, narrow room was dimly lit and musty and smelled like a mixture of sulfur and rotting mushrooms. There were two levels of silver metal cages—small dog cages on top—lining all four walls. As soon as we walked in, all the dogs began howling and clawing at their metal walls. Their discordant cacophony was jarring, and I tensed up. We continued, single file, behind Bill, stopping briefly but frequently to look at each yelping, homeless dog. Then, in the middle of the first row of cages, we came to Milo. Unlike his compatriots, he was not clawing or howling. In the far left corner of his cage, he was curled up in a ball on a bed of rags, his eyes open and watching. I felt my heart thud.

We gathered around him. There was the regal animal who had lulled us into happiness out in the meadow. There was the sphinx-like dog who only minutes earlier had so comforted us, whose gaze had reached out and locked with mine. And here he was, now, all alone on the cold cement floor. He didn't look mellow. He looked sad and forlorn.

"Maybe we can take him tomorrow," Josh said.

"I'll tell you what. I'll bring him to your house tomorrow at two," said Bill, a little too eagerly. "Your vacation begins tomorrow, doesn't it?"

The boys nodded.

"Great," said Bill grinning. "What could be a more fun way to kick off a vacation?"

We said goodbye to Bill and Milo and headed through the cold, dark evening back to our car and off to Chili's for a celebratory dinner. Sitting with my subdued, yet still somehow excited and happy family, I was able to keep any images or feelings or thoughts about Mattie in the background of my mind. Front and center was the image of Mellow Milo, in the meadow, locking his eyes with mine. I can't usually do that. I can't usually control what images, feelings, or thoughts happen. Not at all. Usually, I can't keep my mind from going where it wants to go, when it wants to go there. And trust me, usually, it's not to a good place or at a good time. And yet I *always* try.

Yes, I've been trying, as far back as I can remember. I've told my kids that I want my tombstone to read, "She tried and she tried and she tried." I *try* to do what's good for me; to do what might be helpful for me. And yet, even after my energizing workouts when I felt buoyed and uplifted for some moments or more, I never felt even a modicum of hope about myself and my future. Never did I feel that I had a chance, a chance for a life with less emotional suffering. But that night in the restaurant, the image of a soulful-eyed Milo lifted me up and made me feel like I had a chance. Like *we* had a chance.

Eight

Bill drove up in his red Subaru station wagon the following day at two, as he had promised. He walked in the door with a folded metal crate and a bag of kibble in one hand and Milo's leash in his other hand.

"Sit," he said to Milo as soon as they came into the kitchen, where the boys and I had been waiting. Immediately, Milo sat, back straight, head up. For all I knew, he could have been competing for Best in Show. I was impressed.

Then Bill looped Milo's leash securely around my wrist. He ran his hand over Milo's golden coat, down to the end of his Lion King tail.

"He knows the sit command," Bill said. "But I think you'll all benefit from a dog training course."

He handed me a card. "Here's the number for What A Good Dog. Tell them that you adopted Milo from me. In the meantime, let Milo know this is his home. Make him comfortable. Set up the crate in the kitchen so he'll have a space of his own when he wants it. Play with him. And give him lots of treats. Oh, and take him for some walks. It's a good way for you all to bond. And it's important that he gets enough exercise."

When Bill suggested that we take Milo for walks to bond with him, I assumed we could just as easily bond on the kitchen floor or on the couch in the den. But he had also said that Milo needed walks for exercise. That was another thing entirely. The requirement that I not *do* dog-walking had been the first and foremost contingency I had set forth for the boys before we got Mattie. It had not been a problem because Mattie hadn't needed walks. All she had needed was to be let out in our backyard.

Now it seemed like my worst dog fear was coming true. I couldn't ask the boys to walk Milo. I was grateful they had been sensitive to my needs and acquiesced to getting a dog so quickly, even though it was not what they would have done. I looked at Milo sitting with the boys in the middle of the kitchen where Bill had left us. Without warning, my mind pictured Mattie sitting there in Milo's place, and my heart fell. I shook my head to toss out the image. *Milo was not Mattie. Milo was not Mattie. Milo was not Mattie.* I had to repeat this to myself until Milo, a few feet away, was the only dog in the forefront of my brain. Milo was not Mattie. Milo needed to be walked and taught. I would be Milo's walker. I would be Milo's teacher. I couldn't be with the one I loved. So I was going to *try* to like, if not love, the one I was with. As soon as Bill walked out the door, the boys and I sat down in a circle around Milo and patted him and fed him. "Good boy," we repeated each time we dropped a thumbnail-sized treat down his throat.

Not one to sit still for long, I soon got up and called What A Good Dog. I told the woman who answered the phone that I had just adopted an eighteen-month-old dog from Bill Smith and that Bill said I should enroll him in a kindergarten class. The woman told me that classes would begin in mid-January.

"You need to know," she continued, "that his acceptance into the school depends upon his performing satisfactorily in the hour-long assessment required of all incoming students."

The first available appointment was a week away. I booked it.

"And one more thing," the woman said as I was about to hang

up. "You need to teach your dog name recognition before he can enroll in class."

"Name recognition?" I said. "He has to know his name?"

It had never occurred to me that a creature with a name might not know it. How was it possible that Milo might not know his name?

"Not just know his name," the woman said. "When he hears his name, he has to look immediately at the person who said it."

My stomach clenched. I had loved Mattie. I thought I had appreciated everything about her. I had appreciated not only her sweet and loving demeanor but also, the nontrivial matter, that she was housebroken. But I had not ever given any thought to the fact that when we said, "Mattie, come," she trotted toward us. I had never appreciated that she had arrived in our home knowing her name. This was not something to which I had ever given any thought. But now, Milo's acceptance to What A Good Dog depended on my teaching him his name.

"How on earth do I teach Milo his name?" I said to the woman on the phone.

"It's pretty straightforward," she said. "Get yourself a pocketful of yummy treats. Bite-sized chunks of chicken would be perfect. Say his name and when he looks at you, pop the treat into his mouth."

"What if he doesn't look at me when I say his name? Then what do I do?" It seemed like an obvious question. If he was already inclined to look when he heard his name, I wouldn't need to be doing this.

"If he doesn't look at you, hold the treat near his nose, and when he sniffs it, lure his gaze to you. Then, when his eyes meet yours, say, 'Yes, Milo. Good boy,' and drop the treat in his mouth. You can do it when you take him for a walk. Eventually, through this positive reinforcement, Milo will learn the desired behavior—in this case, recognizing his name."

"Okay," I said. "I hope I can do this."

"You'll be fine," the woman said. "If it isn't working, you can discuss it when you come with Milo for his assessment next week."

"Thanks," I said, hanging up the phone, so distracted and daunted by this unexpected task that I did not wait to hear the woman say goodbye.

Nine

I am not one to procrastinate. I promptly face the inevitable, even when it is something I dread. As soon as I hung up the phone, I began to prepare for our first walk. I found two cooked chicken breasts from Sunday dinner. Our last home-cooked meal before Mattie was killed. I shook that thought off, cut the breasts into small cubes, and scooped them into a plastic sandwich bag. I put on my down jacket, stuffed the bag of chicken in my pocket, and found a pair of fingerless gloves buried deep in a drawer in our closet. Then I leashed Milo, and we were off on our first walk.

We walked out the back door and down the steep driveway. The same driveway where Mattie had been killed exactly forty-eight hours earlier. Chills from within, not from the twenty-degree outside air, ran through me as I traversed the driveway, an image of Mattie filling my mind. For better or for worse, the image was jettisoned as I felt myself being yanked forward toward the street. With his floppy ears up and his tail high, Milo was off and running. I planted both my feet on the driveway to anchor myself.

"Milo," I said firmly. "Stop."

He didn't stop. I didn't know if it was because he didn't know he was Milo or because he didn't know the meaning of the word "stop" or if he didn't care what I said because he wanted what he wanted. And right now, he wanted to run. Yanking the leash again, this time with *both* hands and the full force of my body, I managed to counter Milo's momentum and get him to stop. Keeping the leash taut in both hands, I stepped toward him, and together we continued down the driveway and turned onto the winding, hilly street.

Our street does not have sidewalks. Rising from each side of the street are steep, soggy-leaf-covered hills, densely populated with trees. I stepped along the shoulder of the road with Milo on the other side of me, walking in the bed of leaves. Before I could pull a chicken cube out of my pocket and begin our first lesson, Milo pulled me off the road and onto my stomach. I was stretched out across the cold, wet bed of leaves at the trunk of a tree where a squirrel, moments earlier, had stood sentry. He had fled as soon as he saw Milo bounding toward him.

I picked myself up and brushed myself off. The squirrel chase had been so unexpected and so fleeting that my body had apparently gone into shock. I did not remember feeling a thing. I took a deep breath. It was onward and upward to the top of our hilly street.

"Milo," I said, reaching into my pocket and pulling out what had already become a very cold, soggy piece of chicken. Instantly, miraculously, Milo turned his focus from the tree branch high above in front of him to me. Maybe he did know his name after all.

"Good boy," I said, dropping the mushy morsel into his mouth. "Good boy."

I dragged him back down to the road.

"Milo," I said, a dozen or so steps later.

Again, he snapped his head to look up at me.

Again, I dropped a chicken chunk into his open mouth. He snapped his jaws together and swallowed the chunk. This name recognition thing seemed pretty simple and straightforward. For some fraction of a moment I thought, *I can do this*, and I felt my spirit buoy a little. But then I heard Milo bark, and I felt myself being dragged along the cold, wet leaves to another tree where another squirrel had gone scurrying from a branch. I imagined the tear in my already torn rotator cuff elongating. I had just been to see a surgeon about my rotator cuff before returning home and letting Mattie out, unaware that the UPS truck was turning into our driveway. My shoulder burned. I winced. I winced because of the pain. I winced thinking about poor Mattie. Poor, sweet, dead Mattie.

"Milo!" I screamed, as I pushed myself upright.

My screaming of his name had not been intended as a name recognition lesson or test. I had screamed his name because I was angry. I was angry about being dragged from one squirrel to another. Nonetheless, Milo heard me scream his name and he instantly turned his head and locked on my gaze. I had no choice but to give him a chicken chunk. That was the deal. But that was it. I was done for the day. I had accomplished what I had set out to do. I had taught Milo his name. I was livid with Milo. I was tired of being pulled off the road and dragged through the leaves. And I was livid because Milo was out of control.

We got back into the house just as I heard one of Joseph's friends driving up the driveway. Milo heard the car too. With his leash still on he ran to the kitchen window, jumping up to put his front paws on the sill, where he barked and howled, howled and barked.

"Milo!" I screamed.

Whatever progress I had made with Milo recognizing his name now seemed nonexistent. He continued to howl and bark at the window until Joseph's friend knocked on the back door. Immediately, Milo ran to the door and jumped up, his paws resting at the height of the doorknob, his frenzy of barks and howls becoming more high-pitched and intense as he looked at Joseph's friend through the paned glass window of the door.

"What's going on?" Joseph and Josh said, coming into the kitchen just as I was digging in my jacket pocket for a chunk of chicken.

"Milo," I said, holding the chicken in front of his nose, not wanting to depend on his obedience to lure him away from the door.

Milo apparently caught a whiff because he immediately came down from the door and followed me into the middle of the kitchen. I was still shoveling chicken chunks into his mouth when Joseph let his friend in the door. Before I thought to catch Milo's leash, he left me and the chicken and bounded for Joseph's friend. When Milo reached him, he jumped and wrapped his front paws around the boy's leg and began to hump. And hump and hump and hump.

"Milo!" I shrieked to no avail. "Milo!"

Finally, Joseph grabbed the leash and pulled Milo back, off his friend's leg.

"I'm so sorry," I said to the boy.

"That's okay, Mrs. Abel. I'm sorry about Mattie."

I took the leash from Joseph. As the boys walked out of the kitchen to safety, I pulled Milo to his crate, pushed him in, and latched it. I stood there with Josh, listening to Milo howl and watching him thrash back and forth inside the crate.

"I can't believe this is the dog we nicknamed Mellow Milo yesterday," I said, raising my voice to be heard over Milo.

Josh didn't immediately respond. Then he turned to me. "Mommy, I bet Bill Smith gave Milo some kind of sedative yesterday before we got there."

I stared at Josh. I wondered if maybe he was right. I didn't want to believe it. I thought of how traumatic it must be for Milo to come into a new house and a family of strangers. I wanted to give him a chance. I wanted to be hopeful that he really was the mellow creature we had met the previous day.

"Bill said I should walk him to bond with him," I told Josh. "He also said to walk him for exercise. Maybe that's the problem. He needs more exercise. Maybe I didn't walk him enough."

Josh shrugged.

"Tomorrow, I'll take him for a longer walk," I said. "Maybe that will help."

I didn't know what else to say. It had only been a few hours. Any creature, two- or four-legged, deserves a grace period during a major upheaval. Any creature, two- or four-legged, deserves not to be judged when they are dropped into a new home.

For the rest of the afternoon and evening, whenever a truck rumbled down our street, Milo ran to the living room or dining room windows that face the street and jumped up and howled. When the street was quiet, Milo roamed from room to room. Up the stairs, down the stairs. At one point I put him in the kitchen and closed all the doors. After a minute or two of listening to him hurl himself against the door, I could not stand it. I could not wait him out in the hopes that he would get tired and stop. I opened the door and watched him continue to prowl his new domain.

A couple of times before bedtime, I leashed him up and took him out in the backyard. Much of the yard is lit with spotlights, and as Milo sniffed along on the mixture of snow and leaves, I saw little poops left by Mattie, and I stopped and began to cry. It seemed surreal. Here was evidence of Mattie. Evidence that Mattie had been here such a short time ago. And now? As I was being sucked into a swirling void by my own self-pity and pity for Mattie, I felt a thud. Milo had turned around to face me. He then wrapped his front paws around the top of my right leg and began humping me. I decided to stand there and let him hump until he got tired of humping and stopped. Maybe it was ten minutes. Maybe it was five. Maybe it was fifteen. All I know is that I finally gave up. I couldn't outwait him, even in my dejected state. I pulled my leg back from Milo's clutching, yearning grasp. Dragging him by the leash, I ran into the house sobbing. Sobbing for Mattie. Sobbing for me.

That night when I got into bed, Milo did just as Mattie had done. He jumped in after me and lay down at the foot of the bed. Unlike Mattie, Milo did not put his head down and nestle into a ball and fall asleep. He lay there facing me, eyes open, ears up and alert. I eventually fell asleep under Milo's watchful eye. Each time during the night when my eyes momentarily opened, I looked toward the bottom of the bed, and there was always the same image greeting me. Milo, eyes open, ears up and alert, staring at me. With all the energy he had expended during the day, didn't he need to sleep? Was he like the 1 to 3 percent of the human population who live happily and function well on little sleep? Or perhaps he was waiting for the perfect moment to attack. I told myself to stop being dramatic. I shut my eyes and hoped for the best. Exhausted from my first day with Milo, I fell soundly asleep.

Ten

Rested and refreshed, I jumped out of bed the next morning, determined to make this day with Milo better than the previous one. As I pulled on my clothes, I remembered Josh's comment about Bill Smith sedating Milo. I looked at Milo who sat at attention, watching me. He seemed more like the Mellow Milo we'd seen the day we met him. Maybe he hadn't been sedated. Maybe his aggressiveness the previous day was because he'd been overwhelmed, possibly scared, by so many new things.

"Good boy, Milo," I said.

At this particular moment he *was* being a good boy.

Milo swished his full-fringed tail.

I smiled. Milo indeed knew he was Milo. He knew that being a good boy was a good thing. A thing that deserved a tail swish.

Milo followed me downstairs. No one else was up yet. I filled his bowl with food. While he was eating, I quickly filled a plastic sandwich bag with chicken chunks. Then I bundled myself up in my down jacket, wool hat, and fingerless gloves. Finally, I put Milo's leash on.

It was still dark on this cold December morning. As I closed the back door, I remembered seeing people hunched against the cold walking their dogs when I drove to the swimming pool in my warm car. I had felt glad to be me and not to be them. Doing what

I was doing right now with Milo was exactly why I had dreaded getting a dog before we got Mattie. This is not what I had wanted. But you don't always get what you want.

My goal for this walk was to make it to the top of our street, to the four-way, traffic-lighted intersection where we could cross to a street with sidewalks. There were fewer trees there. Fewer squirrels. No beds of cold, wet leaves. Milo and I would be able to walk like normal, civilized beings along the sidewalk. A woman and her dog out for a brisk, early-morning walk.

I took a long, slow deep breath. The cold air felt invigorating as it passed down inside me. I took another and another. *I can do this. We can do this*, I thought. *This isn't so bad.* These were the hopeful, upbeat things I told myself as we neared the middle of our long, hilly driveway, and I heard a tree branch rustle a few feet ahead of us. I must have heard it before Milo did. A fraction of a moment later, Milo began howling and pulling me toward the branch on the side of the driveway. I stumbled after Milo, catching myself on the tree trunk while he jumped up in the air over and over in front of the trunk, trying to reach the now squirrel-less branch. I caught my breath and steadied myself. I yanked Milo back to the driveway, continuing down to the street. All I needed to do was to make it to the top of the street, across the intersection, and onto the sidewalk. We would be fine after that.

Our walk up the street was not too different from the day before. I called Milo's name. He turned to look at me with military precision. I dropped a treat in his mouth, and we moved onward. Like the day before, whenever Milo heard or saw a squirrel, he sprinted toward it, dragging me behind him, often on my belly.

Finally, finally, damp and cold from my bodysurfing up the street on wet leaves, I pulled Milo to my side when we reached the intersection at the top of the street. The sun had come up while we were wrestling our way up the hill. Looking across the street at the sidewalk and the sparse population of trees, I couldn't help but feel that we had emerged from the dark, into the light. We had left the untamed and arrived at civilization.

"Milo," I said, as the traffic whizzed by, and we waited for the light to change.

He looked. I rewarded him. Yes, I was feeling pretty good. We had made it. I imagined the worst was over. All we had to do was cross the street and walk. Walk and do name recognition. I was standing on the corner with Milo, gazing across the street at the promised land of sidewalks and anticipating our arrival there. Suddenly I was flying through the air. I heard the screech of loud brakes. My entire body hit the ground.

I lay in the spot where I had landed for some moments, taking an inventory of my body. I could move my head. My shoulders hurt no more than usual. The tips of my fingerless-gloved fingers stung. My hips and my knees were sore but not broken. I felt a tug at my hand and realized I was still clutching Milo's leash, which was wrapped around my wrist.

I lifted my head. Milo stood directly in front of me, howling. I turned to my left. An arm's length away I saw the tires and front grille of a yellow school bus. Slowly, gingerly, I stood up and took a deep, steadying breath in the middle of the street.

"Milo!" I screamed as I yanked his leash. I pulled him from the middle of the road to a patch of grass on the other side of the sidewalk.

The bus driver stared at me from behind the steering wheel. The kids on the bus had their faces pressed against the glass and pointed at Milo and me. Behind the bus was a long line of cars whose drivers had been forced to come to an abrupt stop because Milo had leaped into the street, taking me along with him. I was mortified. Every face within these cars had turned to stare at me. I hate being the center of attention. I stood on the grass, holding the leash taut and staring at the ground, trying to stay calm until the traffic began to move and I was once again just another person walking her dog.

When the batch of cars that had witnessed our escapade had fully moved on, I turned to Milo.

"I *hate* you, Milo!" I screamed so hard it hurt my throat. "I hate you so much!"

Milo sat at attention, looking up at me, no doubt waiting to be rewarded with a chicken chunk for recognizing his name.

"You are so, so bad!" I continued in a shrill voice.

Standing there, catching my breath, I imagined going home, putting Milo in the back of my station wagon, and driving the straight, easy route to Main Line Animal Rescue. I pictured myself walking Milo into the office, handing whoever was there the leash, and driving home a free woman. As soon as I imagined myself handing over the leash at the rescue, I pictured Milo curled up on a bed of rags in his cage there. In that moment, as I pictured him on the cold cement floor in his cage, I knew I could never do it. I knew I would never be able to make that trip. Standing there on the patch of grass near the sidewalk, I exhaled a deep sigh, resigned to fifteen years of servitude to this dog who was everything I did not want.

Eleven

For the rest of the morning after our school bus walk, Milo's behavior was not too different from the previous day. He howled at the window whenever he heard a truck or bus. He periodically tried to hump one or another of us. He marched through the house from one room to another, as if he were a soldier patrolling a hostile border.

The boys came and went from the kitchen to their rooms to the den. No one rolled his eyes at me. No one shook his head and said, "This is what you get for being insistent on replacing Mattie so quickly." No one said, "Look at the mess you're in." For that, at least, I was grateful.

After lunch, I decided to try something different for Milo's walk. At the bottom of our street was a dog park. In the fifteen years I had lived in our house, I had probably driven by that park at least once a day. But I had never been down there. There had been no need. In the seven years we'd had Mattie, we had not taken her for a walk even once. I had no idea what the dog park was like, or what you did at a dog park. I was still feeling traumatized by my near-death experience at the wheels of the school bus. It was tragic enough that Mattie had died. If I died or became incapacitated, Milo's own future would be bleak. For everyone's benefit, I loaded Milo into the car and drove to the park.

Milo was standing in the back of the station wagon, ears up, tail up, when I parked the car. Another car arrived just as we did. When a woman got out of her car with five dogs of varying sizes, Milo went wild. He began howling and hurling himself back and forth against the windows of the station wagon. I opened the back of the car just enough to reach in and grab the leash and secure it around my wrist as Bill Smith had instructed. Milo slithered out the door before it was even halfway up. As I slammed the door shut, he was already bounding into the park after the five-pack of dogs, pulling me along behind him.

The park looked like the bottom of a large oval bowl about the size of a football field. There was a pebbled path around the circumference, enclosing a soggy, grassy area where a few dogs were romping together. A brook ran along one side of the path. A steep, tree-filled embankment rose up from the other side. Milo continued to pull me toward the five-pack of dogs. The dogs stopped when we reached them, and everyone sniffed for a while. Then the five dogs turned and continued walking.

"Hi, I'm Anne," I said to the woman holding the leashes of all five dogs. "This is Milo. We just got him yesterday from Main Line Animal Rescue."

"I'm Marion. It's nice to meet you," she said with little expression, not looking or sounding like it was at all nice to meet me.

I didn't know anything about dog park etiquette. But I'm an extrovert. I get energy talking to people. I needed all the energy I could get, so I set my pace to Marion's.

"What kinds of dogs are these?" I said, thinking it was a reasonable conversation starter.

Marion began pointing to one dog after the other, saying either a breed I did not recognize or "mixed breed."

"They are all rescue dogs," she said.

As she pointed, as she spoke, Milo was barking, stalking each and every one of her dogs. I pulled him back. He pulled forward. Back and forward we went, Milo barking the whole time.

I told Marion about Mattie, speaking loudly to be heard above Milo's commotion. Marion nodded and gave me a commiserating smile.

"Milo," I finally said, hoping he would look at me and I could give him a treat. It was as if he were deaf. He just kept barking and pulling. Hoping to quiet him at least for a moment, even if he had not performed the desired behavior of looking at me, I found his mouth and dropped in the treat.

"You really shouldn't do that," Marion said. "You shouldn't reward him if he doesn't deserve it."

"I know," I said, feeling horribly chastised. "Thanks for the tip. I'm really new at this."

We continued together along the pebble path, Milo barking and pulling as Marion and I talked, looking at each other as we did, so we could follow the conversation above Milo's racket. She told me she was a nurse and that she came to the park every day.

"A tired dog is a good dog," she said.

I nodded. Apparently, Milo was not one bit tired.

After we'd walked one full revolution around the path, Marion stopped and turned to me.

"You know, rescues are filled with dogs a lot more deserving than this one," she said, jutting her chin in Milo's direction. "You should take him back and get another dog."

And off she went to make another pass around the park.

I just stood there. Here was a woman who had five rescue dogs, a woman whose profession was caring for people, and *she* was telling me to give Milo back. My shoulders slumped as I turned and walked back to the car, pulling Milo, who was pulling me and barking at the dog park. When I finally got him into the car and had clicked my seat belt, I dropped my forehead on the steering wheel. The image of Milo in his cage at the rescue reappeared in my mind. He lay curled in a fetal position on a bed of rags. He looked so forlorn, so alone. I didn't know if I could live *with* Milo. But I also knew I would not be able to live with myself *without* him if I sent him back to the cage.

As I turned the key in the ignition, I remembered What A Good Dog and our assessment appointment the following week. There was hope. Hope for me and for Milo. When I got home, I pulled out a pad of paper and a pen and began a list. A list of all the things Milo was doing for which I needed help.

Since the boys started school, I had always thought of teachers as allies, and I had never kept secrets from them. If one of the boys was acting out or anxious, I spoke to his teacher and asked for help. Many friends and acquaintances did otherwise. Not wanting to expose their child's dark side, they held back information and worked through issues alone. Now that Milo was one of my boys, I would take my list to our assessment and ask for help.

Later that afternoon, after the dog park, Andy and I took Jonathan and Joseph to see the movie *A Beautiful Mind*, about the Nobel Prize winner John Nash who suffered with schizophrenia. Josh, whose idea of a perfect day is staying home all day in his pajamas, didn't want to go. After the movie, I called Josh to tell him we were going out to dinner and to ask him if he wanted us to pick him up.

"Mommy," Josh said, his voice shaky. "Milo bit me."

"What?" I screamed into the receiver, not because I hadn't heard but because I could not comprehend.

"He bit me," Josh repeated, now sounding like he was succumbing to tears. "On the back."

"How did it happen?"

"I was playing Invisible Football in your room," he said.

Invisible Football was a solo game Josh had invented when he was in kindergarten that consisted of him running back and forth with a football calling out different plays and scores. I don't understand football. I never understood Invisible Football. But sometimes I would find Josh or even Josh and a friend running back and forth in my room, each apparently playing his own game of Invisible Football.

"So what happened?" I said, again.

"Milo came into the room while I was playing. He just sat there in the doorway. I was running back and forth, and as I turned to run back to the other side of the room, he lunged at me, landing on my back, and bit me near my shoulder," Josh said, now clearly sniffling.

"Josh, I am so sorry. We'll be right home."

When we got home, Andy called the pediatrician, and I ran into the den. Josh was sitting on the couch watching a football game. Milo was lying by his feet, asleep.

"It's okay, Mommy," Josh said. "It was frightening right when it happened. But it feels better now. I'm okay."

I walked over to Josh and sat next to him on the couch. There were two tears in his T-shirt and one deep red gash near his shoulder.

I felt terrible. I felt terribly guilty.

"Mommy, really, I'm okay," Josh said.

Jonathan and Joseph came into the den and stood in the doorway, their faces a mixture of concern and uncertainty.

"I'm fine," Josh said, now sounding exasperated at having to repeat himself and, also, because he hates being the center of attention.

Jonathan and Joseph looked relieved. Without even taking off their jackets, they slid onto the couch next to Josh to watch the football game. Milo remained sound asleep by their feet. He reminded me of the large white dog asleep on a bed in the Andrew Wyeth poster on the wall of our vet's office.

I went back into the kitchen. Andy was zipping up his jacket.

"The doctor is calling in an antibiotic prescription for Josh," he said. "I'll go get it and then pick up a pizza for dinner."

"Andy, I feel terrible about Milo biting Josh. But I really don't want to send him back to his cage at the rescue. I hope we can get some help when we go for our dog school interview," I said, sitting down at the table, still wearing my parka.

Andy came toward the table to face me. "I know it isn't easy for you. It wouldn't be easy for anyone to lose a dog like Mattie and then get one like this. Milo seemed like a reasonable dog when we met him. Who would have imagined that we were probably seeing a sedated dog? You're doing the best you can. I know you. You're putting in the work. It's only a few more days until the interview. We'll just have to try to manage Milo until then."

I smiled at Andy. He supported me unconditionally.

"Thanks," I said. "It means a lot to me that you understand the situation with Milo and me. I really don't want Milo to be anyone else's problem. I wanted him. I want to be the one to bear the burden of him. That's why I'm extra upset that he bit Josh."

"Josh will be fine," Andy said. "But I better get him his antibiotic. I'll be back soon."

An hour later when we sat down at the kitchen table, I was relieved and grateful that the conversation was about the football game. No one mentioned Milo. No one said a word to me about the highly aggressive dog who was now part of our family.

The following day, Joseph reached for a container of pea soup that had fallen out of the refrigerator and splattered. As he reached down, Milo came running over and bit him.

"Fuck," said Joseph, standing up quickly and massaging his hand.

"Sorry, Mommy," he said when I turned from the sink to see what had happened.

I ran to Joseph and grabbed his hand, careful not to upset Milo who was now licking up every bit of the viscous green goo off the floor. Milo's teeth had penetrated Joseph's skin. There were two bloody puncture wounds.

"You don't have to apologize," I said, not knowing if he was sorry for swearing or for spilling the soup. "Go soak your hand in warm water. I'll call the doctor."

I was afraid to tell the doctor that our dog had bitten two boys in two days. I didn't know the relevant child abuse laws. I also didn't know if dogs were euthanized if they were considered dangerous. I didn't know if the doctor was required to fill out a form for the township health department. I was determined to give Milo a chance. I was determined to find a way to teach him to be a good dog. We were just starting down that road. But we had not yet begun any kind of rehabilitative training. So I told the doctor that Joseph had been bitten by a friend's dog. As fantastical and coincidental as two brothers being bitten in two days by two different dogs might be, the doctor didn't seem at all suspicious.

"You know what to do," he said matter-of-factly. "I'll call the prescription in right now."

I hung up the phone and looked at Milo, who was now up and alert and patrolling the house. I didn't know what I was going to do with him. I just knew I was going to do whatever I could to civilize and salvage him. I got out my list of Milo's behavior problems.

"Bit Joseph over pea soup," I wrote.

The list was now approaching the bottom of the yellow, legal-sized, lined paper. I had not thought to number the behaviors when I started the list the previous day. "Jumps and humps anyone who comes to our door; out of control on walks (school bus); barks incessantly at trucks, buses, dogs, any loud sounds." I stared at the paper with Milo's line-by-line indiscretions until they became a blur. I wondered if I had subconsciously decided against numbering, because sometimes it's better not to know.

It was time to take Milo for another walk. I couldn't take him to the dog park. I preferred being assaulted by a bus to being reprimanded by judgmental dog park walkers. I suited myself up for another frigid December walk. I doubled the amount of chicken in the plastic bag in my pocket. I hoped that if I increased the number of times I called his name and rewarded him with chicken, Milo would be less likely to chase after squirrels and buses, dragging me behind him.

"Milo," I said, sticking my chapped, raw fingers into the bag of chicken.

He snapped his head and looked at me with his soulful, and now hopeful, eyes.

"Good boy, Milo," I said, thankful that at least he was food motivated.

I popped a chunk of chicken into his open mouth and led him out the door.

I had to wait only four more days until our appointment at What A Good Dog.

Twelve

In the days leading up to our dog school assessment, Milo began to feel more and more comfortable in our house. We, on the other hand, felt more and more terrorized. My list of questions and concerns about Milo kept growing. I started making it a point never to leave Milo home when I wasn't there. When I needed to do errands, I put him in the back of my car and hurried through each stop so he would not get cold while he waited for me. At home, I tried to lure him with chicken chunks as I went from one room to another. I dropped treats in his mouth when we were all together in the den watching television. I just needed to make it, I told myself repeatedly, until I could grab hold of the What A Good Dog lifeline.

To be honest, during our predawn, below-freezing, tug-of-war walks, I often revisited the idea of putting Milo in my gray Volvo and driving him the ten straight miles back to Main Line Animal Rescue. But each time I pictured him on his bed of rags in his cage, I knew I couldn't and wouldn't do it. Mattie hadn't asked to be killed. And Milo hadn't asked to be born. It wasn't his fault that no one had civilized him in his eighteen months on this planet. So, no, I wasn't going to give Milo up. Not voluntarily. Everyone deserves a chance. Even Milo.

Although the list of Milo's behaviors with which I needed help was getting longer and longer, I told myself I had complete faith that Milo was salvageable. I told myself I was absolutely confident that What A Good Dog could help me with Milo. Once when I was waiting for the result of a medical test, a cognitive therapist told me that I should assume it would turn out okay. He said there was nothing to be gained by predicting that it wouldn't. With that advice in mind, not once did I let my mind wander and consider the possibility that Milo was beyond repair. I told myself there was hope. My instinct to survive, my need to be able to live with both myself *and* with Milo, kept me focused on the likelihood that things would work out with him. In spite of the dog-hell I was living in, I was optimistic that Milo and I and What A Good Dog would be able to join forces and fix this unsustainable mess we were in.

What A Good Dog is owned by Mary Remer, the granddaughter of Hope Montgomery Scott, an internationally known Philadelphia socialite and philanthropist. Scott was the inspiration for the 1939 Broadway play and 1940 movie *The Philadelphia Story*, both starring Katharine Hepburn, as well as the 1956 remake, *High Society*, starring Grace Kelly.

Mary grew up on her grandmother's estate, Ardrossan. The estate consists of hundreds of acres and over forty buildings, including "the big house," Hope Montgomery Scott's forty-five-room mansion. What A Good Dog is located in the basement of the big house, which is otherwise vacant except for a small apartment in the back where Mary lives.

Exactly one week after Bill had brought Milo to our house, Andy, Joseph, Josh, and I got into the car with him and left for our much-anticipated appointment. As we began the twenty-minute drive from our house to What A Good Dog, Milo paced back and forth in the rear compartment of our station wagon. It was the week between Christmas and New Year's, so, thankfully, there wasn't much traffic. There also were no school buses or trucks. After a few minutes, Milo lay down. Each time I turned to check on him, I could see his ears up and alert, his head rotating 180 degrees, side to side, back and forth, as he monitored the passing landscape.

We rode in silence. Andy and the boys tend to be quiet in any situation. I am usually more talkative, but I didn't want to share what was going through my mind. All my hopes for Milo's redemption depended on What A Good Dog. And we were headed into our admissions interview.

We turned off the road and passed through the massive stone pillars above which spanned in wrought iron letters, ARDROSSAN. Tucked back along the road to the big house was an occasional stucco and stone cottage, dark and in disrepair. Frequently, in the local paper, there were notices about hearings for zoning variances at Ardrossan, with developers hoping to maximize the number of McMansions they might be able to fit on what was the last great estate of Philadelphia's Main Line.

After about a half mile, we reached the house. It was very, very big and very, very dark. To the left was a black Ford pickup with a woman in the driver's seat. She stuck her arm out the window and motioned us to park beside her.

As soon as Andy parked and turned off the ignition, Milo stood up in the back. I got out of the car just as the woman slid out of her truck.

She was a husky woman in her forties, wearing no-fashion jeans, dirty tan work boots, and a green, nylon bomber jacket with SKYHAWKS lettered in white across the front.

"I'm Gail," she said, planting her feet apart and rolling back on her heels like a cowboy. She did not offer her hand for a handshake.

"Hi, I'm Anne," I said, smiling in a way I hoped was ingratiating. I really needed this woman's help. Milo and I needed this woman's help. Truth be told, everyone in our family was hoping she would offer us help.

I introduced Andy and the boys. Joseph and Josh had come with us, but Jonathan had stayed home to study for his final exams. Then I went to the back of the car to get Milo. Oddly, he was not barking. He was not prowling. Instead, he was sitting in the back, at attention. He jumped down with no commotion and walked in step with me to Gail.

"This is Milo," I said when we reached her.

"Follow me," she said, not acknowledging Milo.

When she turned her back and began to walk, I looked at Andy and the boys. We all shook our heads and shrugged our shoulders. Then we fell into line and walked single file behind Gail.

We followed her through a door, down a flight of cement steps, and through a maze of damp, musty, unlit hallways lined with rodent traps and neat stacks of mismatched patio furniture.

At the first open doorway we came to, she stopped, flicked on the lights, and motioned us in. In the middle of the large, windowless room, on the gray cement floor, was a larger-than-life painting of a white dog with wings and a halo sitting on a puffy cloud. Open folding chairs ran along all four walls of the room.

"Take a seat," Gail said, pointing to the row of chairs along the wall nearest the doorway.

I sat at one end. Josh and Joseph were next. Andy took a seat in the last chair, and Milo lay down on the floor beside him. Gail grabbed a chair and set it down to face us. Then she sat back and put her right foot on her left knee. I felt as if we had been apprehended for a crime and Gail was our interrogator.

"So you got Milo last week," she said, scanning the row of us as she spoke. It was a statement, not a question.

Timidly, tiredly, we nodded yes. It felt like more than a week since Mattie had been killed. It seemed like years had passed since Milo had come into our lives.

"How's it going with you and Milo?" she asked, nodding at us and raising her eyebrows as if she already knew the answer, as if we had done something wrong, and she was daring us to deny it.

I sat up straight, clutching my list.

"He's not at all what we expected," I said, leaning forward. "He's taken over our house. He attacks us. He's impossible to walk on a leash. Our dog was killed in the driveway by a UPS truck last week."

I blinked my eyes. My voice was quivering. I slumped in my seat and tried to dam the tears I felt rising from within me. I looked at Joseph and Josh who were both staring down at their feet, frozen in place.

"Basically," I continued, "Mattie was a twenty-five-pound, breathing stuffed animal. All she did was sleep and give love and take love. A couple of times a day we let her out. That was it. We loved her so much."

"And?" Gail said, looking glazed with boredom. I was jolted back from beginning another one of the Mattie reveries I had been fighting off since she was killed ten days earlier.

"Well," I said, sitting up straight, again, and taking a deep breath. "I spoke to Bill Smith at Main Line Animal Rescue the day after Mattie died. I thought that the only way I could distract myself from being brought down by Mattie's horrible death would be to get another dog. I told Bill I was looking for a small lapdog who doesn't shed. I wanted another Mattie. Bill kept talking about Milo. When we went to Main Line Animal Rescue, Bill had Milo lying quietly on the grass. Milo seemed so calm we immediately nicknamed him Mellow Milo. After patting him and playing with him, we decided to take him even though he is double the size we wanted. It seemed like we needed him, and he needed us."

I paused to catch my breath. I felt Gail's eyes boring into mine. I turned to look at Andy, Joseph, and Josh. They were staring at me, alarm radiating from their faces. I looked down at Milo. He was resting serenely beside Andy.

The silence in the room was deafening. I wanted to scream. I don't know what prevented me from shrieking and running out of the room, up the cement stairs, out the door, and into the dark oblivion surrounding this big house. I wanted to disappear forever. I was exhausted and sad. I was not up to this task. I could not fulfill my promise to myself not to abandon Milo. I didn't know how to do this.

I looked at Andy and the boys again. Joseph and Josh were shaking their heads at me almost imperceptibly. But I knew my boys. I knew they were admonishing me for going public with my complaints about Milo. In the past week, even though Milo had made our house a frightening hell for everyone, I was the one who had been the most vocal about his negative behaviors. It was not only because I am more of a talker than anyone else in the family, but also because I knew I was the one responsible for Milo. I was responsible for bringing him into our house. Now I was responsible for his rehabilitation and redemption. Even if Andy and the boys *wanted* to help, they didn't have the time. They were rarely home. I was the only thing standing between Milo and a lifetime sentence in a cage at Main Line Animal Rescue. I knew it. Andy and the boys knew it. I looked at them again. In the bowels of this disintegrating estate, they were waiting for me to stand up and present my case for getting Milo help. They were waiting for me to save Milo.

But first, I felt that I must tell Gail the truth.

"He jumps and humps everyone who comes in the door, including us," I said. "And when I pull him off and lock him in his crate, he won't stop barking." I was not looking at my list. The words were forming in my brain, and I was speaking them involuntarily. "One time I decided to just stand still and let him hump me until he got bored and stopped. But I gave out before he did. I went running in the house that day to my bed, crying because he was my dog, and Mattie was dead."

I paused and looked at Gail. She stared back, her face devoid of expression. Apparently, she did not appreciate psychological detail or emotional nuance.

I looked at the clock high up on the wall behind Gail. I had only an hour to make my case and secure Milo's future as well as my own. I sped up my pace.

"I walk him twice a day, up to an hour each time, trying to tire him out. If he sees a squirrel, he drags me to the tree, sometimes across a road or street, knocking me off my feet and pulling me along the ground. He goes wild when buses and trucks go by and when he sees another dog. He has bitten both Josh and Joseph. Milo has us all hiding under the bed."

It wasn't everything. But I wanted to give Gail a chance to say something. I assumed she was going to check Milo out for herself to separate the behaviors alleged by an inexperienced, hysterical dog owner from the behaviors he actually possessed. I looked at my family. They were focused on Gail. I looked at Milo. He hadn't moved since we sat down.

"You probably think I'm nuts," I said to Gail. "Look how good he's been all this time."

"I don't think you're nuts. Not at all," she said, sitting up and uncrossing her legs. "He knows what we're talking about. He's internally stressing. I don't know if you know this, but you're the third family Bill Smith has placed Milo with in eighteen months."

I was so shocked to hear this that I just stared at Gail, my mouth falling open.

Finally, I sputtered, "He seems more like a wolf than a dog." It was the first time this thought had occurred to me.

Gail stared at me. "Just because he's out of control doesn't mean he's a wolf," she said. I turned my gaze from Gail to Milo. He did not look anything like a wolf right now. He looked more like a handsome, peace-loving character in *The Lion King*. I looked back at Gail. Staring into her unforgiving face, I resolved that even if I was right that Milo had some wolf in him, so be it. It was just one more problem for us to cope with. It wasn't his fault. He was what he was. I wanted to help him. If I could.

"Milo's behaving so well now," Gail said, interrupting my thoughts, "because he knows I'm going to tell you to give him back to Bill. Bill knew you were vulnerable, and he wanted to unload a hard-to-place animal. He's done this before. It will be a month before Milo exhibits all his negative behaviors. If you keep him, you'll regret it. Once I let my husband keep a dog I didn't like, and I regretted it every day of that dog's life."

Joseph slid himself onto the floor and inched over to Milo and began stroking him. Josh sidled up to me. Andy dropped his hand and was rubbing Milo behind the ears. My first thought was that I was surprised Gail once had, or even still had, a husband, someone who wanted to live with her. She seemed so resistant to human connection. I felt my heart thumping and thumping and thumping.

I sat back in my chair until the thumping eased. I folded up my list and slipped it into my jacket pocket. Then I stood up and zipped my jacket.

"Thank you," I said to Gail.

I walked over to Milo, took his leash from Andy, and walked toward the door. When I turned back, I saw my pack following closely behind me. Whatever underhanded things Bill had done, whatever dire judgment Gail had made about Milo, part wolf or not, these things were irrelevant. I had come to What A Good Dog for guidance, not a prison sentence. Milo was my dog. I was determined not to give up on him. I was determined to save him.

Thirteen

Leaving Gail in the basement classroom, we walked silently and single file through the maze of unlit hallways and up the cement steps. Gail hurried past us just as Josh, who was bringing up the rear, had stepped outside. She didn't say "Goodbye" or "Have a good evening" or "Good luck." She said nothing. The four of us stood huddled together in the darkness, watching her climb into her truck and speed away.

As soon as she was out of sight, Joseph turned to me.

"Mommy," he said, "why did you tell Gail all those bad things about Milo?"

"Yeah, Mommy," Josh said, "why did you do that?"

I just looked at them, stunned. Since we'd gotten Milo, and as he'd revealed himself to be the aggressive dog that he was, I had been grateful that Andy and the boys had not admonished me or blamed me for the mess we were in. They had been on the front lines. He had bitten them, humped them, and barked so fervently that they could not hear each other speak. But now, instead of being relieved that Gail had given us a Get Out of Jail Free card by telling us to return Milo, Joseph and Josh were upset. In spite of the fact that Milo was dangerous to our physical well-being, they were standing in solidarity with him.

"I told Gail all those things," I finally said, "because I need help. We can't continue the way it's been since we got him, and I don't know what to do. I wasn't trying to label him or judge him. I just wanted her to understand who and what he is so we have a better chance of helping him. I thought Gail would hear what I said and give me advice. I thought she'd help me come up with a plan. I don't want to give Milo back. I don't. That's why I dragged us all out to this creepy place."

We shuffled together to the car and got in. Andy started the ignition but didn't move the car. We sat in silence. Milo's déjà vu of the situation from his past two families had him resting quietly in the back.

"What are you going to do?" Andy said, turning to me. "Gail is obviously not going to be part of the solution in helping Milo."

I shook my head and let out a deep, tired but relieved sigh. At least Gail's dire predictions about Milo had not been a deal-breaker for Andy or the kids.

"Mommy, didn't you say Jane called this afternoon and said we should come over after we met Gail?" Joseph asked.

Joseph was right. Jane, the wife of Andy's colleague at the University of Pennsylvania who had put me in touch with Bill Smith the morning after Mattie was killed, had called a few hours earlier. She wanted to know how things were going with Milo. So I had told her.

"We live five minutes from What A Good Dog. Why don't you come over after your assessment?" she'd said, after listening to the saga of my week with Milo.

Now, sitting in the car in the dark, after our debacle with Gail, I turned to look at Joseph and Josh.

"If we go to Jane's, I don't know what time it will be when we get home," I said. My energy, which sinks with the waning sun, was low.

"Joseph has a point," Andy said. "Jane offered. It's only five minutes from here. What have we got to lose?"

When we got to Jane's, I got out of the car and began to walk toward the house. Halfway there, I heard the door of our car slam behind me. I turned to look.

"Mommy," called Josh, who was standing by the back of the car. "Please don't give Milo back."

I just looked at my boy. This was my boy who had wanted to wait to get Milo out of respect for Mattie's memory. He had agreed to take Milo the next day after seeing Milo looking forlorn in his cage. Then he had been bitten by Milo for playing Invisible Football. Now this boy of mine was begging on Milo's behalf. Doing for Milo what Milo could not do for himself.

As I looked at Josh, I saw Milo stand up in the back of the station wagon, pacing back and forth like a caged lion. The back of the station wagon wasn't big; it barely contained Milo. So he took one step across and swung around, another step and swung again. It looked as if he were warming up to hurl himself through the glass.

"Anne," I heard from the direction of the house.

I turned and saw Jane running toward me. When she reached me, she continued walking to my car, which was rocking back and forth, perfectly synchronized with the force of Milo's body against one window and then the other.

"How'd it go?" Jane said as we approached the car.

I shook my head. "Bad. Really bad. Gail told us that we're the third family Bill's placed Milo with and that we need to give him back. We want to keep him, but he's dangerously out of control. And Gail said it will be a month before he exhibits *all* his bad behaviors. I can't even imagine what they might be, given how bad he's already been."

As we talked, Jane's husband, Rich, came out of the house, leaving their pack of five rescue and pedigree dogs inside. The dogs, who watched from a low-hung window, yapped pleadingly to join us. A single bark from a dog on television jolts Milo to his feet and into a barking frenzy. A chorus of five real ones was the starting gun for which he'd been waiting. He backed up to one side of the station wagon trunk and, bending his rear legs and spreading them to make room for his front paws, he positioned himself for a lunge. And with an accompanying howl, lunge he did. Turning his head aside and thrusting his torso forward, he hit the window broadside with a thud. Again and again and again.

Andy and the boys and I, along with Jane and Rich, stood in a tight circle around the side window of the station wagon watching. Speechless.

"Leash walking isn't enough for Milo," Jane said matter-of-factly, drawing our wide-eyed, gaping faces away from the car toward her. "He needs to run around and work off some energy."

I couldn't bring myself to look back at the car. Judging from the frequency and force of Milo's smacks against the glass and his elongated howls, his high-intensity interval training in the back of the car didn't seem to be depleting his energy level.

"You and Andy must have errands to do around here," Jane said, rubbing her arms for warmth. "There's a great Whole Foods nearby. Better yet, why don't you go into town and have dinner. Leave Milo and the boys here for a couple of hours. I'll give them all a quick bite to eat. Then we'll give Milo a workout here in our fenced yard."

I looked at Josh and Joseph. Both were smiling and nodding, excitedly. Andy shrugged his shoulders and nodded his head. "Why not?" he said.

I was shocked. I hadn't expected Jane to step in.

"Okay," I said, turning toward her. "Thank you so much. I'd appreciate anything you can tell me to help tame him. I need all the help I can get."

We followed Jane to the back of the car and watched her open the door and slide her hand into what truly seemed like the den of a raging lion prowling for his next meal.

"Good boy, Milo," she said when Milo momentarily quieted down, apparently surprised that the door to his prison was finally opening.

"Good boy, Milo," she said, as he jumped down beside her. "Milo," she said.

He looked up at her. "Good boy, Milo," she said, pulling something out of her pants pocket and dropping it into his mouth. "Good boy, Milo."

Andy and I stood and watched as Jane and Milo, followed by Joseph and Josh and Rich, left us in the dark and walked toward the backyard.

"Good boy, Milo," we heard. "Good boy, Milo," Jane said over and over, as she dropped morsels of something into Milo's waiting mouth.

When they were out of sight, Andy and I got back into the car. I felt stunned and tired. Most of all, relieved. Andy turned on the car. We just sat there. Silent.

Gail had shown no compassion for us and our trauma of losing Mattie to the wheel of a UPS truck, only to pick ourselves up and be terrorized by Milo. Even worse, she had shown no compassion for Milo. But now, only minutes later, Jane had thrown me the lifeline I had hoped to get from Gail. She had taken Milo from me to assess him herself. I dropped my head back against the headrest and felt myself settling into an unguarded state of being. Exhaustion overcame me. I was tired. Very, very tired. Physically and emotionally. Most of all, however, lying back against the headrest in the dark car, warm air blowing over me from the heating vents, I felt relief. For the first time since Milo had pranced into our house with Bill Smith, I was not responsible for him or the safety and welfare of anyone and everyone around him. For the first time since our fates became entwined, I was not at the mercy of Milo.

Fourteen

Andy and I drove over to Whole Foods Market. We got out of the car and walked through the automatic sliding doors where we stopped and stared ahead at the crush of shoppers jostling one another under the glaring fluorescent lights. Then we looked at each other and, without saying a word, we turned and retraced our steps out through the entrance and back to the car.

I am an inveterate people watcher. Some days when I am home and alone and feel so depressed that I want to drop to the floor, I get into the car and drive to the Whole Foods Market near our house. I park the car, turn on the radio, sit back, and watch shoppers coming and going. I note their ages, what kinds of cars they drive, what they are wearing, if they are in a hurry or sauntering. On their return, I survey the tops of their bags to glean what I can about their purchases. Always, as I sit camouflaged in my car, I feel as if I am an audience of one at an immersive theater. This time as I sat outside the Whole Foods near Jane's house, I was too tired and too distracted to keep my focus on the shoppers.

Andy, who always runs a sleep deficit, soon dropped his head back against the headrest and was snoring lightly, as golden oldies emanated softly from the radio. I must have been lulled into dozing, too, because suddenly I felt the car moving. I opened my eyes and looked at Andy.

"It's been almost two hours," he said, backing out of the parking space. "We'd better get back."

I sat up and shook my head to wake myself. I needed to be alert. I needed to be prepared to hear what Jane was going to say.

I could feel my heart pounding against my ribs. For all I knew, Milo had bitten not only Joseph and Josh but also Jane and Rich and attacked all five of their dogs. Anything was possible with Milo. I braced myself for the return to an endless shift as Milo's caregiver/guard.

As we approached Jane's corner-lot house, we could see that both the front yard and backyard were lit up with spotlights. We pulled into the driveway, and I lifted my head and looked out my window. My eyes widened as butterflies fluttered inside me. The heavy load within me lightened.

There, on Jane's brown winter lawn, was Milo, ears up, tail up, galloping back and forth between Joseph and Josh, both beaming. Joseph tossed a tennis ball to Josh. Milo ran to Josh. Josh gave Milo a treat. Milo opened his mouth again. Josh put the tennis ball in Milo's mouth. Milo bounded to Joseph with the ball clenched in his teeth. Joseph took the ball and dropped a treat into Milo's mouth. Then Joseph tossed the ball back to Josh.

Andy turned off the ignition. Riveted, we sat and watched from the car. I'd never before found repetition so spellbinding. I felt as if I were in a trance or an alternate universe. Or maybe there was a god, and he or she was rewarding me for taking Milo, and we were all together in heaven. Back on Planet Earth, any one of these scenes or all of them together could have been a commercial for Purina Dog Chow. Andy and I got out of the car and stood at the side of the yard watching.

Jane turned and smiled at us. Joseph waved at us. Josh turned and waved too.

"Let's take your mom and dad to the backyard and show them what else Milo can do," Jane said. "*Milo. Come*," she said, elongating both words.

Milo looked at her, then back at Joseph, then Josh, then back at Jane.

"Yes, good boy. Good come," Jane said, in a singsong voice, reaching into her pocket and pulling out a treat.

Milo ran to Jane.

"Good boy," she said with such excitement in her voice that I wondered if she had ever studied acting.

Milo sat at Jane's feet.

"What a boy, Milo," she said, dropping the treat into his wide-open mouth. Milo chewed and waited for Jane, patiently. So very unbelievably patiently I couldn't believe my eyes.

We followed Joseph and Josh and Jane and Milo around the house to the backyard. Milo pranced beside Jane, his expectant, hopeful gaze tethered to Jane's face.

"Attaboy, Milo," Jane said every dozen or so steps and dropping a treat in his mouth every other time.

As we walked, Jane told us that two of her dogs are ribbon winners in agility. I did not know what "agility" was. She told us that agility is dog gymnastics. She also told us that she was an agility instructor at What A Good Dog.

Spread across Jane's backyard were two wide-plank balance beams, a circular Toys "R" Us plastic tunnel, pairs of tall, metal poles, and orange, plastic cones. Joseph and Josh had hurried ahead of us and already placed themselves at opposite ends of the tunnel.

"Come, Milo," Jane said, tempting Milo toward Joseph with a wave of kibble.

"Milo," Joseph called.

Milo looked at Jane and took the kibble. He looked at Joseph and ran through the tunnel in his direction.

"Good boy, Milo," Joseph said when Milo arrived. "Good boy."

Milo opened his mouth. Joseph dropped in a treat.

"Milo," Josh called from his end of the tunnel.

Immediately, Milo disappeared into the tunnel at Joseph's end and emerged moments later at Josh's end, his tail high and wagging.

"Yes," said Josh, taking his hand out of his jacket pocket and dropping a morsel into Milo's waiting mouth.

I was speechless, dumbfounded. I was more than amazed. I was elated. For the first time since we'd had Milo, he seemed more like a dog than a wild creature.

Jane turned to Andy and me. "You can't imagine how many weeks it takes some dogs to be able to do this," she said, smiling.

She was right. I couldn't imagine. Instinctively I felt proud. I felt as proud of Milo as if he were one of my two-legged boys.

"After you left, I worked with Milo for a bit. There's no question he's a dominant, high-energy dog, *and* he's out of control," Jane said as we watched Joseph and Josh send Milo scurrying back and forth through the tunnel. "But why *wouldn't* he be out of control? No one has ever tried to tame him. I can't give you a guarantee, but I'm not sure he *isn't* salvageable. So I called Gail, and she agreed to send someone to your house for a second opinion."

"Oh, Jane, thank you so much," I said, holding myself back from wrapping my arms around her. "Thank you for all of this. We felt crushed after we left Gail. It seemed as if she had already decided about Milo before we got there."

"Well, you're probably right," Jane said. "Milo's reputation, or more accurately his *ill repute,* had preceded him with Gail. The dog community is pretty tight. Gail heard that Bill was having trouble placing him. I feel responsible for Milo being dumped on you since

I put you in touch with Bill. It never occurred to me he would place a dog like this with an unsuspecting family."

"It isn't your fault, Jane. You really helped me out. I needed a dog right away. Milo was so mellow when we met him the first time. Josh thinks Bill sedated him that day."

"It's hard to know why Milo was so calm when you met him," Jane said. "In any case, I'm glad Milo will have another assessment. It's just too bad that Mary Remer can't see him. But she doesn't get involved in ordinary evaluations. She doesn't have time. She's very much in demand with people who need help with high-level show dogs."

Before we got Mattie, I had read extensively about dog breeds and purposely chose a wheaten terrier. The breed met my needs for a low-maintenance dog. Wheaten terriers are loving and well behaved. I was quickly learning with Milo that my life with Mattie had been at one end of the "Life with Dog bell curve," the idyllic end. With Milo, I felt like I had been dragged over the hump of that bell curve to the farthest point on the other side, the hellish side. I hoped with all my being that Milo and I would be able to inch our way a little bit closer to the Mattie side of the bell curve.

When we got home from Jane's house, I already had a voice mail from What A Good Dog.

"Mary Remer will be at your house tomorrow at five," a woman's voice said.

The Mary Remer, dog woman extraordinaire, was coming to assess Milo. I was hopeful that if anyone could help Milo, it was Mary Remer. Then a sense of doom overcame me. Jane had said that Mary did not do "ordinary evaluations." I worried that Mary's upcoming visit meant that Milo's status had been reclassified from "ordinary" to what? "Extraordinary?" But extraordinary in what way? In his badness? In his complexities? He was out of control, but at Jane's, he had shown that he was also a quick and enthusiastic learner. I took a deep, calming breath. Thc important thing, I reassured myself, was that someone had convinced Mary that Milo was not ordinary. That he was worthy of her very valuable time.

Fifteen

The following day, before I stepped out of bed, my mind calculated the number of hours until five o'clock when Mary Remer would arrive. The number of hours until . . . well, I didn't know until *what*. If I had thought about the until *what*, tried to imagine what was going to happen at five o'clock when Mary arrived, I might have stayed in bed with my head under the pillow. If I had seriously thought about our upcoming evening with Mary, I would have realized that she was not going to walk in the door, pop a Good Dog pill in Milo's mouth, and solve all of my problems. I would have had to consider the possibility that Mary would assess Milo and, like Gail, tell us to return him to Bill Smith. But if I had imagined or thought about this possibility, I would not have been able to rouse myself out of bed.

I got out of bed and did what I had been doing every day for the last ten days. It felt more like a decade since Milo had come to live with us. I dressed, fed Milo his kibble, put on my down jacket, stuffed my pockets with chicken chunks, pulled on my chicken-fragranced, fingerless gloves, leashed Milo, and set out the door and up the street. Milo was now perfect at recognizing his name and locking his gaze with mine. Aside from name recognition, we had not made any progress toward taming our walks. Milo still pulled me after every squirrel, every dog, every bus, and every truck.

I would fall. Get up. Fall. Get dragged. It was the dog-walking version of the Bill Murray movie *Groundhog Day*, in which he lives the same February day over and over and over. But the movie's message is uplifting. Individuals with free will can choose to do good. And, although it may take time, it's the only path to redemption. My dog-walking version of this, on the other hand, had no message. Or, at least, no *uplifting* message. Had I been inclined to cause myself more turmoil, I could have come up with any number of ominous messages, all with the theme, "You are such a loser for getting yourself into this mess." But I knew that Mattie's sudden death had pushed me closer—too close—to the abyss of depression. So I kept my mind focused on the here and now. Focused on the physical toil that was Milo.

I had replaced Mattie so quickly with Milo to keep myself from becoming overwhelmed with depression. But with each new day and every new hour, as I dedicated myself to managing Milo and his needs, my mind had been creating a Doomsday spiral. The negative voice in my head had begun to question and attack me. It told me I was wasting my time trying to salvage Milo. I was doing it only because I had nothing else in my life that was meaningful. That the dog I had hoped would save me from worsening depression was doing just the opposite. I heard the voice and listened, despite knowing it was not true. Over and over, I tried to reassure myself that I did not have to attack myself for rescuing Milo. With that in mind, I managed to override the negative voice and not let it stop me from trying to help him.

When I arrived home after our walk, it occurred to me why I had to work so hard to convince myself that my motive for trying to help Milo was not self-serving. I had been told over and over by my parents that I was self-centered. I recalled one of my earliest memories, when I was three years old. I was standing in the living room of our duplex apartment. Facing me, in a wooden upholstered chair set into the curve of the baby grand piano, was my father.

"Anne, you're going to have to start washing your own clothes," he said, serious and firm. "Your mother is tired of picking up after you. You've got to learn to think of someone besides yourself."

The washing machine was in the basement, and I was scared of going downstairs alone. I didn't know how to work the dials, or even how to reach them. I pictured myself dragging a chair over to the machine to boost me up. I don't remember ever doing a load of clothes. But the idea that I was bad—because I thought only of myself and was a burden to others—persisted.

Obedience was very important in my family. My father worked in a lab at MIT next door to an animal experimentation lab. The summer I was seven, he surprised us with a beagle puppy that the lab didn't need anymore. He was so cute and cuddly. "Itsy Bitsy Teenie Weenie Yellow Polka Dot Bikini" was a song I heard all the time on the radio at our neighbors' house. I immediately named the puppy Teenie. I loved this little dog. He was perfect. I would nestle beside him on the living room rug, rubbing his warm belly and patting his soft square head. Sometimes Teenie rolled over on his back for a full belly rub, making me smile. It felt so good to be close to another living creature. It felt so good to be able to make another living creature happy. I was as happy as I had ever been.

Teenie slept in the kitchen of our duplex apartment, a gate separating him from the green-carpeted dining room. One morning I came running downstairs to say good morning to him and found the gate open and Teenie curled up in the corner of the dining room. Before I could go over to him, my father came into the room, and stepped on a big, wet yellow spot on the rug.

"Bad dog!" my father yelled, stepping toward Teenie.

He scooped him up, put him down by the yellow spot.

"Bad, bad, *bad* dog!" he yelled, hitting Teenie on the nose each time he said *bad*.

Then he picked Teenie up and took him into the kitchen. I stayed in my spot in the dining room, afraid to move.

"Bad dog!" I heard my father yell, again.

I heard the door to the basement bang as my father opened it and it hit the kitchen wall.

"Bad dog," my father said.

The next thing I heard was a thud. Then a tiny yelp. I turned to face the dining room wall as I began to cry. I was so frightened for Teenie. I knew what it was like to anger my father. It was something I tried never to do.

My mother came downstairs. "What's going on?" she asked as she rushed toward the kitchen.

"Teenie thought the green rug was grass and he peed on it," I said.

My mother rushed away from me.

I followed her into the kitchen.

"Get out!" she shouted at me.

I went back to the corner of the dining room and sat down, my head in my hands, tears streaming down my face. I wanted to get Teenie and hug him. I wanted to help him and tell him I loved him.

A few minutes later, my father walked out the back door with Teenie in his arms.

"Your father's taking Teenie to the vet," my mother said, coolly and calmly. "What kind of cereal do you want for breakfast?"

I was worried that Teenie was badly hurt. He'd been thrown down the stairs. I wished so much that he'd known that the green carpet was not grass. I was hopeful that when my father came home that evening, he'd have Teenie.

He did not.

Neither he nor my mother said anything about Teenie that night. They sat down to dinner as if it were a regular day. My father reminded me, as he always did before dinner, "You can listen but don't speak." I was afraid to ask them about my perfect little puppy. I never heard them say his name again. For the rest of the summer when I heard the song "Itsy Bitsy Teenie Weenie Yellow Polka Dot Bikini," I cried. I don't remember when I realized that Teenie was not coming home again. Nor do I remember when I realized that Teenie had died.

I was jolted out of reliving the day my father hurled Teenie down the basement stairs and back into the here and now of sitting in the kitchen with Milo, anxiously awaiting Mary's arrival, when the phone and doorbell rang in unison. As I headed for the door, I realized once again that I could not give up on Milo. I could not send him back to the rescue. I could not voluntarily do that to any living creature. I needed Mary's help.

Sixteen

When I reached the door, Milo was already there jumping up and down and howling. I squeezed between him and the door. I pulled it open, and into the mudroom stepped Mary. Instantly, Milo jumped her and began humping her.

I stood back, aghast. We were not off to a good start.

"Do you have a spray bottle and some apple cider vinegar?" Mary asked, kneeing Milo in the chest and yanking him by the collar to a Sit at her feet.

I looked at Mary, then at Milo, then back at Mary. She did not seem flustered, angry, or upset. Even though he had just been kneed in his chest, Milo did not seem angry or upset either. He sat, looking up at Mary expectantly. I was in awe of this woman. It seemed to be standard operating procedure for her to walk into a house, be attacked by a dog, and bring said dog under control, no muss no fuss. No feelings had been hurt, canine or human. It was clear to me, and it seemed clear to Milo. Mary was the boss. I could not imagine ever being able to take charge of Milo like that.

Mary swiveled the upper half of her body to close the door behind her, still holding Milo down in a Sit by his collar. I remembered the vinegar and stepped back to see what I had in the kitchen cabinet.

"I have white vinegar," I said, showing her the bottle.

"That's too strong. Buy apple cider vinegar, dilute it, and put it in a plastic spray bottle. Fill several and put them in convenient places around the house. When you catch Milo in a bad behavior, spray his face."

I looked down at Milo. He wasn't budging. He was staring up at Mary, his tail and spine locked yardstick straight, like a soldier at roll call.

Mary bent at the neck and looked Milo in the eyes.

"Yesssssss," she said to him in a high-pitched, gleeful voice that seemed incongruous with her shoulders-back authoritarian stance and expressionless face.

Milo swept his Lion King tail from right to left against the floor, once.

I joined Milo and stared at Mary as she took a step back from Milo. Mary was in her early fifties. She was lean but not delicate. The skin of her hands and face were coarse and weathered, and she moved with the self-assured, deliberate, straight-legged gait of a martinet.

From the pocket of her blue quilted jacket, Mary pulled a stick of shrink-wrapped string cheese and peeled off the plastic. She slivered a scrap of cheese with her thumbnail, let it roll into the cup of her hand, and presented it to Milo. He licked it up with grateful enthusiasm and then returned to a blue ribbon, statuesque Sit.

Mary and Milo were just finishing their exchange of greetings, and Milo was still at Mary's feet when Joseph came into the kitchen.

"Mommy, it's—" he said, then paused. "Oh, hi, you're Mary?"

Mary nodded a quick, sharp yes.

"There's a phone call for you," he said, in a quieter, more restrained voice.

"Thank you," Mary said, leaving Milo and stepping over to the wall phone. Milo followed her, his shaggy ears up, his tail swaying.

Mary was facing the wall, her back to us, talking into the phone in a hushed tone. Milo sat beside her so he could rivet his gaze to her face.

"Wear the gray slacks and your new black blouse," I heard her say.

I was intrigued that someone was seeking Mary's sartorial advice. I was also surprised that someone who seemed as tough as Mary would have an opinion about clothes. Which I realized said more about my own judgmental and narrow-minded labeling than it did about Mary.

Mary's phone call displeased Milo. He began barking incessantly. He was no longer sitting in a perfect Sit. He was standing on all four legs. He exhaled deeply, lowering the front of his body toward the floor in a perfect, yet rigid, downward dog. Then he rose up and simultaneously inhaled and yelped. The gasping, rasping sound lifted the hairs on my arms. He reminded me of an athlete who knew how to maximize strength by inhaling when contracting a muscle and exhaling when releasing. I didn't think serious athletes combined exhaling with yelling. It occurred to me that it should be difficult if not impossible to inhale and yelp at the same time. But I watched and listened to Milo do it over and over again.

I needed to do something. A woman who was doing me a favor by coming to my house was being verbally assaulted by Milo as she tried to talk on the phone. An image of him physically assaulting her popped into my mind. Instinctively, I stepped forward, bent down, and grabbed Milo's collar.

Milo looked at me out of the corner of his eye and growled. Without turning away from the wall, without pausing her conversation, Mary shooed me away. Seconds later she placed the receiver in its cradle and turned to face Milo. In less than a second, Milo jumped Mary. A fraction of a second later, Milo humped Mary. Then, in what seemed like one more fraction of a second, Mary picked up her leg and thrust her knee into Milo's chest with the instinctiveness of a healthy reaction to a doctor's reflex test.

"One way to deal with this is management," she said, guiding Milo toward his crate and locking him in. "If you know you're going to be on the phone, and that's a time he acts up, put him in his crate first."

I shook my head. When Bill had given me the crate the day he brought us Milo, he had told us to use the crate as private space for Milo. He had not mentioned anything about using it as a jail. I looked at Milo in his crate. He stood, filling the entire interior space. Crating Milo did not seem to be a perfect solution. Within seconds, he was howling. He was angry, very angry. Perfect solution or not, I was relieved. This was the first time since Milo had been with Jane that I was not responsible for his behavior. I didn't have to dance about ineptly trying to get him under control. I looked at Mary.

"I'm going to a party from here," she said, unzipping her jacket and hanging it across the back of a kitchen chair. "When we're finished, do you mind if I bring in my clothes from the car and change in your bathroom?"

Now I realized this wasn't just a Mary Remer house call. It was a Friday night house call while she was en route to a New Year's Eve party. I was grateful beyond words that Mary had come. I was also surprised that she was thinking and talking about her party as Milo's barking was becoming more frenzied, more frightening. I could not imagine what he would do now if we opened his crate. I did not want to imagine what he would do to punish us for locking him up. But Mary was looking at me as if we were the only two in the room. I was awed by her equanimity.

"Of course, anything you want," I said to Mary in answer to her question. "I really appreciate your fitting us into your schedule."

"Do you have a blanket we can drape over the crate?" Mary asked, indicating for the first time that she had not been oblivious to the sounds emanating from Milo's crate. I ran upstairs, grabbed a comforter, and ran back down and gave it to Mary. The blanket trick worked. I looked at Mary, my eyes popping open, shaking my head in disbelief. This woman was a dog-wizard.

I called Andy and Joseph and Josh into the kitchen and Mary told us all to sit down at the table.

"Don't you wish you went to a school that taught with rewards rather than punishments?" she said to the boys.

"They do," I said, unable to join the boys in their agreeable, rhetorical yes. Fifteen years earlier, when we visited the pre-kindergarten of the Quaker school the boys attended, the admissions director said, "We look for the good in every child." Thirty-two child-years later, we hadn't been disappointed. I was excited to have found a school for Milo with a similar philosophy.

"You should always have treats handy in your pockets," Mary said. "If Milo is lying quietly, tell him he's a good boy and give him a treat. Manage him so he's set up for success, not failure. If he acts out when you're on the phone, put him in the crate and throw a blanket over it before you make or answer a call."

Although we were all nodding yes, I could not imagine hearing the phone ring and jumping up to corral Milo into his crate before I answered. What I could imagine was missing a lot of phone calls or, alternatively, being bitten. But I did not say anything. We didn't get that many calls. Besides, we had voice mail.

From the kitchen, we all followed Mary into the large center hallway and formed a circle. For two hours, Mary worked with Milo and us. We followed Mary's instructions to make him sit, stay, and lie down. With nibs of Mary's string cheese, we lured Milo into each behavior and then rewarded him again when he completed the behavior. It took only a few sets of luring for each new behavior before Milo was responding immediately to our commands.

"Down," said Andy.

When Milo was down, Andy gave him the cheese. Then Andy said, "Stay."

"Do that again," Mary told Andy. "Then, when he's doing his Stay, look away from him. See how long he stays when you break your gaze with him."

It was absolutely phenomenal. Soon, Milo was sitting in a Stay at Andy's feet, at my feet, for up to a minute, just waiting. Just waiting *patiently* for a minuscule sliver of string cheese. Even though the amount of cheese we gave Milo was tiny, he caught on so quickly to everything Mary dreamed up that we went through several sticks of cheese. I had not felt this happy, this hopeful, since before Mattie was killed. In the time we had been in the center hallway, Milo had transformed from a terrorizing dog into the Disney dog Bill Smith had promised.

Finally, Andy, Joseph, Josh, and I could not bear to thumbnail another bit of cheese with our raw fingers. Enough was enough. We came, we saw, we conquered. Now we were exhausted and ready to quit.

"Good boy," Mary said, rewarding Milo one more time.

She stepped closer toward us, decreasing the size of our circle, and began to speak to us. But we could not hear her. We were too distracted because Milo was not happy. He wanted to continue with his education. First, he sat beside Mary and barked at her. When she ignored him, he began to hump her.

My heart sank.

"This behavior calls for a time-out," Mary said, taking Milo by the collar and putting him in the kitchen and shutting the door. We stood with Mary outside the door. After a minute, Milo's barking stopped.

Mary turned to me. "Where does Milo sleep at night?"

"At the bottom of our bed," I said.

"No. He cannot do that. Maybe someday. Maybe. Maybe not. But not now," Mary said. "He needs to be continuously reminded that he is not your equal. He can sleep on a dog bed on the floor in your room if you want. Or in his crate. But not in your bed."

I grimaced. Having Mattie sleeping by my feet had been one of the joys of having a dog. It was soothing to me to feel her warm body through the blanket. It was soothing for me to feel Milo's warm body too. But I wanted to succeed with Milo. I would do whatever Mary said.

We stood a few more moments in the hall in silence. All was quiet in the kitchen. Mary looked at us and smiled.

"Let's go in the kitchen," she said.

Joseph opened the door and saw Milo eating a stick of string cheese he had found in the pocket of Mary's jacket that was draped over the kitchen chair. Joseph reached down to take the cheese away from Milo. Milo bit Joseph's hand. We all stared at the indentations Milo's two upper fangs had left on Joseph's hand. We looked at Mary.

Mary did not shake her head at this disappointing turn of events. Nor did she roll her eyes at us to indicate Milo was really, truly a wolf in very handsome dog's clothing. She showed absolutely no sign that Milo was doomed.

"Milo really wants to be part of your family," she said, turning to us.

I just stared at her. I was trying to figure out how she had come to this conclusion. I was trying to remember our two hours in the hall. I was trying to remember if, at any point, Milo had somehow revealed to Mary his profound affinity for us. Had Milo taken Mary aside and told her this? And what was I going to tell the pediatrician this time? I hoped he had a "Don't ask, don't tell" philosophy. I looked at Mary and shook my head.

"There's no question," Mary said in a calm, even voice. "Milo's biting Joseph isn't one of the top ten good dog behaviors."

"Do you think he's salvageable?" I asked, not sure I wanted to hear her answer.

"What I can tell you," Mary said, "is that he's an out-of-control, high-energy dog. Try to hang on with him for a month. Call me if you have any problems or questions before class begins in two weeks. At any rate, call me the day before the first class."

I smiled and thanked her. Mary went into the bathroom and emerged in black slacks and a sleeveless black, form-fitting top. She put on her blue quilted jacket and walked out the door. I watched her back up her blue BMW convertible and speed away.

Indeed, as I had suspected, Mary Remer had not come to our house with a Good Dog pill. Nevertheless, for two solid hours Milo *had* been a good dog. It wasn't a lot, considering that afterward he had bitten Joseph. Bitten him again. Still, the two hours Milo *had* been good was not *nothing*. He had shown that, with the right management, he might be redeemable.

After Mary drove away, everyone left the kitchen except for Milo and me. I sat down at the kitchen table and began to review the events of the evening, beginning with Milo jumping and humping Mary when she first walked in the door. Then my mind began rolling through the scenes in the hallway of Milo sitting, lying down, and staying.

I felt something at my feet. Milo had followed me to the table and was lying on the floor beside me. I patted him. He lowered his head to the floor. I bent down and patted his golden coat some more.

"Good boy," I said. "Good boy."

Then I pulled a leftover stick of string cheese from my pocket and thumbnailed a few slivers.

"Good boy, Milo," I said, putting the cheese in front of his nose. "Good boy."

He lifted his head and pulled the morsel out of my hand with his tongue.

"Good boy," I said again, offering another morsel of cheese.

Milo took the cheese, swallowed, and looked up at me.

A feeling of lightness filled me. I much prefer rewarding to punishing. And rewarding Milo, as Mary had said, just for being calm and quiet, felt good. Being nice to Milo felt good.

It was a start.

Seventeen

I have tried more than twenty antidepressants for my treatment-resistant depression. None of these medications mitigated my overwhelming sense of melancholia. Aside from the actual time I spent nurturing my children, the only thing that alleviated my emotional and physical heaviness, my sense of hopelessness and despair, were vigorous workouts. Sometimes the workouts helped more, sometimes less. Any relief, no matter how minimal or fleeting, was better than nothing.

Up until the month before Mattie was killed, after dropping the boys at school, I swam a mile at the Y next door to their school before going home and sitting down at my desk. By early afternoon, I was listless and depleted. I wanted to slide off my chair, under the desk, and curl into a ball. Instead, I went into our basement and worked out on an exercise bike. When I finished, I felt invigorated and able to greet my kids with a smile and to listen to what they had to say when I picked them up at school.

Unfortunately, for some months, my shoulder had become increasingly painful during my swims. An orthopedic surgeon told me I needed to stop swimming and do physical therapy for my rotator cuff. If it didn't heal on its own, I would need surgery. In the meantime, I had to give up swimming.

After we got Milo, I realized that having to give up my morning swim was not all bad. Instead of swimming I was now walking

Milo in a grassy, weed-infested field near the boys' school. With an abundance of community parks and woods, there was no reason anyone would come to this field for a walk. Except Milo and me.

No doubt, this field would not have been Milo's first choice for a walk. For Milo, any place would be better for a walk than this field. Not only were there no people, but also no dogs, no trees, no squirrels, no birds, and, of course, no school buses or cars. There was nothing even remotely tempting for Milo to make a mad-dash chase. Which is exactly why we went to this field for our walks. We went once in the morning and then again in the afternoon. It was boring, but it was safe. And since Milo's welfare depended on my being ambulatory, I was doing us both a favor by choosing the unremarkable field over a very remarkable street. To help with the tedium, I wore a headset and listened to NPR. Periodically, I commanded Milo into a Sit, Stay, or Down, rewarding him each time. If Milo was ever disappointed to be walking in the secluded, frozen field, he didn't show it. He scurried along with his nose to the ground, ever hopeful, no doubt, of sniffing out something worth chasing.

As tedious as it was for me to spend an hour traversing the deserted field with Milo, the morning walks had a positive aspect. They gave me a modicum of continuity and stability by keeping me on a similar schedule as when I had been swimming. Walking Milo filled what would otherwise have been a gaping hole in my day. Additionally, I was moving my limbs and breathing in the invigorating cold air. Now that we were in the field, and Milo was not dragging me after squirrels, people, dogs, or buses, my heart never reached anything near its maximum workout level. But something, anything, was better than nothing.

If I had not had Milo, if Mattie had not been killed, I doubt I would have thought about trying to lift my mood by walking in the morning. If I had, I doubt even more that I would have actually done it. I don't like walking. I don't like communing with nature. I don't like walking empty sidewalks.

But now I *did* have Milo. Mattie *had* been killed. It wasn't a choice. I had to walk Milo for an hour each morning. My instinct that I needed another dog ASAP after Mattie was killed had not been completely misguided. I did need something to distract me from my grief. I also needed something to distract me from my torn rotator cuff and my inability to swim. Something to get me out and about and moving around. At least a bit.

Drum roll. Trumpets. Enter, Stage Center: Milo.

Eighteen

I am proof that nurturing is an instinct. For me, it feels like something genetic from a distant ancestor, as it is certainly not something I inherited or learned from my parents. My parents systematically dismantled any sense of self. What I liked or what I was interested in was of no importance to them. It was not until I moved away from my parents that I realized that how they made me feel was not normal.

When I was sixteen, my mother sent me to Israel to work on a kibbutz as part of a program sponsored by Histadrut to get American kids to move to Israel when they became young adults. I didn't want to go to Israel for the summer. I was terrified of being homesick. I went because I had no choice. I went to please my mother.

My mother's goal, however, in sending me to Israel was not for me to ultimately move there, but to continue my indoctrination of all things Jewish and to ensure that I found myself a Jewish husband. The more Jewish I felt, the more likely I would be to marry a Jewish man. She'd been warning me for as long as I could remember, "If you don't marry someone Jewish, I'll disown you." As a child, I didn't know exactly what "disown" meant, but whenever she said it, I imagined myself floating alone in a dark outer space.

My mother's edict that I marry a Jewish man had nothing to do with me or my happiness. It was all about her and her ego. She wanted the world to see that she had raised me right. She had raised me to marry a Jewish man. She would not be one of the many mothers she told me about who had let their daughters date non-Jewish boys, only to be heartbroken and ashamed when they married one. No, my mother was going to get what she wanted. A Jewish son-in-law.

I was placed on a kibbutz along with four other American kids. It was 1970. None of the kibbutzniks spoke English. I had gone to an afternoon Hebrew school my entire life, so I knew a modicum of conversational Hebrew. Immediately, adults and kids were asking me to translate. I quickly became friends with the kibbutznik children. When we weren't out in the fields working, they took me on trips to nearby cities, or we just hung out together on the porch of our house. I felt as if I belonged. I felt validated for being me. I even had a kibbutznik boyfriend. Oded was a handsome boy of few words, much respected by his peers. He dreamed of becoming a fighter pilot in the Israeli army. I loved spending time with Oded and the other kibbutznik kids. I loved going with him to visit his parents. I loved sharing stories with him. I didn't realize it, but over the ten weeks I was on the kibbutz, I had begun to find the real me.

Of course, I'd not been looking for the real me. I didn't know that the me I had been for sixteen years was only a shadow of the real me. Back then, I did not realize that I was downtrodden or depressed. I did not realize that the dictates of my mother, her put-downs and treatment of me, were outright abusive and not at all normal. I did not realize that, for the first time in my life, in Israel, I was blossoming into who I was meant to be. I was writing every night in a journal, something I had never done before. I was meeting new people, people who thought I was as interesting as I thought they were. I was so happy. I did not know enough to compare my ebullient, curious state of mind on the kibbutz with my muted, fearful, restrained state of mind at home.

At the end of the summer, my parents picked me up at Logan Airport in Boston, and together we drove the two hours to our house on Cape Cod. I wasn't tired at all. I didn't feel jet-lagged. I was bubbling with stories. Not remembering the house rule, not remembering "listen but don't speak," I burst with words and gushed with emotions. Happy, joyous, sixteen-year-old-in-love emotions, and stories about returning to Israel and the kibbutz and Oded in ten countable months. I was so excited that it wasn't until later that I realized neither parent had said a word. Not one single word.

My first day home, I went grocery shopping with my mother at the A&P. When we walked through the sliding glass doors into the fruit and vegetable section of the air-conditioned store, I immediately spotted a shrink-wrapped Styrofoam tray of grapes. I picked it up and, chuckling, I said to my mother, "It's so funny to see just one bunch of grapes. We used to go and steal bucketloads of grapes from the Arab fields near the kibbutz."

When I finished speaking, she walked away without saying a word. It wasn't because she was appalled that we stole from Arabs. She hated Arabs. She could not stand seeing me happy and on my way toward independence. All I remember after that episode in the fruit section of the A&P is lying in my bed, sobbing into my pillow. I sobbed for the entire two weeks between my return from Israel and the beginning of my senior year in high school.

I cried in my room upstairs, while below, family life went on. Neither parent came in to see me or say anything. But my plan to go back to Israel motivated me to get back on my feet and go to school the Tuesday after Labor Day. Every week, I wrote to Oded in Hebrew on the delicate blue US airmail paper that folded neatly into a self-adhesive envelope. And I made neat piles of his green Israel-issued airmail paper on my night table.

I counted down the months until I would graduate from high school and be on my way back to Israel for the summer. In the meantime, as long as I did what my parents wanted me to do, they ignored me. I kept quiet at dinner. I did my homework. I didn't mention Israel. They had not said I *couldn't* return there the following summer. So it seemed to me that going back was okay with them.

One night, a few months after I got back from Israel, I was sitting on my bed, leaning against the headboard with my knees bent and my legs functioning as a table, doing my homework, when my father appeared in my doorway, startling me.

"Your mother just told me you aren't taking math this year. If you don't make up for this, your life won't be worth living. This summer you'll take calculus in summer school. And if you want us to pay for college, you'll go to engineering school next year and major in chemical engineering."

"Dad, I'm going back to Israel next summer."

His ice-blue eyes glared at me.

My father isn't someone you argue with. So I was surprised to hear myself saying, "Dad, I've never gotten above a C in math."

"Your mother and I know better than you. You're not going back to Israel. You're taking calculus."

I was heartbroken. He had shattered one of only two dreams I had ever had in my life. The first dream was to return to Israel. The only other dream I had left was that someday I would accomplish enough of the things my parents set out for me to do that they would finally love and accept me. I truly loved and respected my parents. I wanted to do whatever I could, at any cost, to get them to love and respect me back.

I didn't go back to Israel the following summer or for years later. I took calculus instead. And I majored in chemical engineering in college. At the beginning of each semester, I'd go to the library, open a textbook, and say to myself, "You can do this." But by the middle of the first page, my mind was numb.

Once, in a new math course, I leaned over to the boy sitting next to me and said, "What's that squiggle he keeps drawing on the board?"

The boy looked at me, his eyes popping out of his head, and asked, "You don't know what a partial derivative is?"

I was determined not to give up. I was determined to get through the program and please my parents.

At the end of my senior year in college, the day final grades were released, I anxiously went to the registrar's office to see if I'd passed my courses and would be able to graduate. I was excited beyond belief when I saw that I had, and I couldn't wait to tell my parents.

I ran to the nearest phone booth, slipped a dime into the slot, and called my father. "Dad, I did it. I'm graduating. I am a chemical engineer."

Uncharacteristically, he chuckled. Then he said, "Now I can write that article for *Science* about teaching a monkey to be a chemical engineer."

I felt like he'd kicked me in the stomach. I fell back against the wall of the phone booth to keep myself from folding onto the grimy metal floor.

Once, I had quietly told my father I didn't like studying chemical engineering.

"If you don't like it, it means it's good for you," he said with a smirk.

"Then I must be the healthiest person alive," I answered.

It always seemed odd that my father had taken a sudden interest in me in high school and was concerned enough about my future to take time away from his work to redirect my education. Decades later, I realized that, just as my mother had set my father on me when I was three years old for being self-centered and not picking up my clothes, so, too, had she sent him to my room when I was sixteen to inform me about my future as a chemical engineer. She didn't want me returning to Israel. She didn't want me living across the globe where she would not be able to control me.

My self-worth was destroyed by the combination of my parents' harshness and their dictating my life. As a parent, I came to believe it was of the utmost importance that my children not only learn who they were and what interested them, but also that they develop the self-reliance to pursue these passions. I wanted them to have the confidence to take a chance and not be devastated if they failed. "What's the worst that could happen?" was one of the questions I asked when the boys were afraid to reach for something they thought was beyond them.

I was determined to help my children find their passions and learn how to pursue them. I would not be dictatorial or controlling as my parents had been with me, instead urging my boys to do whatever it was that interested them. Whether it was dinosaurs, Transformers, rocks, baseball, or pets, I went full force in encouraging them. Anything they delved into was a chance for them to learn how to find their places in the world.

Nineteen

When I envisioned being a good mother, I had not really thought about what the tangible results would look like. Soon into this endeavor, all three of my boys seemed to be thriving. It's not only that they got good grades. I also regularly received "Special Reports" in the mail about one or another of my sons from their school. The "Special Reports" were not part of report cards or formal assessments. I had heard other parents mention them with much consternation as reports detailing some unacceptable behavior of their children. However, the ones I received were always about something my boys did in class that was above and beyond what was ordinarily expected. It was not about their academic achievements, which were always at the top of the class. It was usually about a kind deed they quietly did for a classmate who was struggling at home or at school. A tense classroom situation between students that they stepped in and diffused. Leadership that they exhibited in a low-key, even humorous manner. I was always surprised when I opened my mailbox and found one of these reports. I was surprised not only that I received them regularly, if somewhat randomly, but also that I received them for all three of my very different sons. I did not feel that there was one right way for them to be. I did not want to force them to be anything except what *they* wanted to be. "You can be whatever you want, as long as you are honest, responsible, and able to support yourself in whatever lifestyle you choose."

My determination to help my children find their passions morphed into a resolve to help myself in the same way. I also realized that to be the kind of mother I hoped to be, I needed to build self-respect and develop my own interests just as I hoped my boys would do.

I had worked for two years as a chemist after receiving my chemical engineering degree. Not surprisingly, I didn't like manipulating equations Monday through Friday from nine until five any more than I had in college. Next, I got an MBA at the University of Chicago, hoping that marketing would be more to my liking. It was, but not by much. I worked as a marketing consultant in Boston. I struggled to keep my eyes open and my mind alert as I went from one spreadsheet to another, from one profit and loss statement to the next.

After a few years, we had to move from Boston to Philadelphia for Andy's job. I decided to stop working until I could figure out what it was that I wanted to do. I didn't want to do anything. Nothing seemed interesting to me. Everyone around me seemed passionate about what they did. With pencil and paper in hand, Andy was happy for hours manipulating equations. One of my new friends taught autistic children, and though the school superintendent wanted to promote her into an administrative job, she didn't want to give up the work in the classroom that she loved. Another friend, a corporate lawyer, was fascinated with the puzzle of piecing together financial deals. A third made teddy bears and had converted her dining room into an aviary for stray birds.

All I liked to do was watch people and imagine their lives. I had done it my entire life. I watched people in cafeterias, airports, supermarkets, and waiting rooms. At Back to School Night, I didn't listen to what the teacher was saying about the curriculum. Instead, I imagined her in her living room, in college, at a party. Would we have been friends in college? Would I like her life? When the exterminator who sprays our house once a month stood in the kitchen chatting about the weather, I tried to picture his apartment and how he dressed when he wasn't in his green uniform.

Watching people and thinking about them was the only thing I liked to do. It didn't seem like a career goal or even a path. Then I read Ann Beattie's novel *Picturing Will.* The protagonist, a photographer, wanders in and out of parties, homes, and lives taking pictures. *That's what I want to do*, I thought, excitedly. *Be an official fly on the wall.* I enrolled in a two-year photography program at the Community College of Philadelphia. I loved it. Mostly. Well, partly. I loved the assignments requiring us to photograph people on the street or take formal portraits in the studio. I loved getting to know my subjects as I shot through a roll of film.

Each of the people I photographed and caught in the act of their daily routine and memorialized in an eight-by-ten-inch image seemed special to me. They were people doing their jobs, doing their best. Everyone was trying. Everyone was hoping. In one way or another, for one thing or another.

I was hopeful that I was on the right track. I loved presenting people with their photographs. As I progressed from one class to the next, I found I hated the mechanics of the camera. Agonizing over shutter speeds and apertures distracted me from what people were saying. I also didn't like spending time in the darkroom fiddling with exposure times and dipping my fingers in chemical baths. After two years, when one of my well-meaning classmates said, "You should spend more time in the darkroom," I knew photography was not for me. I had spent enough years doing what I "should" do. I had spent too much time in my life being miserable as I worked toward a chemical engineering degree, a business degree, hoping that once I got the degrees, my life would improve. But it hadn't. So when I realized that cameras and darkrooms were not for me, I knew I needed to find something else.

Almost immediately, it came to me. I wanted to learn to write so I could write stories about people. I enrolled in an adult education writing course at the University of Pennsylvania. I enrolled in another. I began writing "The Homefront" column for a weekly newspaper. I wrote about public schools versus private schools, a mailman, a school bus driver, suburban racism, Mattie, soccer, and even a love letter to Andy for a Valentine's Day issue. I loved the challenge of coming up with topics, week after week. I enjoyed researching and interviewing. Shortly before each deadline, I enjoyed the adrenaline rush as I pieced together the beginning, middle, and end of my story. The day the paper appeared on the stands, it was exhilarating to open it up, turn to "The Homefront," and see the ideas and thoughts that had been floating in my head for a week, all there in black and white below my name. Also, I loved friends and acquaintances talking to me about my stories. What they agreed with. What they didn't agree with. I liked being part of a conversation with people who, unlike my parents, believed I had something to say.

After two years, at the age of forty-four, I enrolled in the MFA program in creative writing at the New School for Social Research. I loved the curriculum, the teachers, and the students. I was interested in what they said and wrote. My classmates and teachers seemed interested in what I said and wrote.

I was so excited that, shortly after I began the program, when I saw my father, I forgot not to speak. I forgot to be scared. Instead, I began to tell him about my classes and about the faculty, which included many famous writers. He listened to me gush for a few minutes. When I paused to take a breath, he spoke before I could continue.

"I know what the problem was," he said. "I know why you didn't like chemical engineering. It's because you didn't have good teachers."

I just stared at him, my mouth agape. He didn't get it. He liked manipulating equations and scientific formulas. He didn't understand that I disliked it. My father could not step outside of himself and see me. He could not hear what I was telling him about myself.

But I could hear myself. I had learned to listen to myself. To validate what I was feeling rather than to dismiss or judge it. I liked meeting people. I liked talking to people. I liked hearing the stories about how they navigated their lives. How they coped with adversity. How they celebrated their victories. I liked writing people's stories and shining a light on them so others could see them too. Just as I found it gratifying to validate my children, so, too, did I find it gratifying to validate the strivings of other people. I set up shop as a freelance writer after I received my MFA. I was finally finding my way.

My parents never congratulated me on receiving an MFA. A month after graduation, I sent my parents a copy of my first published piece. A week passed. I didn't hear from them. I called and asked if they had read it.

"I'll read something you write when you win a Pulitzer," my father said.

My mother answered the same question with silence.

Twenty

Two days after Mary Remer's visit to our house to evaluate Milo, winter vacation ended. Jonathan returned to Harvard. Josh and Joseph went back to school. Andy left for work. Home alone for the first time since Mattie had been killed, I went upstairs to my desk to work on a freelance story that was due in a week. It was not Mattie who followed me there, of course, but Milo. When I sat down and clicked on my computer, he was not happy. I knew this because he stood beside me and barked incessantly. I picked up a spray bottle mixture of apple cider vinegar and water on my desk and I sprayed him just as Mary had shown me. Milo crouched and growled. I jumped back. He lunged, missing me by a fraction of an inch.

Satisfied that he had made his point, after lunging at me, he took a few steps back. I sat back down at my desk and began tapping on the keyboard. Milo barked again. I wanted to cry. I do not like noise or disharmony. I did not want Milo to bite me. I could not think of what to do to appease him except to literally feed the beast. I knew it was wrong. I knew I was encouraging, even teaching, the absolute wrong behaviors. Even law enforcement agencies sometimes pay a ransom to rescue a hostage. I envisioned myself as a hostage and dropped a stream of treats down Milo's throat. After his windfall of treats, he lay down at my feet and went to sleep.

I sneaked out of the room and hurried about throwing out the spray bottles of vinegar I'd placed all over the house. I valued Mary's expertise. But after being lunged at by Milo for spraying him, I knew I couldn't risk my safety by trying to control him this way. Remembering that Mary had also said to reward Milo with treats whenever I found him lying quietly, or just not being bad, I replaced the vinegar bottles with bags of treats. I loved positive reinforcement. I loved being kind to Milo and encouraging his good behaviors. I found myself buoyed each time I stopped and rewarded him for not being bad. It was uplifting. It gave me a moment here, a moment there, of relief. Each time I rewarded him for good behavior, I hoped it was the beginning of our baby-stepping together along the Life with Dog bell curve.

Perseverance is one of the only positive things I took away from my challenging upbringing. I never give up. I keep putting one foot in front of the other until I accomplish my goal. To do otherwise was not an option because it would incur my parents' wrath. It was this mindset that had gotten me a chemical engineering degree. Similarly, I remained committed to the plan Mary Remer had proposed, that I stick it out with Milo for at least a month. I began the fourteen-day countdown until obedience school began.

Each passing day was a struggle. A chaotic, exhausting, terrorizing struggle. I told myself not to judge. I told myself not to feel hopeless. I told myself that we were in a holding pattern. All I needed to do was keep myself and everyone around me and Milo unscathed until the first day of school when I could grab onto the lifeline that was Mary and What A Good Dog.

During my two-week countdown, a carpenter was working at our house. He was a large man in his mid-twenties, who wore tan, steel-toed work boots, hunted, and had a German shepherd at home. He was a man who exuded confidence. Milo followed him quietly from room to room, ears up, tail up, rubbing up against the carpenter's jeans, trying to nuzzle at every opportunity. It was clear to me that what Milo wanted, what Milo needed, was a man whose every step was solid and self-assured. A man whose very being commanded respect. Not a middle-aged woman who wanted nothing more from her dog than to give love and take love. The week before the beginning of dog school, I asked the carpenter if he would like to take Milo.

"No," he said, simple and to the point, not needing even a moment to think.

I had tried. For Milo and for me. I really did want to help Milo. I really did want him to have a nice life. Preferably not with me. As I guided him away from the carpenter, I was glad Milo had not understood my question or the carpenter's answer.

My attempt to give him to the carpenter made it clear to me that even though I cared about Milo, I did not love him. Perhaps it was a classic case of Stockholm syndrome, in which a hostage feels deep sympathy for his captor and forms a deep bond. Even though I felt this bond, I knew I did not love him.

The day before dog school began, with great relief, I called Mary as she had told me to do.

"His barking has gotten worse with buses and trucks, and now he's also barking at cars. His aggressiveness when he sees other dogs seems worse too. I don't want to think of what he'll do tomorrow in a room filled with them," I told Mary when she asked for an update.

"When you get to Ardrossan, wait in the car," she said without hesitating.

I was reassured that my updates about Milo did not seem to worry her.

"The other dogs and their moms will be waiting on the grass nearby. I'll get them all inside, and then I'll come out for Milo. I have a full bag of tricks. If Milo can't handle the class, I'll go through my bag and find another one to try on him. But meanwhile, if I ask you to leave, I don't want . . ."

I waited for Mary to finish her sentence. But she didn't. With her shoulders-back, head-high stature and well-articulated, unpadded sentences, her silence came as a surprise to me.

Then I realized that, as confident and forthright and comfortable as she was with dogs, perhaps she was not as comfortable handling the emotions and behavior of dog *owners*.

"You don't want me to be embarrassed if you ask me to leave," I said, tentatively, quietly, in case my logic about Mary's unfinished sentence was wrong.

"Exactly," she said, sounding relieved.

"I won't," I said. "I realize this is about Milo, not about me. I just want to do what I can to help him."

"Okay, good," Mary said. "I just wanted to give you a heads-up that I might have to send you and Milo out of the room, and not to take it personally."

"I appreciate your concern, Mary."

"Okay, and don't forget to bring lots and lots of really, really good treats. I suggest going to the deli counter and getting inch-thick, cubed sirloin or other cuts or types of meat. Milo is very food motivated."

When we hung up, I leaned my head against the wall. Mary's confident commitment to Milo bolstered me. It was a relief to know that his fate hadn't been entrusted to me alone. I was even a bit excited about starting What A Good Dog. Someone had once suggested I take Mattie to dog school. We went to one class and quit. I didn't like it. I wasn't interested in controlling Mattie, in teaching her behaviors and tricks. She was perfect for me, just the way she was. But with Milo, I was intrigued by the notion that we might be able to make this wild animal into a nonthreatening pet.

I lifted my head up from the wall and turned around. I looked down and saw Milo in his plush brown dog bed, curled on his side in a fetal position, his four oversized, furry paws meshed together near his belly. Never could he cocoon like this at Main Line Animal Rescue. I imagined his frayed nerves healing. As I sat down and watched him, a soothing contentedness spread through me. It wasn't love, but it felt good.

After hanging up with Mary, I headed to the supermarket and pulled my number at the deli counter. I was number ten behind people racing from work to buy dinner to take home. No one in my family was a fan of deli meat, so I had never stood in a line at a deli counter before. But I wanted Milo's school experience to be a positive one. When my number was finally called, I handed over my ticket.

"I'd like inch-thick slabs of lean roast beef, turkey breast, and honey-cured ham," I said, repeating what Mary had told me to get.

I typically bought prepackaged meat. I didn't know much about cuts of meat or custom deli counter products. Although Mary said to get one-inch cubes, I was planning to cut the slabs into cubes myself. Even with my limited knowledge of meats, it seemed that requesting slabs would draw less attention than requesting cubes. My goal was to get what I needed and get out with as little fanfare as possible.

"Ma'am, are you sure that's what you want?" the man behind the counter said.

"Uh-huh," I said, nodding.

"Do you know what that is going to look like? Because I can show you a sample," he said, not moving.

"No, that's okay, but thank you," I said.

"Just a minute," he said, holding up one finger. "Let me get my manager."

This was exactly what I had been hoping to avoid. I wished I were a turtle so I could pull my head into my shell and make believe I was not here. I thought of hurrying out of the store. But too much was at stake with these meats. I stood at the glass counter and waited, cringing but resolute.

The manager appeared with his employee and the two of them smiled at me.

"Ma'am," said the manager. "I understand you would like some one-inch slabs of meat."

I nodded.

"We're happy to give you any cut you want, but no one has ever requested one inch of anything."

Shopping at Staples for my children's school supplies, even in the mad rush of September, was less arduous than this. I had wanted to avoid explaining my need for inch-thick, eight-dollar-per-pound meats. I did not want to become an upper-middle-class, suburban-grocery legend. But I was weakening under this unexpected pressure.

"I want it for my dog," I said, unable to keep myself from wincing.

The two men stared at me. Neither one said a word.

I needed to fill the silence. I needed to justify myself to these men. I needed to make one last effort to maintain a modicum of dignity and keep myself from evolving into the subject of a tale regaled by one employee to the next, shift after shift, year after year.

"My dog has problems, and I'm trying to tame him," I said, my voice rising as if I were asking a question. As if I were asking permission.

The two men turned from me to each other. I couldn't tell if they were communicating with subtle facial expressions. In any event, I was relieved that they had nothing more to say. At least not to me. I was thankful that the customer is always right.

Twenty-One

The day of our first class at What A Good Dog finally arrived. I felt as if I had been waiting for this day for much longer than two weeks. Living with Milo, the minutes dragged on while the days flew by. I felt as if I'd had Milo forever. Every moment of my day, every cell of my body was focused on Milo. When I was not wrestling with him on walks or unsuccessfully ignoring a barking frenzy I could not mollify, I was giving him treats for lying quietly, for not being a dangerous nuisance. I really hoped he was not damaged beyond repair. I had become enmeshed with this beautiful, out-of-control dog.

On the drive to What A Good Dog, Milo barked and howled as usual. I followed the long road toward the parking lot on the side of the big house and the basement classroom. The parking lot looked like a Volvo dealership. Eleven of the fourteen cars glistening in the noonday sun were late-model Volvos. A gaggle of blonde moms, all dressed in Lululemon leggings and hoodies, stood on the nearby grass with their optimally bred, blonde labradoodles, goldendoodles, and cockapoos. Some of the women stood alone. Others stood in pairs, their dogs by their sides.

I parked my mud-splattered, ten-year-old Volvo across the parking lot from the grass and rested my head against the headrest. I let the sun streaming through the windshield warm and soothe me. Suddenly, I felt a heavy thud and heard a bone-chilling howl.

Milo had seen the dogs on the grass and was hurling himself into the back window, hoping to join them. A chorus of excited barks rose from the golden dogs on the grass. Pulling at their leashes, they had formed a straight line and were staring up at Milo. I wanted to slink down in my seat under the steering wheel and disappear.

Mary and an assistant appeared together at the center of the parking lot. The enthusiastic choir on the grass came to a halt. Milo's frenzied solo baritone resonated.

"Okay, everyone," Mary called in a strong, deep voice. "Lead your dogs in a controlled manner into the classroom."

A jumble of moms and dogs funneled up from the grass to the parking lot toward Mary and onward into the basement of the big house. They were led by four goldendoodles, who like the cool clique at middle school, had already banded together up front. Like a drill sergeant studying her new recruits, Mary stood stick-straight with pen and clipboard in hand, watching each new student and mom scurry past her.

When all the students had disappeared into the building, Mary began to walk to my car where Milo was becoming even more vocal about his being ostracized from the fun, and I was cringing more and more. I took one very deep breath and got out of the car.

"Do you want me to take him in?" Mary said.

We were standing together at the back of the car. Milo, out of his mind with fury, crouched in the rear compartment of the station wagon, facing us and spewing a mixture of growls and howls.

"No, I'll do it," I said.

When my sons were born, I followed the advice of experts and resisted the new-mother urge to be territorial. From the beginning, I forced myself to hand the infant to Andy and walk away, letting him fumble his way toward competence without the added stress of my shadow. I never intended or even wanted to be Milo's guardian. Of course, with Milo, nothing went as I planned. Although he terrified me, I was the one at home most familiar with him. No one in the family dared or wanted to assume any responsibility for him. I had become Milo's sole caretaker, meeting all his needs, including keeping him and all those around him safe. So when Mary asked if I wanted her to take Milo into the classroom, I felt protective of him and unwilling to hand his leash to Mary, even though I knew her to be a well-meaning expert.

There was another reason I wanted to stick with Milo. In high school when I went to Israel for the first time, I was told that if I didn't begin speaking Hebrew the moment I stepped off the plane, I would become increasingly intimidated by the fluency around me and be less and less likely to speak Hebrew as time went on. It seemed to me that if I let Mary take Milo now, at the beginning of our first class, her finesse with Milo would make me even more insecure and nervous about taking him when it was time for me to step in.

Mary's eyes widened in surprise, but she nodded and stepped back a half step.

With my right hand, I slowly lifted the trunk door a crack. I then slid my left hand through the narrow opening and grasped Milo's leash. Milo lowered his head and pushed his long slender nose through the opening, ready to pounce and chase after his classmates.

"Milo, wait!" I shrieked, as if something as benign as the tone of my voice were enough to get Milo not to do what Milo wanted to do.

His triangular head and then his torso followed his nose and squeezed through the slit of the opening I had created with the trunk door. Using the back of his neck, he pushed the trunk door fully open. Just as I grabbed his leash with both hands, his hind legs pushed off from the deck of the trunk and propelled him, leapfrogging through the air, like a swimmer off the block when the gun goes off at the beginning of a race. Milo pulled me, running behind him. I couldn't decide if I wanted to laugh or cry or just go berserk. Before we got to the entrance to the basement, I somehow managed to catch his collar and yank him to a stop. A tentative stop, for sure. With each yank I gave Milo, he gave me two or three or four or five back. I felt myself tipping forward. I felt my feet inching in Milo's direction. I turned back to Mary, who had closed my trunk door and was now hurrying toward us.

Mary and I sandwiched Milo, like guards escorting a high-security prisoner. Our game of leash tug-of-war was now a game of body tug-of-war between Milo and me. For every forward lunge Milo made toward the scents and sounds of his classmates, I gave a yank of almost equal force in the opposite direction. His barking was interrupted only by his gagging—when he lunged, I yanked.

We approached the wide-arched opening to the classroom with the other dogs, the same room we had been in with Gail.

"Don't go into the classroom. Keep going farther down the hall," Mary said. "There's a separate room at the end that connects to this one. That's where I want you and Milo."

Milo didn't want a separate room. He stopped at the arched opening to the classroom, spread his four legs for ballast, and howled to his classmates. I handed the leash to Mary. I was relieved to be able to relinquish responsibility for my larger-than-life dog.

"Milo, come," she said, holding the leash short and taut and redirecting him with one very controlled but forceful tug. Voilà! Milo stopped barking and was walking forward at Mary's side.

"Yes, what a boy," she said dropping a sliver of string cheese into his mouth.

With his eyes focused on another piece of cheese Mary was holding at waist level in front of him, Milo was distracted by the one thing he lusted after more than dogs.

"Yes, Milo, good boy," Mary said, recasting her spell and rewarding him with a speck of cheese every few steps as he trotted by her side, tail up, ears up. I stopped mid-step. I wanted to fully and consciously absorb every moment of this magnificent, beautiful show.

When Mary and Milo turned left and out of sight, I ran after them.

"It's amazing. You make it looks so easy," I said catching up with them in the room that would be ours and only ours for the next hour. "Do you want a boarding student?"

"That wouldn't help you," she said, making it clear she did not find my lighthearted comment funny.

Dog school, Lesson One: Never again speak facetiously to Mary.

"Training a dog, especially a dominant, alpha dog like Milo, is about establishing a hierarchy where you're number one, and in the context of your family, Milo is number six, after Andy and the boys."

Milo, sitting at Mary's side, was motionless, except for the up-and-down, side-to-side shifting of his eyes, as he tracked Mary's treat-feeding hand.

"Dogs are pack animals, and a dominant dog wants to be the leader of the pack," Mary said, her brown eyes wide and focused only on me. "A pack can be one person, two persons, a dog, a bus. It doesn't matter. For an alpha dog, life is a continuous challenge to be number one." She handed me the leash. "And your life with Milo will be one of continually reinforcing that it's you who are number one."

I was discouraged by Mary's proclamation. *I* was the alpha? *I* was the boss? *I* was *his* boss? That was not who I was. My relationships, household rules, even my clothing and decorating styles were informal and minimalist. To each his own, I believed, as long as each was respectful of others. Live and let live. Any alpha I might have had in me had been destroyed by my parents.

A blonde woman in her mid-thirties appeared in the open archway between the classroom and our room.

"This is Carolyn, my assistant," Mary said.

Mary did not introduce me to Carolyn. Apparently, Carolyn already knew who I was. We exchanged smiles.

"Carolyn is going to stand near the opening to the classroom with a spray bottle of vinegar and water," Mary said. "If Milo becomes aggressive in here, or comes into the classroom, Carolyn will spray him in the eyes."

Carolyn held up her plastic spray bottle. I nodded and winced.

"Spraying him might not be a good idea," I said, worried about Carolyn's well-being. "I did it once to Milo, and he lunged at me."

"Milo will not lunge at Carolyn," Mary decreed.

From Mary's mouth to God's ears, I thought.

I looked down at Milo. He was still completely focused on Mary's treat-feeding hand. I looked at Mary.

"I want you to do in here what we are doing in the other room," she said. "When I call your name, I want you and Milo to come into the room, not going farther than a few feet from the archway. Circle around, and then go out the way you came in. The rest of the class will be in the other part of the room. Carolyn will be between you and the other dogs with the spray bottle aimed at Milo. If he begins to get aggressive or misbehave, she'll spray."

Outwardly, I nodded. Inwardly, I recoiled, mortified. I felt as if Milo and I should each be wearing orange jumpsuits with PRISONER written on the back like the inmates doing highway cleanup under the watchful eyes of their armed guards.

I looked down at Milo, my partner in crime. He was no longer watching Mary's treat-feeding hand, as if at any moment she would be dropping a morsel his way. His nose was to the floor, no doubt smelling the scents of the other bad dogs who had been sequestered in this room before him. Investigating, a step here, a step there, Milo pulled me behind him. Instinctively, I followed.

"Anne, stop!" Mary called.

Startled, I came to a complete halt. I looked at her, bewildered. I didn't understand why she was upset. I was not doing anything bad. I was not doing *anything*.

"Anne, stop him and yank him back to you," she said. "Then push him down to a Sit, since that is what I told him to do earlier. He must stay in the Sit until he's told otherwise. He can't get up unless *you* say he can. *You're* the leader. You're *supposed* to be the leader. Right now, Milo's the leader."

Milo wagged his tail when he heard Mary say his name. I, on the other hand, hung my head. Milo might have been enjoying this, but I was not. But my enjoyment was not why we were here.

"Sit," I said to Milo as Mary watched.

Milo sat. First, he looked at Mary. Then he looked at me. When he looked at me, I dropped him a one-inch cube of honey-cured ham. Satisfied, or satisfied enough, Mary turned to leave the room. Then she stopped and turned back to me.

"After class, wait here for me," she said, and then she left.

Carolyn followed her, stopping in the archway between the two rooms. The What A Good Dog sentry, she positioned herself with her back against the side of the arch, her gaze like a hawk's, alternating between Milo and me in our room and the rest of the students in the classroom.

I heard Mary ask the "moms" in the other room to sit down in the folding chairs, their dogs sitting by their sides.

"I'd like to go around the room," she said, "and have each of you introduce yourselves and your dogs."

I was relieved. Being bad, being ostracized had its privileges. My worst moment of any adult ed class or workshop was the first day when the teacher asked everyone to say who we were and why we were there. An inveterate fly on the wall, I loved hearing other people's stories. But my curiosity was overpowered by angst, as person-by-person my turn approached and, like a fly in ointment, I was stuck. My father reminded me every night at the dinner table, "You can listen but don't speak." So speaking up, speaking out, or putting myself forward as someone worthy of talking to, or otherwise deserving of space on this planet was not something I was comfortable doing.

Indeed, solitary confinement with Milo at What A Good Dog had its advantages. I was relieved that I would not have to stand in front of the blonde Lululemon moms and their golden purebred dogs and make an elevator pitch about Milo and me. I was grateful that I would be spared from the ordeal of introducing us.

By the time the words of the women in the other room reached me, they were reduced to an indecipherable drone. So Milo and I used the time to practice Doggie Push-ups, something we learned from Jane.

"Sit," I said, luring Milo with a treat.

"Stand," I said, doing the same.

"Down." Treat. "Stand." Treat.

One Doggie Push-up was completed. We did it again. "Sit." Treat. "Stand." Treat. "Down." Treat. "Stand." Two reps perfectly executed.

Next, I tried giving him a treat only after completion of the four-step exercise. My inch-cubed honey-cured ham, combined with Milo's love of meat, made him a quick learner. He performed perfectly. There was no frustration for either of us, only rewards. Milo liked taking. I liked giving. Together, in solitary confinement, we were contentedly creating a few minutes of mutual harmony.

"Anne," I heard Mary call from the other room.

Mid-push-up, my limbs and breathing came to a halt. Maybe there was an Anne in the other room. Milo completed his push-up.

"Anne, bring Milo to the doorway and introduce yourself."

I looked down at Milo whose mouth was open, waiting for the cube of ham he deserved for his perfect execution of another Doggie Push-up. I pulled a cube from my pocket and dropped it down his wolflike gullet. Then I shortened my hold on his leash and shuffled toward the archway between the two rooms. Carolyn took one step back into the main classroom to make room for us. She positioned her spray bottle of vinegar in front of her at waist level, Milo's eyes her unobstructed target. Milo's ears were up. His tail was up. He was pulling me forward, excited to be joining his classmates, finally. My heart was pounding. I cringed. My 110-pound body was the only thing standing between a one-dog frenzy and a multi-dog melee. Carolyn pointed the spray bottle at Milo and pulled back on the lever. I yanked Milo to the other side of me and positioned myself as a shield between Carolyn's spray and Milo's eyes. I did not let myself imagine what might happen when Milo saw a roomful of dogs. I took one last step and one last breath. Then Milo and I stepped into place under the arch, in full view of the moms and their dogs.

Twenty-Two

Knowing full well that it was physically impossible for me to dig my feet into the cement floor for added stability, I dug my feet into the cement floor for added stability. I was holding Milo's shortened leash with two hands now. I felt my hands shaking. Milo pulled at his leash. I pulled back. I pulled back with all my might. I remembered my treats. As I quickly considered if I should take a chance holding the leash with only one hand, my left hand—operating on automatic pilot—was digging into the pocket filled with one-inch cubes of honey-cured ham. I felt my feet being pulled from the center of the archway ever so slightly toward the classroom, just as I grabbed a handful of ham out of my pocket.

"Milo," I said, putting the ham close to his nose so he could smell it.

I felt the pulling stop. I looked down at Milo. I dropped the cubed ham into his fully extended jaw. He swallowed and opened his mouth again. I dropped him another. And another. One by one, I quickly dropped him my handful of ham. He was fully focused on me. He seemed to have forgotten that he was in a room full of dogs. I switched hands on the leash, dug into another pocket, and pulled out an overflowing handful of one-inch-cubed roast beef. I could feel adrenaline surging through me. When it came to fight or flight, I would always fight. Right now, right here, I felt as if my adrenaline was fueling me with superhuman energy and coordination worthy of an Olympic Gold Medal.

"I'm Anne," I said to the group, as I dropped a steady stream of inch-cubed roast beef into Milo's busy mouth. "This is Milo."

I had done what I came to do. I had said what I had to say. I began to swivel on my heels and turn.

"Anne, can you tell us more about Milo?" I heard Mary say.

More? Was she *trying* to start a bloody brawl on our first day of class? Was she out of her mind? But at an early age, I'd been trained to do what my parents told me to do. I turned back to face the class. I had stepped a few inches back toward the archway from where we had been moments earlier. Carolyn repositioned herself and her spray bottle and was trigger ready. Perfectly aligned with the new coordinates of Milo's eyes, she was mirroring every one of our micro-movements as we stood between the classroom and our cave.

"Milo is a mixed breed," I said. "We got him at Main Line Animal Rescue a few weeks ago."

I could now feel the bottom of the plastic bag of inch-cubed roast beef. With the confidence of a woman high on adrenaline, I decided *I* must take control. Not of Milo. Of Mary. I didn't wait for Mary to dismiss us.

"Milo, come," I said, turning and dropping my last chunk of roast beef into his mouth.

Mercifully, Milo obliged me and turned and walked beside me back into our room.

"Thank you," I heard Mary say above the thump, thump, thumping of my very strong, athlete's heart.

Thank you for nothing, I thought.

"Milo is a very, very smart dog," I heard Mary say as we retreated.

Unlike the moms whose introductions were spoken too softly for me to hear, Mary's voice was loud and clear. I liked her saying

Milo was "smart." I was momentarily buoyed by her telling his classmates and their moms that he was smart. But I did not understand why Mary was talking to the class about Milo. Teachers of two-leggeds were always circumspect about divulging information about a student with another parent. It seemed the same respect for privacy should exist between a four-legged and his teacher.

"Anne is Milo's third family in eighteen months," Mary continued. "He probably outsmarted his first two."

Enough already, I thought. A mix of emotions was swirling inside me. On the one hand, Mary had not said that Milo had been so bad, so out of control, that his first two families had given him up. She said Milo had probably "outsmarted" them. Which reinforced the idea that Milo was smart, and I was someone with great respect for intelligence. Mary's comment made me feel proud of Milo. It also made me feel a bit proud of myself. Although it wasn't as if my genes had anything to do with his being so smart.

On the other hand, I also felt ashamed for Milo that everyone in the class knew he had been kicked out of two families in under eighteen months and was now testing how far he could go with me, Family Number Three. This was not a dog that other moms would welcome into their circle or invite over for playdates.

Suddenly, I felt myself being pulled by Milo back toward the archway and the classroom. I stopped and gave him a full-body yank in the opposite direction, back to the center of *our* room. I heard a mix of chairs being moved and chatter in the other room, which is probably why Milo had been heading in that direction.

"Anne," I heard Mary call. "I want you and Milo to come here into the main room and practice leash walking."

I pretended I did not hear her. Instead of going into the classroom, I went to my backpack up on a high window well and took out a bag of one-inch-cubed turkey to replenish my depleted supply.

Then I did in our room what I heard Mary directing the other moms to do in the classroom. Milo definitely recognized the sound of the rustling turkey bag. He was by my side even though there was slack in the leash. Round and round we went. Every five steps, every ten steps, every fifteen steps I rewarded Milo with a treat, increasing the steps between treats. Milo trotted beside me, his gaze on mine.

"Anne," I heard Mary call, again. "Come into the main room and continue your leash walking."

I couldn't ignore Mary anymore. I grabbed another bag of treats from my backpack. I held Milo's leash taut. Together we advanced toward the archway. I was nervous. A month of living with Milo had me expecting only the worst. Carolyn met us as we walked through the archway into the classroom. With less than a foot between her and us, she followed step-by-step as we walked the width of the room, turned, and walked back.

"Again," Mary called.

Milo continued to be more interested in the cubed turkey chunks than in the dogs in his peripheral vision. He moved with me, our steps perfectly synchronized. We did another complete pass around our 10 percent of the room.

"Again," Mary called, like the drill sergeant that she was.

I felt my body relaxing. This was not hard, not at all. Then I heard one high-pitched bark from the other end of the room. I felt a tug in that direction on the leash, as Milo took one step away from our invisible circle, and toward the sound. I looked up and saw Carolyn, now an inch away from us, cocking the trigger of her spray bottle. I yanked Milo back into orbit. As I did, Carolyn pulled a paper towel out of her pocket and held it in front of the spray mechanism to absorb the water-vinegar mixture she had readied for Milo. I felt as if Milo and I had dodged a bullet. I could almost feel the two of us falling to the floor, dead. Or at least, blinded.

"Anne," called Mary. "Good redirection of Milo. You can go back into your room, now."

I hurried Milo out of the classroom to safety. I was trembling. I could not imagine what would have happened if Carolyn had sprayed Milo, or if Milo had broken formation and run. I looked at Milo. He was looking up at me. "Sit," I said to him.

He sat. I treated.

Milo and I spent the rest of the hour alone, together, in solitary confinement. Here at school, in our own room, Milo caught on so quickly to each new command that I actually felt myself becoming bored. Bored with Milo was a new feeling for me. A good feeling. We practiced Sit, Stay, Down, Stay, Up, with Mary's bellowing instructions coming to us from the other room. With the luxury of boredom, I relaxed a bit with Milo, also a new experience for me. In my slightly bored, relaxed state, in our safe, secluded room, I suddenly saw Milo not as a dangerous, out-of-control, onerous nuisance for whom I was solely responsible, but as a stunningly beautiful, graceful creature who was having a terrific time doing what I was telling him to do.

"Good boy, Milo," I said repeatedly, almost singing my praise. "Good boy."

I noticed that even when I didn't give him a treat, when I used only the tone of my words to express my delight with him, he wagged his tail and locked his gaze into mine, happy just the same. I was so proud of him. Proud of myself. I realized that, for the first time since I'd had Milo, probably for the first time in his life, Milo was proud of himself. My heart opened for this cast-off creature who had never been given a chance.

My reverie was popped when I saw Carolyn approaching us. Immediately, I panicked and looked down at Milo to abort whatever bad behavior he was doing to bring Carolyn our way. But he was doing exactly what I had last told him to do. He was lying by my feet, looking like a beautiful but misplaced Egyptian sphinx. I looked back at Carolyn.

"You and Milo are fine," she said, obviously reading my glaring nonverbals. "Mary wants me to remind you to wait here at the end of class. She wants all the other dogs to be safely gone before you take Milo out. She also wants to speak to you."

I heard Mary dismiss the class. My fingers were raw from all the treats I had doled out. I did not feel like continuing with training while we waited. I worried about what Mary was going to say. I was worried that she would say I did not have enough control of Milo or that he was too far gone to continue with class. Even worse, I was worried that she would say he was so far gone that she did not have another trick in her bag she could try on him. I leaned against the wall, nervous. In the past hour, I had been so absorbed by the moment-to-moment drama and then at the end by the joy of watching Milo being so well behaved and happy, I had forgotten that this first class was likely an official test for us. A test we might have failed. I should not have let my guard down. It would only make the fall from Mary's grace even worse.

I held Milo's leash tightly as we waited for the class to leave and get safely into their cars, protected from Milo. I didn't know how long it would be until Mary came in, but I surely didn't want her to catch Milo pulling me around the room as he explored. I didn't want her to see me—see us—doing anything bad. I wanted her approval. I wanted her to let us stay in the class. I wanted and needed her help.

"Milo, sit," I said.

He sat. I treated.

"Milo, down," I said.

Again, he went down. Again, I treated. Over and over, we did this. Milo was happy for the treats. I was happy to be able to keep him under control so that when Mary entered the room, she would like what she saw.

After some indeterminate amount of time during which I was lulled into a trance by our sit-treat-down-treat routine, Mary walked through the archway. Immediately, I felt Milo pull. I yanked him down and, with my cold fingertips, dug a cube of something out of my pocket and slipped it into his mouth.

"Good boy, Milo," I said. "Good boy."

Milo swished his tail to the left, to the right, and back to center.

"Anne," Mary said, now standing directly in front of me. "I think you and Milo did quite well today. I am particularly pleased that Carolyn did not have to spray Milo. It's much better for him to have only positive feelings about school. Rewards, not punishments, as I explained when I came to your house."

My entire body relaxed. I felt so loose, so relieved, so exhausted that I felt like sliding my back down the wall behind me and collapsing on the floor. But Mary's eyes were so focused on mine, it was as if our connection were keeping me upright.

"I noticed that when you were introducing yourself and Milo to the class, you were continuously feeding Milo treats."

I nodded. As best as I could recall, in that particularly harrowing episode, one of many in the emotional roller-coaster hour that was class, it was instinct that had prompted me to pour treats down Milo's throat. The instinct to survive.

"I was terrified that Milo was going to go berserk in there," I said, shaking my head in regret. "I didn't know what else to do."

I felt crushed. Mary had called me in to introduce myself and Milo to the class as a test. A test that I had failed. I felt bad for myself for being a failure. I felt even worse for Milo whose existence depended on me.

"No, not at all," Mary said. "That was exactly the right thing to do."

My ride on the emotional roller coaster that was What A Good Dog continued. Hearing Mary say that giving Milo an abundance of treats was the right thing to do, I felt myself rise from the ashes and soar. I had done it right! I had not screwed up Milo's chances of redemption. Like two rising, entwined phoenixes, our lives had been renewed.

"This is exactly what I want you to do with Milo this week as homework," Mary said. "One way to break dogs of bad behaviors is to desensitize them to the particular triggers that set them off."

I stared back at Mary. I had no idea what she was saying. I did not understand her canine psychology jargon and certainly not her canine psychology principle of trigger desensitizing. Plying Milo with treats as I spoke to the class had not been a premeditated tactic based on any knowledge I possessed. I had not been channeling anything but terror. Terror that I was the only thing standing between Milo and mass carnage.

"Milo has many things that trigger out-of-control, aggressive behaviors in him," Mary said, understanding that I did not understand. "People, cars, squirrels, dogs, school buses."

Instantly, I remembered being flat on my belly in the middle of the street an arm's length away from the front grille of a school bus.

"You need to expose Milo to one of these triggers and distract him with treats. Eventually, if it works, he becomes desensitized to the trigger. At first, especially for a dog who is highly food motivated like Milo, he will learn to associate the reward, a treat, when he sees or hears the trigger. So the trigger will evoke a positive response in him. In time, the trigger will become so commonplace to him that he will not even notice it."

Again, I found myself just staring at Mary. This time I understood what she was saying. But I could not believe that she was serious.

"So let me get this straight," I said. "For homework you want me to take Milo to a crowd of people and give him treats to distract him from wanting to attack them." I could feel the sarcasm rising from my tongue and coating the words as I formed them and sent them Mary's way.

Although I could not tell from Mary's unchanging expression if she had heard my sarcasm, I was immediately sorry that I had been flip with her. We were on the same side. We were on the same team. We were Team Milo's top-ranking players.

"I'm sorry," I said. "I didn't mean to be dismissive of your plan. It's just that . . ."

"I understand," Mary said, nodding. "I can see how this seems like a disaster waiting to happen. But trust me. It works."

"You're the boss," I said, hoping to sound agreeable.

"No, you're the boss," Mary said. "Never forget that when you are with Milo."

I looked down at my dog. He looked at me. He looked at Mary. He'd been in a quiet Sit, listening.

"Good dog, Milo," I said. "Good Sit."

I dropped him a treat.

"That's it," Mary said looking at me, not Milo. "You've got this."

I rolled my eyes and grimaced.

"Give yourself a pat on the back," Mary said, almost forming a smile. "I really think that with time and work you'll get to a point where you can manage Milo."

I smiled, this time genuinely. It was the first time someone had said anything positive about my future with Milo, about his future with me. Not just someone, but someone with expertise and experience. Someone who knew Milo. Someone who knew me.

Carolyn appeared in the archway.

"Everyone's gone," she said to Mary.

"Okay, Anne, you can take Milo to your car, now," Mary said, looking at me. "Good boy, Milo," she said looking down at him. Milo flip-flopped his feathery tail, no doubt expecting a sliver of cheese. Mary gave him a quick rub behind the ears instead. I waited for Milo to somehow let Mary know he was displeased by the motley reward. I tightened my grip on his leash and planted my feet firmly. Instead, Milo swept his tail back and forth, clearly pleased with Mary's ear rub.

Twenty-Three

It was five degrees and gray the morning after our first class. There was not a ray of sunshine to be seen. In addition to my usual outdoor winter walking gear, I pulled on thermal underwear, snow pants, and a ski hat that had slits for my eyes. I drove to the frozen, tundra-like field where Milo and I walked mornings and afternoons. Our walk on this freezing morning was uneventful. I scurried along beside Milo, not paying attention to who was leading whom. I deserved a break from my role as dog educator. As much as Milo liked learning, he deserved a vacation too.

I am a firm believer in The Slippery Slope Theory of life. Whether it was arduous daily workouts or arduous daily tasks such as dog-walking, I am loath to shave off even a minute of time when I am not feeling up to the task. One minute here, one minute there, and before you knew it, you were sitting on your butt doing no minutes at all. Day in, day out, I pushed through to the last fraction of a second. But on this five-degree day, my chicken-tossing fingertips went from uncomfortably frozen to numb. I began to worry about frostbite. More practically, my feelingless fingers were unable to grasp the chicken cubes in the bag to give to Milo. Step after step, he looked up at me expectantly. Step after step, I disappointed him. After forty-five minutes, with another fifteen minutes to go, my body involuntarily walked toward the car. I tugged Milo. He didn't budge. He wanted to stay. I felt bad. I felt guilty. What if I were sliding down that slippery slope? What if tomorrow I decided I wanted to do only thirty minutes? *Sometimes*, I told myself, *restraint is the better part of valor*. I didn't believe this. Not at all. I felt bad about shortchanging Milo. I felt guilty about not fulfilling one of my obligations. But I was cold. Very, very, very cold.

I took off my fingerless gloves and, with my feelingless fingers, I chiseled off a frozen cube of chicken.

"Into the car, Milo," I said, opening the back of the station wagon and holding out a treat.

Milo saw the treat and jumped into the car. He turned around and sat, mouth open.

"Good boy, Milo," I said, dropping another frozen chicken cube into his mouth.

I shut the door and, huddling in my down jacket to retain my body heat, I got in the car and drove home.

A few hours later, shortly after lunch, I checked the thermometer outside our back door. It was seven degrees, merely two degrees warmer than it had been in the morning when I had followed my instinct to survive and aborted our walk fifteen minutes early. Contemplating our afternoon walk around the field before I picked the boys up at school, I was not hopeful that I would be able to last even forty-five minutes.

Milo was pacing back and forth across the kitchen. He knew he was due another outing. I did not want to disappoint him. I also did not want to think about how much more difficult it would be to manage him if I did not follow through with the routine we had established. I imagined him pacing, his unbridled anticipation of the walk rising with each advancing minute of the day. I imagined his unchecked disappointment going deep within him, digging up triggers that even he, heretofore, had not known pissed him off. *Really* pissed him off. The indignity of being cheated out of a walk would be enough to make any terrifyingly out-of-control, alpha dog even more so.

Leaning back against the kitchen wall and closing my eyes, I let out a deep, resigned breath. Afternoons were always the most difficult time of the day for me. My energy was at its lowest, and I had more trouble pushing away my negative thoughts. Isolation made my depression worse. Before Milo, I worked out again in the afternoon, and if I felt particularly bad, I would go out to Starbucks and sit down at a table and watch people or sit in my car at Whole Foods and watch people there. Being a fly on the wall and seeing people lifted my spirits and gave me energy. Now that I had Milo, going to these places was not an option. I had to take him for his afternoon walk.

I opened my eyes and stood up straight. It was so cold, gray, and unpleasant outside that I could not imagine anyone else roaming the streets. Surely, it was for days such as this one that squirrels spent the fall collecting acorns. Any squirrel with any hope of surviving the winter would certainly know that today was not a day to be out and about. Any squirrel worth his or her bushy tail would know that today was a day, *the* day to stay huddled near his or her stash of acorns, under a bed of leaves, deep beneath the snow. It was also too late in the day for people who walked their dogs once a day. And too early in the day for people who walked twice. It was also too early for the school buses to be rumbling to pick up their passengers and take them home. If ever there was a time that I might be able to eke out a street-walk with Milo in relative safety, this was it. Maybe the walk would even give me a boost of energy. If my suppositions were wrong, if the street was a bevy of activity of squirrels, dogs, people, and buses, I could admit defeat and retreat.

I loaded my pockets with bags of treats. I encased my body in layers of insulation. I leashed Milo. We were off. Milo trotted a few feet ahead of me down the driveway. I hurried to catch up. I imagined that Milo remembered our walks down the driveway and up the street when he had first come to live with us. I imagined that he was excited about finding squirrels, dogs, people, and cars to chase. Without seeing another living creature, we made it the half mile to the top of the street, to the intersection where Milo had pulled me onto the street in front of the school bus. We crossed the street and continued walking straight, now on a sidewalk. I did not have a destination in mind. I was taking it one block at a time.

Milo was behaving less aggressively. Every block I called his name and rewarded him with a treat. I felt as if I were strolling, as if I were taking a spring afternoon walk with a sweet, low-maintenance dog. I drove down this street, past these houses, multiple times a day. I recognized the cars in the driveways, the swing sets and sandboxes and outside decor. When I was driving, I went too fast to see inside the houses and collect clues about the lives of the inhabitants. On this gray and dismal afternoon, the inside lights were on. Milo was walking so agreeably that I was able to look into living rooms, kitchens, and family rooms. There were people preparing meals, mothers and children playing, and in one living room, a woman sitting peacefully in a chair reading. I wished I could trade places with any one of them. I had become that person I always pitied. I was the person out in the cold, walking her dog. When we first got Milo, and he was pulling me into the trees and streets during walks, my only feelings about dog-walking were dread and terror. Today, even though Milo was well behaved on our walk, I realized that I really did not like walking dogs.

I was surprised when we got to the end of the street. I looked at my watch. I had been so engrossed looking at the people in their warm houses that the thirty minutes seemed more like ten minutes. It felt good to be defying the weather and be out and about. I didn't feel like going home. Across the street was a shopping center with a free-standing Bed Bath & Beyond. The street-level, sliding glass doors of this Bed Bath & Beyond opened to a small lobby with an elevator and escalator to the store on the upper level. I thought of our People Desensitizing homework and decided that the Bed Bath & Beyond lobby would be a perfect place to do it. It was warm and never crowded. When we arrived, I could not believe my luck. The store was well into spring already, with a glass-top patio table and plastic-webbed chairs set up in the lobby in the middle of the room.

"Milo, sit," I said when we reached the table.

He snapped his lean butt into place on the lobby's gray tiles.

"Good boy," I said, dropping a cube of ham into his uplifted, open jaw.

I took off my jacket and mittens and hat, laid them on the table, and sat down in the chair beside Milo. Directly in front of us was a blank white wall. To the left of the wall was the down escalator. To the right was the elevator.

"Good boy," I said to Milo, giving him a ham cube.

He looked at me. I treated him. He looked at me again.

Beyond Milo, to his left, I saw a slight, gray-haired woman kneading her gloves snugly around her fingers riding down the escalator. Milo's gaze was still turned right, toward me.

"Good boy, Milo," I said, rewarding him with one cube, two cubes, three cubes for keeping his gaze tethered to mine.

I felt my heart thumping and adrenaline surging. What I was doing was not prudent. On the other hand, I rationalized to myself, getting into a car and driving was not prudent, either. A drunk or texting driver could go out of control at any time. Yet, multiple times a day, I took my chances and risked my life by getting into my car and driving. It was a calculated risk I was willing to take. Watching the gray-haired woman descending the escalator, headed our way in the Bed Bath & Beyond lobby, I made another calculated risk. I was prepared to use this woman as Milo's first subject. I continued to rationalize, telling myself that this was no different from a patient on whom a new doctor performed his or her first surgery. *Someone* had to be first.

"Milo, you don't want to eat this lady who is coming down the escalator, do you?" I said, dropping ham cubes into his mouth as the woman neared the bottom of the escalator.

I was speaking to him so plainly and logically, from so deep in my heart, that I almost expected him to shake his head, no. No, he did not want to eat the woman. He did not seem to hear her as she stepped off the escalator. He was still focused on me, swallowing the steady stream of ham I was pouring into him.

The woman's bag rustled as she stepped off the escalator. Milo's body tightened and he turned toward the woman. I tightened my one-handed grip on his collar.

"You don't want to eat her, do you, Milo?" I said in a calm, soft voice belying my pounding heart, as the woman approached.

Milo was now leaning back to ready himself for a forward spring. I squeezed a cube of ham between his clenched teeth, into his mouth. He swallowed. I felt his entire body relax and soften.

The woman passed us, uninterested, oblivious to the intense picnic taking place in the lobby. I continued feeding Milo as I watched her walk through the sliding glass doors. When she was on the sidewalk and the doors closed behind her, I wanted to pick up Milo and do a dance of joy with him.

"What a good boy you are, Milo," I said, remaining in my chair, grinning. "What a good boy you can be. You didn't eat that lady. I'm so proud of you."

Elated by our mutual success, I stopped feeding him for a few moments to rub him between the ears. As I resumed with the ham treats, I was awed by how well I had come to know Milo in such a short time. We had spent so much time together, my eyes trained on every muscle and limb of his, always prepared to counter any attack he might initiate. I'm a goal-oriented person. Success, in and of itself, is a motivating reward for me. Each time Milo showed signs of improving, I felt a deep sense of accomplishment. Taming wild dogs wasn't a goal I would have voluntarily undertaken. But now that it had been foisted upon me, positive results were gratifying. I pictured Milo and me from above, sitting at a patio table, together, in January in the lobby of Bed Bath & Beyond, and I smiled.

I saw a college-aged boy coming down the escalator. He sneezed. Milo turned from me abruptly, his body tense.

"Milo," I said, forcing a treat through his clenched teeth. "You don't want to bite this nice boy."

His body tightened even more. I squeezed another treat into his mouth. Milo leaned back, ready to lunge.

"Milo," I said again, simultaneously tightening my grip on his collar with one hand and shoving a third cube of ham into his clenched jaw with the other. His body softened, finally, and he turned to me, his mouth open for more treats.

"That's a handsome dog," the boy said, coming toward us and stopping to pat the top of Milo's head. "What kind is he?"

I had come to this lobby to teach Milo not to attack strangers, not to socialize him to make small talk with them. That was a behavior lesson for another day. Another lifetime.

But the boy was standing in front of us, waiting patiently for me to tell him Milo's breed. It was important for me to act calm. I knew that Milo could sense what I was feeling. I knew he could tell if I were tense or relaxed.

"He's a mix," I replied to the boy, keeping my hand discreetly moving in and out of my pocket with treats. "We just got him from a rescue."

"Good for you. It's really great of you to save him," the boy said, nodding his head to affirm what he was saying. "He's a lucky dog."

The boy's words made me feel deceitful. My reason for getting Milo was nothing but self-serving. I hadn't done it to help anyone but myself. I'd kept him only because I'd have felt worse if I hadn't. Yet out and about on this frigid, gray day, sitting with Milo in the lobby, talking to the friendly college boy, I found myself wondering who was saving whom.

"I bet he has some husky in him," the boy said, standing back and studying Milo like a painting.

As we talked, I slowed down the rate with which I was giving Milo treats. Milo's demeanor remained calm.

"He really is a beauty," the boy said, excitedly, coming toward us again to rub Milo behind the ears. Milo moved. My heart stopped. Before I could do anything, Milo was sidling up against the boy's leg, just as he did with our young carpenter.

"Someone called him a Heinz 57," I said, catching my breath as I remembered Mary's description of Milo.

"Well, I think he's so handsome he should be his *own* breed," he said.

I laughed. Josh had suggested that we tell people he's a psycha, from the root word "psychotic." I thought of telling the boy this. But I didn't.

"Thanks," I said instead, not sure if that was the appropriate response. It was not as if I'd created Milo's looks. "His looks saved his life."

"Well, good luck," the boy said, pulling gloves out of his jacket pocket. "I think rescue dogs are the only way to go. You're one lucky dog, Milo."

Chills ran through me. I thought of how close I had come to giving Milo back. I thought of how downtrodden I'd felt being pulled through wet leaves by this dog. But now, here we were together, a woman and her beautiful rescue dog enjoying an afternoon outing.

Milo and I watched the boy walk outside through the sliding glass doors.

"He was a nice boy, wasn't he, Milo?" I said, looking down at my beautiful, one-of-a-kind dog.

When he heard his name, Milo looked up at me, his soulful eyes locking with mine. I popped him a ham cube.

It was time to go home and pick the boys up at school. I was surprised that, unlike most afternoons when I took Milo to the meadow where it was just the two of us, today I felt full of energy. I realized that my contact with the people in the Bed Bath & Beyond lobby had contributed to this energy.

"Good boy, Milo," I said, standing up from my chair. "This was really fun. Here's one more treat just for being you."

Twenty-Four

Milo and I returned to Bed Bath & Beyond every day for three weeks. We even went on Saturday when the lobby was a hub of activity, shoppers coming and going. Within a week, all I had to do to keep Milo seated and calm as the unsuspecting public passed by our stakeout was rub him behind the ears and say, "Good boy, Milo. Good boy." By the second week, I didn't have to do even that. Sitting beside me, his back straight, in a statuesque perfect Sit, Milo was downright regal.

"That's a beautiful dog," I heard over and over, as shoppers took time out of their errands to pat Milo on the head.

I realized that letting people approach and pat Milo was a perfect way to expand our People Desensitizing. Milo liked being patted. Each time someone approached us, he wagged his tail. Instead of being afraid and going on the offense and lunging, Milo was learning to like people. When it was clear that he was growing more comfortable with people in the Bed Bath & Beyond lobby, I decided to change the settings of our People Desensitizing sessions.

Next, we embarked on School Bus Desensitizing. Every afternoon, we went to the boys' school fifteen minutes early, just as the school buses were arriving. Driving into the school, we were often sandwiched by a school bus in front and a school bus behind, causing Milo to howl and hurl himself apoplectically around in the back of my station wagon. With my pockets stuffed with bags of treats, I walked Milo on a short, tight leash and positioned us beside the school's traffic director.

"Hi, I'm Anne," I said to this man I'd seen twice a day, every day for over a decade when I dropped off and picked up my kids. "I need to try to desensitize my dog to school buses."

As I spoke, I could feel Milo gagging as he tried to simultaneously bark and lunge while I held him back.

"Is it okay if I stand here with you and try to get him accustomed to buses?"

"Sure, I love dogs. By the way, I'm Bob."

"Nice to meet you in person after all these years," I said with a smile.

The buses were rolling in and lining up. The first in the shiny yellow battalion idled along the curb directly in front of the entrance to the school building, the others taking their places, snaking behind them.

"Milo," I said, turning my attention to my seething dog and dropping a stream of treats in his open, howling mouth. "You don't want to attack these buses."

Over and over, I filled his mouth with treats and I told him he didn't want to attack the buses. Milo was not buying it. He took the treats, swallowed and howled and pulled. When the last of the buses had come and gone, I said goodbye to Bob and, exhausted, headed to the car where Joseph and Josh were waiting.

"Milo," the two boys called out excitedly as we came into view.

"How did bus desensitizing go today?" Joseph asked, rubbing Milo behind the ears.

"Actually, Milo," Josh said, "those buses really piss me off too. Way too loud. Talk about noise pollution."

Any onlooker of a certain age, someone not privy to Milo's

backstory, would see our chipper group piling into my station wagon and undoubtedly be reminded of Lassie!

Day after day we went back and stood with Bob. By Monday of the second week, I found that Milo was calm enough for Bob and me to talk. Bob was an avid Eagles fan. So were my boys. As I dropped treats into Milo, I was able to repeat to Bob things I had heard the boys say and keep the conversation going. The following day, we talked about Milo. The day after that, the weather. By the middle of our second week, Milo learned to sit placidly on the grass between Bob and me. We patted him as the buses came and went. Parents followed in their cars, waving to the three of us. Increasingly, with each day, Milo became calmer and calmer, accepting pats from Bob and me and an occasional treat. By the end of the second week, it was hard for me to remember how crazed Milo had been whenever he saw a school bus. He even stopped barking and getting upset when he was in the car and saw one. I found that our shared, harrowing desensitizing experiences made me feel more and more connected to Milo. We weren't just sitting together in my study sharing the same air. We were sharing intense emotions as well as achievements. When Milo succeeded, I succeeded, and we both felt good.

Twenty-Five

When I was growing up, my favorite thing was to be in the same room as my parents, listening to them talk. They never included me in their conversations, and they were not at all nice to me. But I didn't care. I liked being around them. I hoped that eventually, if I did everything they told me to do, they would accept me and be kind to me.

My mother had always insisted on giving me a birthday party, inviting my friends and their mothers. The day would go well enough—until the party ended. When the last guests had gone home, my mother would turn to me and glare.

"Tomorrow is *my* day. Do not spoil it," she'd say in a low growl. Her anniversary was the day after my birthday.

For the sake of appearing like a good mother to my friends' mothers, she'd made a pretense that, at the very least, I was special on my birthday. It was all for show. By dinnertime, she could no longer continue the charade.

As an adult, then as a mother, I continued to try to gain my parents' respect and love. I never succeeded. I loved them, but if they loved me, they did not know how to show it. Finally, after decades of trying to be included in their family, I gave up. I found that the toxicity of my relationship with them was more painful to me than the hurt I felt from their alienation. By the time we got Milo, I had stopped visiting them, and our weekly phone calls had become semiannual, if that. Even though I had given up on my parents, I was not going to give up on Milo.

Unlike my parents, Milo didn't hurt me deliberately. Sometimes he just lost control. Sometimes he behaved as if I were just another wolf in his pack who needed to be dominated. Until Milo came to live with us, no one had ever taken the time to teach him how to behave around people and to connect with them. As Milo and I worked together, I experienced more and more moments when I felt that Milo and I were connecting with each other. When he looked at me and his tail went back and forth, my heart melted. Milo was happy to see me and loved being with me. I had never experienced anything like this with either of my parents. They were never happy to see me.

I began to take Milo in the car with me everywhere I went when it wasn't too hot or too cold. Grocery shopping, doctors' appointments, to pick up the boys. Initially, I took him with me so I could fit in a desensitizing session or a walk before or after an errand. Later I took him just for fun. For Milo and me.

"Okay, Milo," I would say when I turned off the ignition, cracked open the windows, and turned to look at him behind me lying in his fleece dog bed in the back of the station wagon. "Mommy is going into the grocery store to buy Milo some yummy treats. I'll be back soon. You be a good boy."

Milo, who by now was trained to look at me whenever he heard his name, would turn his head toward me. I was surprised how good it felt to be talking. Not just talking but talking to someone who was listening.

Then I'd lock the car door, go to the back of the car, and wave at him. When I returned, I always gave him a treat or two. Soon, whenever he saw me coming toward the car, he would stand up and swing his tail 180 degrees. While I was gone, Milo sat in his beautiful sphinx pose, his head up, his eyes roving from window to window. In a short time, I stopped giving Milo treats when I got back to the car. He no longer stood up when he saw me return. Instead, his torso and head remained still, and his tail did a slow, regal wave. Each time he wagged his tail at the sight of me, I felt my mood brighten. It felt so good to know that my presence made Milo feel happy. I loved feeling appreciated by Milo. I wished my parents had even once been able to give me this feeling.

Twenty-Six

It was hard to believe that the terrifying Milo Bill Smith had brought to our house three months earlier was the very same Milo who now so often made me feel appreciated and needed. We were definitely making progress inching our way toward the normal section of the Life with Dog bell curve. But we still had a lot of work ahead of us.

Though I'd been brazen, even imprudent, in my efforts to desensitize Milo, there was a challenge in Milo's training that I had not yet been able to face. The thought of bringing Milo face-to-face with another dog still terrified me. I felt more comfortable with people than I did with dogs. I had more experience reading the nonverbals of people. Until Milo, I really had not spent any time trying to understand the inner workings of a dog's mind. So I had fewer qualms about desensitizing Milo to people than to dogs. If things went awry, the person would know to pull back. I would only have to extricate Milo. On the other hand, if Milo got out of control with a dog, it was likely the dog would behave in kind. The image of two dogs going for each other's jugulars, and the jugulars of anyone who came between them, kept me from working with Milo on Dog Desensitizing.

During weeks two and three of dog school, I had suffered through sixty boring minutes, alone with Milo in our room at What A Good Dog. A few times each class, Mary called us into the main classroom. During those times, Milo and I circled around the top 10 percent of the classroom uneventfully, as I shoveled treats into his mouth. Always, Carolyn accompanied us with her spray bottle mixture of water and vinegar mere inches away.

By our fourth week of class, despite the fact that Milo was no longer aggressive toward people or buses, he still howled and hurled when he saw a dog through the car window. I tried to arrive at dog school a couple of minutes after the rest of the students and their moms had gone into the building. But there were always one or two moms and dogs hurrying in late who would ignite Milo's fury inside our car. This did not seem to be lost on Mary, who was still escorting us to our room. I assumed this was why, despite Milo's progress with all other behaviors, she still sequestered us in solitary confinement.

During the fourth class, Milo and I worked in our room on the behaviors Mary was bellowing in the main classroom.

"Sit."

"Stay."

"Down"

"Up."

"Leash walk with no tugging."

I was feeling increasingly bored and frustrated. Milo caught on to each new behavior in one pass, and then we just kept doing them over and over. I was glad Milo was a quick learner. I just wished the situation were different and we could be learning with everyone else where there would be so much more for me to see. As the minutes slogged by, I felt the tedium and isolation weighing me down. I decided it was time to ask Mary for help desensitizing Milo to dogs so that it would give us a chance of joining our classmates sooner rather than later. As the idea of asking Mary for help was still settling in my mind, I heard Mary call my name.

"Anne, come to the archway with Milo and stand there."

I assumed this was another invitation to come into the classroom and walk around a few times near the archway. We'd already done it twice that day. Usually, we met Carolyn at the archway and continued, without pausing, to circle around the room. I was puzzled, now, that she wanted us to *stand* in the archway. As eloquently stated by the nineteenth-century poet Alfred, Lord Tennyson, "Theirs not to reason why, theirs but to do and die." So I moved toward the archway with Milo, determined to try do whatever Mary, my alpha person, told me to do.

Milo and I stepped into the archway.

"Milo, sit," I said, giving him a handful of treats when he did. "Good boy, Milo."

Carolyn, not surprisingly, was inches in front of us, her spray bottle aimed and cocked.

"Anne," Mary called out. "I want you to walk with Milo on your right, around the circle, and stop when you get back to the archway. Then, when you're ready, I want you to walk down the middle of the room to me, and when you reach me, I want you to tell Milo to sit and stay. When you hear me say, 'Okay,' you can release him."

I stood in the archway, shoveling treats to Milo. I could not get my feet to move. Without moving my head, my eyes made a sweep of the circle of blonde Lululemon moms and their dogs. They had pulled back in their chairs and were tensely clutching their dogs close, ready to become human shields to protect them. My mind was racing with images of the mayhem that was likely to occur if I followed Mary's commands. I would have felt better if Carolyn had a clone to sandwich Milo and me with a second spray bottle.

Theirs not to reason why. Theirs but to do and die.

"Come, Milo," I said, taking a step forward.

Milo stood up and moved beside me.

"Good boy, Milo." I dropped him a treat.

Carolyn was on my right, next to Milo, stepping backward as we moved forward.

"Good boy," I said continuously as we moved around the circle. "Good boy, Milo."

Milo looked at me, then straight ahead. His tail and ears straight up.

"Good boy, very good boy," I said in a singsong voice every time he looked at me.

Milo was not much more than a yard from the dogs in the circle. Oddly, he did not seem to notice them. I kept my eyes down and focused on Milo. As we made our way around the circle, I noticed that when he did look away from me, he quickly snapped his head back toward me and looked up. I could not imagine what was going on in my dog's head. I expected that at any moment he would pull me stumbling after him as he lunged for a dog. I looked at Carolyn. Like a sniper trained on her target, she was crouching toward Milo slightly, even as she walked backward. I tightened my already tight fist around Milo's leash. As I did, I noticed that there was slack in the leash. Milo was not pulling at it. It was hanging loosely between us as we made our way together back to the archway. My body was tense. I remained on guard. I remained vigilant to every movement in Milo's body from the tip of his slender nose to the tip of his Lion King tail. Everything could change in a fraction of a second. I thought of pulling the leash taut. But I didn't want to disrupt Milo's exemplary behavior. I needed to trust him.

"Good boy, Milo," I said, when we reached the archway.

I turned and faced the classroom.

"Sit, Milo," I said, and he did. I dropped him a treat.

I felt as if we had stepped through this archway another lifetime ago and that our trip around the circle was a dream. For a moment or two, I stood unmoving in the archway. I wanted to savor this dream. I wanted to remember it. From the circle, I heard the scrape of a moving chair and I awakened from my dream.

I saw Mary on the other side of the room. She might as well have been on the other side of the world. I wanted to turn and retreat into our solitary confinement cave. I would never complain again about being sequestered there. I looked at Mary again. I took a deep breath, and as I exhaled, I stepped forward. Milo stood up and moved forward with me, the leash still hanging loosely between us.

One step, two steps, three steps, four.

"Good boy, Milo." Treat. "Good boy." Treat.

I planted my foot. I took a step. I planted my foot. I took a step. Slowly, deliberately, I led us across the room. Finally, after an eternity, we reached Mary. There was a dog and mom sitting inches away on the other side of Mary. Carolyn or no Carolyn, bad things could happen fast.

I turned to Milo. "Sit, Milo," I said, my stomach clenched, my body as taut as the leash was loose. I locked my gaze into Milo's. Before my eyes, before the eyes of Mary and every other two-legged and four-legged in that classroom, my dog snapped his butt down with the precision of a Westminster show dog.

"Stay," I remembered to say.

I was so stunned I could barely get the word out.

Milo sat, back straight, ears up, his gaze tethered to mine. I didn't treat him or say anything. I didn't want to break whatever spell some fairy godmother had cast on him. Milo sat there before me, beside Mary, his eyes fixed on mine.

"Okay," Mary said, softly.

That was my cue. My cue to release Milo from his Sit.

"Good boy, Milo," I said, dropping three chunks of chicken into his mouth.

He was still swallowing when I fell to the floor, wrapping my arms around his torso and nuzzling my head into his. I didn't care if I was breaking the rules. I didn't care if my decorum was not that of an alpha. My dog was a champion. I could not have felt prouder of him. I thought of us in this very room with Gail. I remembered her saying that if we did not give Milo back, we'd regret it for the rest of his life. I gave Milo another hug and popped him another treat. I couldn't remember the last time I'd been this happy.

"Very good, Anne," Mary said. "Good boy, Milo."

I had forgotten Mary was there. I was oblivious to everyone, even Carolyn. It felt like there wasn't anyone else in the room with me, like there wasn't anyone else in the world with me except Milo.

"I was terrified when you called us in," I said to Mary, my heart still racing. "I thought you were crazy."

"Yes, I could see that," she said. "But I noticed earlier in the class today and last week, also, that when you came in and circled near the archway, your leash was slack. I noticed Milo wasn't pulling and trying to redirect you. I sensed that you had established control over him, even if you didn't realize it."

I just looked at her, shaking my head in disbelief. "You're right. I didn't notice it until just now when we were circling the room. I thought of tightening the leash, but I decided I needed to trust him."

"Your intuition to leave the leash slack was right."

I was sure Mary had not only six senses but possibly seven, eight, nine, or ten. I was in awe that she could read so much from so little. I looked down at Milo. He was schmoozing with the dog beside him. They were sniffing each other, tails and ears up.

I looked at Mary.

"Milo was frustrated. He was acting out because he wanted to *play* with the dogs," she said, smiling. "He couldn't have done this a month ago. But your desensitizing him to people and buses reduced his overall anxiety. So now he doesn't feel the need to be the aggressor."

I nodded in agreement. It seemed like a stretch to believe this, but I was happy to feel that way, just the same.

"From now on you'll be in this classroom with everyone else," Mary said.

For the rest of class Milo was a star pupil. Mary even used him as her example dog for some of the new behaviors.

After class, I felt carefree and festive. To celebrate Milo's achievement, we went to a dog boutique near What A Good Dog. The floors were hardwood, the products high-end, the staff knowledgeable dog lovers. Bowls of treats were scattered around the shop. I scooped them up and doled them out as Milo and I meandered the wide aisles. Somebody approached with their dog to stand behind us in line at the cash register. Before I could drop my dog toys and grab Milo by his collar, the two dogs were circling and sniffing, their tails high and wagging. Milo wasn't being aggressive. As Mary said, he just wanted to play. When we got back to the car, I presented Milo with a pig's ear from my bag of purchases. He lay down and began gnawing it, enthusiastically. My heart soared.

I left Milo with his pig's ear and went next door to an artisan bread shop, famous for its generous samples. A few minutes later I walked out, a bread in a bag and savoring, nibble by nibble, a buttered slice of warm cinnamon raisin challah. I stopped at the back of my car. Milo looked up, and when he saw me, his feathery haute-couture-worthy tail swept steadily behind him, reminding me of the distinct, measured handwave of royalty. Then he returned to work gnawing his pig's ear. I felt myself falling in love. It wasn't love like the love I'd felt for Mattie. No two loves are alike, after all. But there was no denying it. I was now in love with Milo.

Twenty-Seven

The morning after Milo's triumphant performance at What A Good Dog, I decided to go to the dog park at the bottom of our street. We hadn't been there since Nurse Marion with her five rescue dogs had decreed that I should return Milo to the rescue and get one of the many dogs there who she said were "more deserving" than Milo. I wondered if Nurse Marion would be at the park today and what she would say if she saw Milo and me now. I also wondered if she were as judgmental and unforgiving with her patients who were ornery because of their pain and fear.

When we got to the park, there were five cars scattered across a parking lot that looked like it could hold twenty. As soon as we turned into the pebbled lot, Milo stood up in the back of the station wagon, ears up, tail up. It was as if he remembered being here and he knew we were here for him.

"Milo, sit," I said as I opened the station wagon's back door.

Milo sat, locking his hopeful, expectant eyes with mine. I felt my body relax. For a moment I stood and stared at my very happy dog.

"Good boy," I said, giving him a treat.

I skipped beside Milo as he pranced from the parking lot into the park. Every few steps, I gave a quick tug to the leash, and Milo obliged me and slowed down a bit. There were two people walking together toward Milo and me near the entrance, each with two small dogs scurrying, unleashed nearby. I let go of Milo's leash, hoping he would realize that if he wanted to interact with the dogs, he did not have to be aggressive.

"Good boy," I said, giving him a treat, the leash at my feet.

He looked at me, took the treat, but was clearly distracted by the approaching people and dogs. As he moved toward them and they toward him, I scurried behind, ready to grab the leash if Milo began to cause trouble.

But he didn't. He absolutely did not. As the two women passed us, Milo sniffed each of their dogs and each of the dogs sniffed Milo. The women did not seem to notice Milo or what was going on. Or, if they did, they assumed it was regular dog communication among regular dogs. They smiled noncommittally when our eyes met, without slowing down for even one step. Clearly, Milo and I were nothing out of the ordinary. I let out a deep sigh. It felt so good to be ordinary and have an ordinary dog. I took off Milo's leash.

After Milo and the four dogs finished their introductory sniffs, the four little dogs hurried after their owners. Milo didn't follow them. The dog version of speed dating had not rendered a match. Milo's feelings didn't seem to be hurt. His tail up, his ears up, he stood tall, surveying the park. Then he followed in the direction of the two women and four dogs, and I followed him.

We quickly caught up to them. We quietly passed them. Milo's four legs were skipping, barely touching the ground, before lifting off again. Usually, when Milo was moving, I was being pulled behind him. Except for his butt, I had never before been able to study him in motion. Now, as he skipped along the oval path, I marveled at the contoured muscles of his lean, still underweight body. His every movement seemed effortless as he traversed the park, skipping and gliding.

Halfway across the park, he stopped for a moment and stared ahead. At the end of the oval, I saw a black poodle walking beside a man. I was so intimately familiar with the inner workings of Milo's brain and the movement of each of his muscles and body parts that even watching him from behind as he stood motionless, staring ahead, I knew he had his sights set on the black poodle. Before I thought to catch up with him and grab his collar, he was off. Not skipping and gliding—but flying. I was so caught up in the beauty of him in flight that I didn't hurry after him. I forgot to worry about what would happen when he landed beside the black poodle.

Hurrying to reach him, I could see Milo and the poodle circling each other and sniffing. Their circling and sniffing seemed more thoughtful, more intense than Milo had done with the four little dogs at the entrance of the park. The man with the black poodle, in his mid-sixties and wearing a black leather bomber jacket, had stopped walking and was watching the two dogs introduce themselves to each other. He was still standing there, watching, when I got to them.

"They seem pretty interested in each other," I said, after standing with him for a minute or so of silence.

"Yeah, they do," the man said. "Anise isn't usually interested enough in other dogs to stop moving for this long."

I nodded. I felt like Milo had been released from prison the day before, and this was his first social interaction. I didn't want to spoil things for him. He'd done the time for his crime. He deserved a clean slate.

Milo and Anise began moving together around the path, neck-and-neck, nose-to-nose. The man and I followed.

"I'm Anne," I said.

"Hi, I'm Alan," the man said, offering me his hand.

"Anise is a poodle?" I said, stating what I thought was obvious.

"A *French* poodle," Alan said, sounding miffed.

Based on nothing, I had assumed that all poodles were French poodles.

"How old is she?" I said, trying to find neutral ground.

"Eighteen months," Alan said.

"I can't believe it—that's exactly how old Milo is."

I felt as if I were back on the playground with my toddler boys, looking for companionship for them and maybe for me too.

Milo and Anise were now running in small circles. One after the other. They went in one direction a few times. Then, all of a sudden, they turned and went in the other direction. Milo and Anise began to expand the size of their circles, inching their way into the middle of the grassy meadow inside the oval walkway.

"Where did you get Anise?" I asked.

"I got her from a breeder in Maine."

"Maine?" I said, wondering why anyone would go so far for a dog.

"Yeah. It's where I had to go to get a pedigree poodle with an impeccable bloodline," he said, sounding matter-of-fact. "I'd have gone a lot farther for a dog like Anise."

Milo and Anise were now circling back toward us. Circling. Changing directions. Circling some more. A man with a golden retriever walked past us. His dog seemed oblivious to Milo and Anise. Milo and Anise did not stop for a moment to check out the dog.

Alan stopped to watch Milo and Anise, his face squinched.

"I've never seen her do this . . . this, I don't know, I have never seen her behave this way," he said, shaking his head, as if this new behavior of Anise's was not a good behavior.

"I think they're having a lot of fun," I said. "They're certainly using a lot of energy. A tired dog's a good dog."

I believed what I said. I also didn't want Alan to think Milo was a bad influence on Anise. We'd already been shunned by Nurse Marion. That was enough.

"How did you find Anise?" I said, hoping to distract Alan.

He looked at me. He looked back at the two frolicking dogs. He hesitated. Then he turned back to me and began to walk.

"I did a lot of research. I studied bloodlines of dogs back six generations on both sides. Finally, I found this breeder in Maine. Once I got on her list, I had to wait two years."

I could not imagine anything for which I would wait two years. Even children are only a nine-month wait. Alan continued talking about the dog shows Anise's ancestors had won, the events, the years. He went into such depth about the trophies awarded to Anise's family going as far back as her great-great-great-great-grandmother *and* -grandfather. As I listened, as I tried to keep track from one generation to the next, it was all I could do not to let my jaw hang in disbelief.

Alan's delineation of Anise's family tree was so detailed that it took us a full revolution around the park to get from beginning to end. I listened to the particulars of Anise's relatives, but I did not retain the details in my brain. I got the point. Anise not only looked like a regal black poodle, she *was* a regal black poodle. Alan had the papers to prove it.

Now Milo and Anise were running the full length of the field. Anise was leading Milo. Then Milo passed, and Anise followed. When they reached the end, the two dogs jumped into the air, facing each other, their front paws reaching out, as if trying to hug.

If I felt elated watching Milo and Anise, I could only surmise, from Alan's long face, that he was horrified. I looked back at the field where Milo and Anise were now running across the park, away from us. One leading. The other leading. Again, when they got to the end, they jumped into the air, chest to chest, front paws up and out. When they landed on the ground, Anise rolled over Milo. Milo rolled over Anise. They sprang to their feet and did it all over again. It was like watching two dancers performing a ballet. Anise, the black swan; Milo, the golden prince. It was breathtaking. To me.

"I haven't seen you here before," Alan said, shuffling along.

"No, we just got Milo recently. This is only our second time here."

"Where did you get Milo?" Alan said, seeming to perk up. "What breed is he? Is he a Briard?"

I didn't know what to say. In my wildest imagination I could not have pictured Milo playing so beautifully, so elegantly with another dog. I did not know what kind of breed a Briard was or what it looked like, but the way Alan said the word I sensed he was attempting to give it a French accent. I was sure that if I said Milo were a Briard, also of French origin like Anise, Alan would be more accepting of Milo. He might be more willing to overlook Milo's high-octane effect on his once demure, reserved, and still very royal dog.

I'd be the first to admit that Milo had some undesirable character traits. Okay, a lot of undesirable character traits. But I was absolutely not sorry or regretful that Milo was not a purebred anything, but rather a mixed breed, a Heinz 57, maybe even a psycha. I was not at all ashamed that Milo was an old-fashioned mutt. A beautiful, athletic, and smart mutt. His family background did not make him any less deserving than Anise with all her entrenched blue blood coursing through her.

"Actually, he's a mixed breed," I said, answering Alan's question, unable to lie, even for Milo.

Alan didn't say anything. He didn't nod, yes, or shake his head, no. Clearly, this was not the answer he had hoped to hear.

"We got Milo at Main Line Animal Rescue right before Christmas," I said, deciding to finish Milo's origin story there.

I could feel Alan's disappointment. For almost eighteen months, he had been coming to the park with his black poodle princess. In synchronized steps, Anise's four for every two of Alan's, they had walked the path together. Now, out of nowhere, Milo had come along, jumping, running, twirling, rolling, gliding, flying Milo. Two lost lovers, reunited at last. Instead of stepping properly about the park with her proud dad, Anise had tossed decorum to the wind. Every ounce of her graceful, energetic, and enthusiastic being was now perfectly synchronized with Milo.

When we reached the path to the parking lot, Alan clipped his leash on Anise.

"We've got to go now," he said, sounding resigned to the new world order.

"It was nice meeting you and Anise," I said.

He gave me a sad smile. "I'm sure we'll see you soon."

I felt his pain. His hopes and dreams for Anise had come crashing down on him the moment she first sniffed Milo. I suspected that Alan had two-legged adult children who had taught him that humans grow up to be their own people. People with their own thoughts about their future. From his resigned, sad smile I also suspected that Alan had learned that the wisest thing to do with adult children was to accept them and love them and hope for the best.

"I hope we *will* see you soon," I said.

Milo and I watched Alan and Anise get into the car and drive off. I looked down at Milo. He looked up at me.

"Should we go around the park again, Milo?" I said, taking him by the collar and gently turning him toward the park.

He stood for a few moments. There were other dogs walking and romping. Then he turned to look at the parking lot.

"I agree," I said. "Let's go home. We'll come back tomorrow at the same time and see if we can find Anise."

I leashed Milo and together we walked up the path to the car.

"Good boy, Milo," I said, giving him a treat when he jumped into the back of the station wagon and turned around and did a perfect Sit.

I was amazed when I realized it was the first treat that I'd given him in the thirty minutes since he'd met Anise. My boy had been so fully engaged with Anise, so fulfilled and happy, that he had not needed or wanted anything more.

Twenty-Eight

I took Milo back to the dog park at the same time the next day, hoping to see Alan and Anise. I was disappointed when I didn't see Alan's black Audi sedan when we pulled into the lot. Milo, who had stood up in the back of the car when we pulled in, was no doubt also hoping to see them. I decided not to tell Milo that they weren't there so he could hang onto his happy hopefulness a little longer. I scurried with him from the parking lot into the park.

"Milo, sit," I said when we reached the park, in a half-hearted attempt to remind him who was boss.

"Good boy," I said when he sat.

I took off his leash. As soon as I unclicked it and freed him, he was off. His burst into the air was so unexpected that I almost fell backward. I could not imagine where he was going or what he was chasing. I began to panic. Wherever he was going, he was going to get there well before I was. I watched him spring from his hind legs into the air, fly forward, land on all fours, and then do it all over again. His balletic athleticism was so wondrous that I forgot to be worried. I didn't run after him. I just stood and watched, awed by my golden bullet of a dog. As he reached the middle of the grassy area, I saw what looked like a black bullet shooting toward him. It was Anise! They came together in an airborne swirl, their front paws outstretched. I was stunned that Milo had spotted Anise, a black dot, across the equivalent of a football field. And she had spotted him.

While Milo and Anise ran and chased and twirled and rolled, I hurried along the pebble path toward a woman with short black hair, probably about sixty, who stood watching them. She seemed so totally engrossed in the performance on the field that I assumed she was Anise's mother.

"Hi," I said, when I reached her. "They're pretty amazing, aren't they?"

"They are. They really are. I've never seen anything like it. I've never seen Anise like this. I didn't know she had it in her to be so lively and energetic."

"I'm Anne," I said. "I met Anise and Alan here, yesterday."

"Hi, I'm Barbara. Alan's my husband. He told me about Milo and Anise."

We turned from each other to watch the two dogs. A few other people on the path stopped to watch as well.

I turned back to Barbara and said, "I got the feeling, yesterday, that Alan wasn't too happy about Milo and Anise. Well, mostly I thought he wasn't too happy about Milo. He seemed dejected when I said Milo is a mixed breed and not a Briard."

"Yeah, he wasn't exactly thrilled about Milo. Alan puts a lot of stock in labels. He likes his cars, wines, and dogs to be luxury brands, even when we can't afford it."

I liked Barbara's forthright, honest description of her husband.

"I wasn't completely up front with Alan yesterday," I said, wanting to reciprocate Barbara's honesty. "Milo has quite a checkered past. We're his third family in eighteen months. We were basically duped into taking him, and I've spent the last few months doing nothing but trying to make him a nonthreatening pet. So I don't hold it against Alan that he's not pleased about this."

"I think it's great," Barbara said. "It's great for them to work off some energy. And they really seem well matched. Alan will come around. He always does. I know it's a cliché, but it seems appropriate here. Alan's bark is worse than his bite."

I laughed. I liked Barbara. I liked her openness and nonjudgmental acceptance of Milo.

"Okay, I'm glad to hear it," I said. "Because I really love seeing them like this."

"Oh, Alan's already softening," Barbara said as we began to walk along the path, following Milo and Anise who were dancing together at the other end.

"Alan told me how Milo had catapulted Anise into a ball of uninhibited energy."

"I'm glad to hear that," I said to Barbara.

After I had spoken, I wondered if Alan had meant what he had said in a good way.

"Did Alan say anything else?" I asked.

Barbara looked at me and smiled. "Alan said to me, 'At least I think Milo's Jewish.'"

I laughed. "I don't know how Alan figured out that we're Jewish. We didn't talk about religion yesterday. But he's right."

"I don't know. Alan seems to have a sixth sense about these things," Barbara said, smiling. "Ten years ago, our son married a woman who isn't Jewish. It took Alan some time to get over his disappointment, but he did. Everything is fine, now. I'm sure that if Anise wants Milo, Alan will come around about that too."

Barbara and I quickly and easily fell into conversation about ourselves. Before Anise, Alan had had a French bulldog who'd died four years earlier. Barbara had never warmed up to that dog. She found him unattractive, and he drooled a lot. Anise was much more to her liking.

"Sounds like Alan's a bit of a Francophile," I said to Barbara. "He seemed disappointed that Milo was not a Briard."

"Point taken," Barbara said, laughing. "The only place Alan's willing to travel to besides golf resorts is Paris."

We walked and talked and watched the dynamic duo for thirty minutes. Then Barbara called Anise and leashed her up.

"It was really nice meeting you and Milo," Barbara said. "Alan or I come here either this time in the morning or in the afternoon around four. Don't worry about Alan. He's probably already come to terms with Milo. And I think Milo's great. He's a really beautiful dog. He's lucky to have found you."

Milo and I watched Barbara and Anise leave the park and get into Barbara's red Honda sports car.

"Anise is a nice girl, Milo," I said, looking down at my forlorn dog. "Don't worry, we'll see her again soon."

Every day for a week, we saw Anise with either Alan or Barbara. Anise and Milo danced and played and tussled. If a dog came near, hoping to join the fun, they were out of luck. Milo and Anise were oblivious. Which was just as well. I couldn't imagine another dog being as poetic in their play as Milo and Anise or having their stamina.

At the end of the week, Barbara told me they were going to visit their daughter in Massachusetts. The next day it was so sad when we got to the park and Milo realized there was no Anise. It was also not good for me. I liked walking with Barbara and Alan. I liked their stories, and they seemed to like mine.

Without Anise and her parents, Milo and I were left to walk around the path alone, together. Milo was not interested in dogs smaller than he was. If we passed one, he would sniff for a few moments, but then he moved on. He spent more time sniffing out the bigger dogs. One dog after another would bow down or chase Milo but not be able to keep up with him. Once that happened, once it was established that Milo was the alpha, Milo lost interest in that dog. Meanwhile, the humans at the park, some alone, some in pairs, didn't seem any more interested in me than Milo was in their dogs. They smiled at me as we passed. Occasionally, we did a lap together. But that was it. Milo missed Anise, and so did I.

Twenty-Nine

It appeared to the world that I was learning to manage Milo. I was making a pretense of being Milo's alpha. Mary explained, unequivocally, that Milo needed an alpha mom. Every bit of alpha I might have had was crushed during childhood. I knew Milo needed me to be an alpha, so I did my best. I sensed that he wanted to be a good dog. That he loved me. But Milo didn't know how to control the part of him that I suspected wanted to run with wolves. On the outside, he looked like his own mellow designer breed dog with the coloring and soft coat of a short-haired golden retriever and the lean, athletic physique of a large French poodle. I tried to maintain the outward appearance as Milo's alpha. By the middle of March, two months after we began classes at What A Good Dog, anyone who saw Milo prancing around the park would have agreed with Bill Smith's assessment that Milo was a friendly, happy family dog who liked to frolic and play. But in reality he was not. Not always.

Early on, Milo reminded me of a wild creature with his aggressive, food-motivated, stalking behaviors. Milo's family tree likely included some aggressive dogs, genetically predisposed to stalking prey. I didn't talk about it. I didn't want to scare people. A smart alpha dog can be trained to live in a civilized society, as long as they have an alpha person leading them with consistency.

A few days after we got Milo, I had been in line at Whole Foods behind a woman who was buying marrow bones. The cashier asked her what she was going to do with them.

"Bake them and give them to my dog," she said. "They keep her busy for hours."

The following day when I took Milo to the vet for his checkup, I mentioned the bones.

"Gristle isn't good for dogs and neither is marrow," the vet said. "Boil the bones. Remove the gristle and marrow. Then they'll be safe for you to give him."

I don't like to cook. The only real cooking I did was on Friday nights when I popped chicken in the oven, and also when I made chicken soup for Passover. But since Milo had walked into our house, I had been doing a variety of things for him that I did not like doing. Walking, dog school, 24/7 behavior modification. So I decided to add cooking marrow bones to the list.

I went to Whole Foods and bought ten three-packs of marrow bones. I got the two cauldrons I used to make chicken soup from our basement. I filled them with water, and when they came to a boil, I dumped in the bones. Watching them simmer, I decided that without the gristle and marrow, the bones would not be of much interest to Milo. So I filled two large bowls with dry kibble, added water, and let them sit until the kibble had absorbed the water and turned to mush. After the bones had simmered for a few hours, I dumped out the water and waited for them to cool down enough for me to hold them. I pulled off as much gristle as I could with my hands and used a knife to scrape off the rest. With my now raw, scratched fingers, I scooped and scraped the marrow out of the center of the bone.

The thirty bones, now free of gristle and marrow, were ready to be built back up. In an assembly-line manner, I held each bone in one hand, scooped some kibble mush with the other, and stuffed it into the hole that had previously contained marrow. I stuffed and compacted as much mush as I could into each hole. I smeared peanut butter around the exterior of the bone and then rolled it in the kibble mush, to coat it. When all thirty bones had been stripped, stuffed, smeared, and coated, I dropped each one in a plastic sandwich bag and put them in the freezer.

Each day when it was time for me to go into the basement and work out, I pulled a frozen bag from the freezer.

"Milo, it's time to go exercise," I said, holding the bag for him to see.

Even though I was disciplined about working out and never missed a day, my heart sank lower and lower each minute as I headed into the basement to the exercise bike. Walking down into the basement with Milo, his tail high in happy anticipation of his bone, distracted me from the dread of my looming workout.

"Sit," I said, when we got downstairs.

Milo sat.

"Good boy. Down."

Milo went down.

Each day before I gave him the bone, I gave him a series of commands to remind him that I was the boss.

"Wait," I would say when I finally put the bone down in front of him.

For a number of seconds, he and I locked gazes, the bone on the ground between us.

"Okay, Milo. Good boy."

As soon as I said this, Milo would pick the bone up, lie down in his bed in the corner, and begin gnawing on it. I felt so good seeing him enjoy it that I couldn't help but let out a deep, calm breath and smile. The gratification I got from watching Milo with the bone made the time and effort I spent purchasing, boiling, scraping, stuffing, and smearing worth it, raw hands and all. I believe I enjoyed the bone as much as Milo did. Pedaling my way to the end of my workout, I occasionally looked at Milo on his bed, the bone between his oversized, furry front paws, and I felt a surge of energy go through me. It took Milo less time to clean his bone than it took me to work out. When he was done, he pushed the bone off his bed, put his head down, and went to sleep. No sleeping creature looked more angelic than Milo.

One day, after a month of workout bones for Milo, I had a dentist appointment and had just enough time to work out and get there. I grabbed a bone from the freezer and hurried into the basement with Milo. I was distracted, worried about being late. I didn't want to take the time to go through the usual commands with Milo. I put the bone down on the rug between us and noticed my shoe was untied. As I bent down to tie it, I saw Milo leaning backward, his brown eyes wild and fiery. Instinctively, I stood up and backed away from him until I felt myself up against the wall. I watched as Milo sprang forward into the air and lunged for me. His body taut, he stood on his hind legs, his front paws pinning me to the wall, and bit my upper arm. My heart banged against my ribs, and my body was quivering. Still flattened to the wall, I saw Milo step back and prepare for another lunge. I stood there afraid to move. Afraid that any movement from me would make him even angrier and more dangerous. I watched, helpless, as he lunged a second time, landing eye level with me, his front paws sandwiching me. I held my breath, bracing myself for a second bite.

I was terrified that he would clench down again on my upper arm. We stared at each other. It felt as if my heart ricocheted between my spine and my rib cage. I was determined not to look away. I had no idea how much time had passed. Suddenly, Milo's eyes lost their wildfire. His body softened. He dropped to the floor. My heart was still banging against my ribs, my quivering body held upright by the wall behind me. I didn't move. Milo walked back to the bone in the middle of the room, which was still on the rug where I had put it. He turned around and faced me, his head lowered, tail and ears down. He didn't pick up the bone. He didn't sit. He just stood there and looked at me, his eyes peeking out through the narrow slits of his partially closed eyelids. I had never been the victim of a violent crime. As I stood against the wall, silent and still, watching Milo, I felt as if I could imagine the helplessness and terror of seeing your assailant attack.

I rested against the wall, watching Milo, not wanting to move until I was sure he would not attack again. He kept his head, ears, and tail down, still peeking at me through his eyelid slits. I moved one foot. He didn't react. I moved another foot. He remained standing.

"Milo, sit," I said, as I approached.

He snapped his butt down.

"Milo, down," I said.

He lay down.

Gail had said, during our What A Good Dog interview, that no amount of management, no amount of reward, no amount of love would keep Milo from sometimes forgetting his training. Nothing would stop his aggression in certain circumstances. He was not completely tamable. When I finally felt safe enough to take my eyes off him, I looked at my arm. There were four distinct teeth indentations on the top of my arm and two on the bottom, but no blood. I kicked the bone away from him, picked it up, and hid it in a high cabinet. I wasn't going to reward him for his lunges and bite. I also wasn't going to punish him. I had the sense that he knew he had been bad. Very, very, very bad. Milo's apparent remorsefulness, however, wasn't what kept me from punishing him. Locking eyes with Milo, I remembered I had skipped the commands when I gave him the bone. I had not said, "Sit, Down, Wait." Then I had stooped to tie my shoe, putting myself into a submissive position. I had caught Milo off guard and triggered the untamable part of him to take control and attack me. I didn't think it would be fair to punish Milo because *I* had forgotten to do what was necessary. I had forgotten that I always needed to be making an effort to be Milo's alpha.

Any alpha I might have had did not survive my childhood. Not only did my father throw my beagle puppy, Teenie, down the stairs and kill him, he also verbally abused me on a regular basis. Every night at dinner he told me I was not allowed to speak. When he walked by me, as often as not, he yanked my bangs, causing my head to snap forward. But I loved Milo. And I so much wanted to be a good dog mom to him that I tried to bring to life whatever dormant alpha in me had survived. When I became a mother, I had three children who didn't need an alpha mom. My combination of empathy and a desire to help them express their own individuality was sufficient. Mattie, like my sons, had not needed an alpha mom. With Milo, I realized I needed to find some alpha in me.

We are all a combination of nature and nurture. Nature is what we are born with. Nurture is everything else—good and bad—that happens to us. How we are nurtured colors and shades, heightens and lessens the characteristics with which we are born. Mattie was easy to love. She even taught us to share love with Family Hug. Milo was *not* easy to love. But Milo taught me to understand and appreciate his individuality. That may be what unconditional love is.

My desire to receive love from my parents was so strong that I tried to reshape my own being to conform to what I thought they wanted. But even if I had been able to achieve that, it would have been approval, not love. They weren't able to give me even that.

When I was growing up, all I wanted was to be with my parents. I had given up hope that they would ever listen to me. But I still wanted to be with them. Even as an adult, I longed to connect with my parents.

Andy's first job out of graduate school was as an assistant professor at Harvard. We lived a mile from my parents. After six years, he was denied tenure. That meant that we would have to move. I dreaded leaving my parents. I was still hopeful that by staying near them, I had a chance of gaining their acceptance and love.

Job offers came in from all over the country. I wanted Andy to choose the school closest to Boston. I lobbied for him to go to Columbia University in New York City. Andy wanted to choose the school with the best reputation, which was Northwestern University outside of Chicago. We compromised on The Wharton School of the University of Pennsylvania in Philadelphia.

Unexpectedly, we were able to buy a castle-like house made of stone. I never would have dreamed that such a beautiful house could be mine. The Boston housing market had exploded in the six years we lived there, and the Philadelphia market had been depressed. The day Andy and I went to Philadelphia to sign papers, we went to the house with our new key. The previous owners' kitchen phone was still working. I picked up the receiver and tapped in my mother's 800 work number.

"We did it. The house is ours," I said. "It's more beautiful than I remembered. But, Mom, I would rather live in a hut near you than in this house in Philadelphia."

There was a long silence.

"Mom, are you still there?" I asked.

I don't know how long I held the phone to my ear.

Then my mother spoke. "Anne, I'm too busy to listen to your problems."

She slammed down the receiver.

I called her back immediately. Her secretary answered.

"Anne," she said apologetically, "I'm sorry, but your mother told me not to put your call through to her. She said she doesn't want to speak to you."

I hung up the phone and dropped to the floor. I had wanted to connect with my mother and tell her how much I loved her. I thought I was saying the nicest thing a daughter could say. My nature was to reach out to my mother. My mother's nature was to slam me down and disconnect.

Thirty

Milo loved his new life. He reveled in our trips to the dog park. He paced with excitement in the back of the station wagon, his Lion King tail high, each time we turned down the road to What A Good Dog. He pranced alongside me down into our basement where he savored his peanut butter–encrusted, kibble-stuffed marrow bones while I worked out. He even loved getting in the car and going on errands with me. Sometimes shopkeepers would come out to see Milo in the back of my car. He was such a beautiful dog, and he looked so regal, his head up and rotating, seeing all that there was to see. When he saw me come out of a store, his floppy ears straightened, and his tail made a full sweep behind him.

I often did errands after our morning walks. On rainy days, my hiking boots were caked with mud, my raincoat dripping.

"Just back from the dog park?" salespeople asked.

I smiled.

"Is Milo in the car? Can I come say hi to him?"

Milo never disappointed the fans who had been following his transformation. Always, he gave one slow, dramatic sweep of his tail and perked his ears up into perfect triangles. Everyone smiled. Including me.

It wasn't just Milo's love of life that captivated me. It was also the zest, enthusiasm, and excitement with which he went about his day. He was curious about everything and anything that moved. It could be a colony of ants on the back step or a deer passing through our yard.

One day, I walked into my bedroom with Milo and saw a large black spider scurry under the bed. Milo saw it too. For me, the spider was a problem. But for him, it was the perfect toy. Milo lay down beside the bed, his nose tucked under it, stalking the spider. He lay nearly motionless. I watched him and waited as he watched the spider and waited. Suddenly, Milo began jabbing his oversized, furry front paw under the bed. Jabbing forward and retreating. I was sure he would not succeed. His paw just wasn't long enough. He didn't seem frustrated. He was enjoying the hunt. Then he sidled his prone body a few inches closer to the wall and began jabbing his paw from his new vantage point. Within a minute, the spider came scurrying out from under the bed. Milo sprang to his feet, barking and howling, chasing the poor spider until it ran out of the room and up into a ceiling vent.

"Good boy, Milo," I said, beaming. "You didn't give up. You kept on trying. I'm so proud of you."

I had taken several meditation classes and had never been successful at keeping myself in the moment. But with Milo, I was always in the moment. Consequently, disconcerting moments like finding a spider under the bed often became moments of exhilaration.

One week in late March, the weather was unseasonably warm, and a bevy of bees had found their way through the cracked cement in our stone wall and made themselves at home. The worker bees flew out of the wall, did whatever it is worker bees do, and then they flew into the wall to return to their families. Milo sat by the wall, barking and swatting at the bees as they came and went. His attention was focused on only one thing: the bees. I was fascinated by his prolonged attention span and his ability to focus on a task.

The UPS man—yes, *that* UPS man—had parked his truck on the street and was walking up the driveway with our package. He dropped the package at a door twenty feet away and waved. Milo looked at him for a moment, ceased his barking, and then turned his attention back to the bees and resumed his barking. Clearly, the bees were more interesting prey for Milo than a single, brown-uniformed UPS man.

This was only the second time I had seen him since he killed Mattie. The first time I had seen him was three weeks after she died.

"I hope you don't mind that my boss kept me on your route," he had said to me then. "I asked him to move me. I told him it wasn't right for you to have to see me again after what I did. But he said it wasn't possible." As he spoke, his gaze had darted downward, sideways, and upward. Never had his gaze met mine.

"Accidents happen," I had replied. "Even though we lost Mattie, now Milo, a rescue dog, has a home." I didn't go into any details about how out of control Milo was. I hadn't wanted him to feel worse than he already did.

Now, two months later, I thought of walking over to the UPS man and telling him about Milo stalking the bees. I thought it might make a fun story. I decided against it. I didn't want to push my luck. I didn't want Milo to turn his sights from the bees to the UPS man and attack him. Instead, I waved at him and smiled.

Milo swatted with his left front paw, then his right. He stood, he sat. He barked and barked. Then I saw his right front paw hit a bee and I heard a high-pitched, curdled shriek. Milo pulled his paw back. With his tail, ears, and head down, he turned around and walked toward the house. Milo knew how to fight. He also knew when to admit defeat. Whatever Milo did, he did with all his physical and emotional might. He tried to make every moment of his life a moment he wanted to be in. His enthusiasm was contagious. I had fun just watching Milo be Milo. A very happy Milo.

Thirty-One

After his show-dog-winning performance during class at What A Good Dog, Milo had been wholeheartedly accepted by his classmates and their moms. Now that everyone knew he was not a threat, he had become a bona fide member of the class. He did not have to feel frustrated about being excluded. Each week, when we turned into the parking lot of the school, he stood up in the back of the car, his ears and tail up. He no longer went berserk or even barked when he saw the other dogs waiting on the grass.

Milo was the most enthusiastic student in class. During Mary's demonstrations of new behaviors, Milo's eyes tracked her every move, his head following her as she moved. When it was time for Milo and me to work on any new behavior, Milo picked it up so quickly that I couldn't help but wonder if, during the demonstration, he had not only been following her actions, but also her words.

Being in the classroom with everyone else was better for me than being sequestered in our solitary-confinement room. Still, dog school was tedious. I didn't like being an alpha to anyone. I did not get a thrill seeing another creature follow my every command. But Milo was so engaged, so quick to learn, and so happy that I found myself perking up and enjoying myself each time he surprised me anew with another perfectly executed behavior.

At the end of our sixth class, I joined the end of the line of other moms who wanted to talk to Mary.

"Good boy, Milo," Mary said, when we got to her. "I'm very proud of you."

Milo, who sat beside me, whooshed his tail.

"I just want to tell you, Milo and I are going to be missing some classes," I said, when Mary looked at me. "I'm having rotator cuff surgery next week. I don't know how long it will be before I'm able to come back with him."

"You have to cancel your surgery," Mary said, looking alarmed. "Rotator cuff surgery is a big deal. It takes a long time to rehab afterward. Milo will miss too many classes."

I wasn't having the surgery for fun. It wasn't something I wanted to do. Moving my arm was painful. Not only when I swam, but when I raised it. I couldn't believe that Mary was telling me to compromise my health so Milo could continue with school.

"If he misses too much," I said, "we'll take the class again."

"You can't do that. Milo would be bored doing that, and he'll lose interest. It will be hard to motivate him."

I just looked at Mary. It was hard for me to imagine a situation, any situation, in which Milo would not be motivated by a moist cube of meat. I did not think Milo would mind repeating Dog Kindergarten. I didn't agree that it would stunt Milo's emotional, social, or academic development. Milo was a confident dog. He had a strong sense of self. I didn't think his morale would suffer if his classmates graduated from Dog Kindergarten and he had to repeat it. If Milo was disappointed about repeating, I would explain to him that it was because of my surgery and had nothing to do with him.

"You know," Mary said, her brown eyes wide open, "Milo is gifted."

Gifted? Milo? My three two-legged sons were smart and hard-working. None of them had ever received below an A-minus on a report card. I could count on fewer than a hand's worth of fingers how many times the three of them, combined, had come home with A-minuses. Not once had a teacher said that one of my two-leggeds was "gifted."

I didn't know if I should laugh at Mary or tell Milo how proud I was of him. Staring back at Mary, I knew that laughing was not the way for me to go. I patted Milo on the top of his head.

"If you won't cancel your surgery, the next best thing is to ask Jane if she can fill in for you and bring Milo to class until you're able to come back."

"I could never ask Jane to do that," I said, shaking my head to make my point clear.

"I'm sure she wouldn't mind. She's a real dog advocate. She'd do it for you. Even more, she'd do it for Milo."

"Let me think about it," I said, wanting to get away before Mary came up with any more plans that I wouldn't like. "I'll talk to my husband. But I don't think so."

"Milo really needs this class," Mary said, getting up and walking us toward our car. "He's come a long way from the dog I met three months ago on New Year's Eve. But he has a long way to go. I don't want him to regress."

Driving home from What A Good Dog, I was smiling as I thought about what a laugh Andy and the two boys would have at dinner when I told them about my crazy conversation with Mary. They would think it as ridiculous as I did that Mary said Milo was gifted and would be bored repeating Dog Kindergarten.

At a red light on the way home, I turned around to look at Milo in the back of the station wagon. I watched his head rotate 180 degrees as he surveyed the traffic. A school bus rumbling beside us did not elicit a peep out of Milo. I shook my head in amazement, in awe of how far Milo had come since Bill Smith had foisted him on us. A triptych of images from Milo's early days appeared in my mind. In the left panel, our family huddled outside Ardrossan, distraught and hopeless, after Gail had admonished us that if we did not give Milo back, we would regret it for the rest of his life. In the middle I saw Jane's backyard later that evening with Milo running on command, back and forth inside the plastic Toys "R" Us tunnel. In the right panel was Mary in our hallway on New Year's Eve teaching Milo to follow commands.

As I went over and over these images in my mind's eye, I found myself reevaluating what Mary had said to me after class. Maybe she was overstating things. Maybe she was a dog-centric woman who was putting Milo's well-being over mine. On the other hand, she, with Jane, had given us our first ray of hope that Milo might be salvageable. And, as the days turned into weeks, Mary had not given up on Milo. Step-by-step, one behavior after another, she had told me what I needed to do to get Milo under control. I had been skeptical. More than once, I had been terrified that if I did what Mary said, mayhem and tragedy would ensue. Walking Milo around the circle of dogs in the classroom and People Desensitizing in a crowd were just two of the things Mary had told me to do that, at first, I had thought were bad ideas. I had ignored my own reservations, disregarded my dire predictions. With a quaking body, I had shut down my anguished brain and done what Mary had told me to do.

Looking at Milo in my rearview mirror, I felt myself smiling. His ears were flopped forward and, ever curious, he was still turning his head to survey the sights all around him. Suddenly, the conversation in my head about what Mary had said after class changed. Mary had not led us astray since New Year's Eve when she'd walked through our door and been jumped and humped by Milo. On the contrary, in less than three months, her astute guidance had transformed Milo from an out-of-control dog to a mostly manageable work-in-progress dog. If Mary thought missing class because of my surgery would be detrimental for Milo, who was I to say she was wrong? Regression was not an option. There was too much at stake if I ignored Mary's advice and Milo regressed. Aside from the safety and well-being of Milo and the world around him, which in and of itself was not at all inconsequential, I knew *I* would be devastated and disheartened and, yes, bored to have to start over with Milo.

I began another conversation with myself. I really didn't want to postpone my surgery. I had waited three months to secure this date. I had waited many more months before that not only unable to swim but also in frequent pain. I was not comfortable imposing on Jane, even though Mary had suggested it. All I knew about Jane was that she was busy with dog activities. She taught, she trained, she took classes, she took her certified therapy dogs to visit patients in hospitals. Jane had more than enough to do without taking Milo to Dog Kindergarten. By the time I pulled into our garage, my head felt like it was going to explode from the disparate opinions vying for dominance. I wasn't comfortable sacrificing my physical health. I also was not comfortable sacrificing Milo's hard-won well-being.

I needed King Solomon. I needed someone with the wisdom, fairness, and common sense of the ancient king. When I got home, I picked up the phone and tapped in Andy's number.

"Is everything okay?" he said when he answered. I don't usually call him at work.

"Yeah. More or less. But . . ."

"Great minds think alike," he said, jumping in when I hesitated.

"What are you talking about?" I asked.

"Or maybe your ears were burning and that's why you called?" he said, laughing.

"Andy, enough with the clichés," I said.

"Rich just left my office as the phone rang with your call," he said. Rich was Andy's colleague and Jane's husband.

I waited to hear what was going on.

"This is like playing that game Telephone," Andy said. "From what I understand, Mary Remer talked to you today about having Jane take Milo to classes while you're in surgery next week and the weeks after when you're rehabilitating."

"Yes, she did," I said, too absorbed in my thoughts about my conversation with Mary to wonder how Andy already knew this. "That's why I'm calling you at work. I won't go into all the details now about what Mary said. But she was adamant that if Milo missed classes, it wouldn't be good. At first, she said I should postpone the surgery. When I said that wasn't an option, she suggested Jane take Milo to classes. I told her that wasn't an option, either. I can't impose on Jane like that. I don't know, Andy. I just don't see a solution that works for everyone and it's really bothering me. Why is everything with this dog so complicated?"

Andy is less emotional than I am. His decisions are based on logic, not feelings. I felt relief, dropping the mess of what to do with my surgery and Milo's education on Andy.

"You're right," Andy said. "It does seem that everything about Milo is surprisingly complicated. But believe it or not, at this point it's all been worked out."

"What are you talking about?" I said, feeling annoyed and confused.

"Like I said, this is kind of like playing The Telephone Game. After you left school, Mary called Jane and told her the situation. Then Jane called Rich and asked him to tell *me* to tell *you* that *she* wants to take Milo to class. Jane thought you'd be more comfortable and willing to agree if you heard it from me."

"What?" I asked. "I just left there thirty minutes ago."

"I guess the drums of the dog world beat loud and fast," Andy said. "Rich was in here for quite some time making the case for Jane stepping in for you with Milo."

I stood in the kitchen with the phone to my ear watching Milo on his bed watching me. It was as if he knew we were discussing him.

"What do you think?" I said to Andy, no longer feeling annoyed.

I was touched that Mary cared enough about Milo to call Jane. I was also moved by Jane's empathy for me. She understood my reluctance to impose on her. Rather than making me uncomfortable by calling directly and putting me on the spot, she had created a chain of people who were comfortable speaking to each other, one to the next.

"Anne, you really need to go through with the surgery. Mary and Jane seem to know what they're saying and doing. They seem as concerned with Milo's well-being as you are. It's almost as if you're the boots on the ground with Milo, and Mary is the five-star general charting the course."

I didn't know what to say. My parents had continually reminded me that I was an imposition on them, and they admonished me that I should not trouble other people.

"Anne," Andy said, "I really think that if Jane didn't want to do this, she wouldn't have gone through this much trouble to make her point. She wouldn't have bothered Rich. She could have just called you. If you'd said no, she would have been able to tell Mary she had tried. Listening to Rich, it also seems to me that Mary and Jane, and even Rich, are really impressed that you have hung in with Milo. That after being conned by Bill Smith, you didn't give Milo back. Mary may be the one with the plan of attack for salvaging Milo, but you're the one doing it. I just don't think many people would be willing or able to take on an animal like Milo."

"Andy, you know that I kept him only because I would have felt worse if I'd given him back. It was for me, not for him," I said, reluctant to have my self-serving behavior glorified.

"Anne, at this point it really doesn't matter why you stuck with him. What matters is that he's getting better. Think of it as Jane doing a favor for Milo, not for you. Her taking Milo to class while you're having surgery and rehabbing is good for Milo. It will keep him from regressing. You've put so much into him already. It would be a shame for Milo to slide back to where he started. It would be a shame for everyone. You've got us all rooting for him now."

I hadn't taken my eyes off Milo on his bed while I talked to Andy. He had put his head down and closed his eyes as we spoke.

"Okay," I said to Andy, with a deep sigh. "It makes me uncomfortable imposing on Jane, but I really care about Milo. I don't want to shortchange him or screw up his chances for a good life. He's trying really hard. As uncomfortable as it makes me feel, I'll agree to it for Milo."

"I'll catch Rich before he goes home and tell him," Andy said.

"Tell him how much I appreciate it and that I'll call Jane tomorrow."

I felt relieved and grateful. Most of all, I felt connected, connected to a group of caring people. People who wanted the best for Milo. People who were willing to take the initiative and put themselves out in order to give a wayward animal the chance to have a good life.

As I savored Mary and Jane's compassion for Milo, I found my mind detouring from Milo to myself. For a moment, a brief but very real moment, it occurred to me that Mary and Jane were showing compassion not only for Milo but also for me. I thought of my father telling me when I was three that I was self-centered. He said that my mother was tired of picking up after me, and that I needed to wash my own clothes. Unlike my parents, who abused, thwarted, and undermined me, Mary and Jane wanted to help me. Mary and Jane weren't worried only that Milo would regress if he missed classes because of my surgery. They were also concerned that if Milo regressed, my quality of life would diminish as well. Mary and Jane were stepping in for me as much as for Milo. It felt sublime to be on the receiving end of such kindness.

Thirty-Two

The day of my surgery, Andy stayed with me at the hospital until I was taken into pre-op. Then he went home and got Milo and took him to Jane's. When I woke up, Andy was waiting for me. The plan had been for Andy to drop me off at home before he made the thirty-minute drive to Jane's to pick up Milo. I was still feeling the euphoria of the anesthesia, and I had a vial of Percocet in my pocket, so I insisted on going too.

Jane saw us pull up and came out to our car with Milo.

"Milo, sit," she said.

Milo sat.

"Good boy!"

Treat.

"Milo was a very good boy at school today," she said to us through the open car window. "Weren't you, Milo?"

Milo swish-swashed his tail and stared up at Jane with hopeful anticipation of a treat.

Jane kept her hand in her treat pocket. Milo had eyes only for Jane. Fortunately, I was not an envious person. Jane put Milo in the back of our station wagon, gave him a goodbye treat, and we were on our way home.

The next two weeks were uneventful. Andy took Milo to the dog park down the street before he left for work. One of the boys did the same after school. On Wednesday mornings, Milo's class day, Andy drove thirty minutes in the opposite direction of work, to drop Milo at Jane's house before turning around and heading to his office. After class, Jane brought Milo home to me.

The pain from my shoulder was minimal. What was difficult was the frustration that arose from having to keep my left arm in a sling. For me, energy begets energy. Being sidelined while I healed left me lethargic and more depressed than usual. The doctor had said that after two weeks I could take the sling off when I was home. By the time two weeks passed, I decided to expand the definition of "home."

"I'll take Milo to the park this morning," I said, when Andy picked up Milo's leash. "I can't stay home any longer. I'm going out of my mind."

"You're making a mistake," he said, leashing Milo.

"It's *my* shoulder and I cannot go on like this," I said. "I need to get out of here."

Andy shook his head. "You're right, it is your shoulder. But I don't want to hear about it when you're in pain because the surgery didn't work."

"Deal," I said, taking the leash from him.

I'm less prudent than Andy. I was willing to take my chances. I wore my sling to the park to make sure I didn't forget and try to use that arm. We were the only ones there. I was a bit lonely and bored, but it was much better than being lonely and bored at home. It felt so good just to be outside and moving that I did it again in the afternoon. I decided that the following day I would take Milo to school myself instead of having Jane do it.

The most difficult part of handling Milo in class was that I had to do double duty with my good arm, holding the leash and doling out treats. Milo did not pull or tug. He responded to every command. Sit, stop, circle, down. His mouth open, waiting for his treat after he completed each one.

After class, Mary asked me to wait until everyone had left so she could speak to me. Milo was definitely performing at the top of his class. I felt the same motherly pride I felt with my high-achieving, well-behaved sons. I couldn't imagine what Mary wanted to discuss with me.

When the last students had straggled out, Mary came over to Milo and me. He and I were sitting together, me on a chair, Milo by my side.

"Don't get up," Mary said, as I started to rise. "Good boy, Milo," she said, dropping a sliver of string cheese in his mouth. "Anne, I'm running a class called Manners One beginning tomorrow. I think it would be really good if you and Milo could be part of it," she said, sounding as if she were issuing a command rather than making a suggestion.

I stared back at her. We had only a few more classes to go. I had been seeing my freedom at the end of the long road of rehabilitating Milo.

"Manners?" I finally uttered.

Mary wanted me to teach Milo manners? Was I going to have to insist that he somehow convey a "Please" or a "Thank you" when appropriate? It was one thing for him to learn not to lunge at strangers or jump and hump them. Now she wanted my dog to learn etiquette?

"It's not what it sounds like," Mary said. "Good dog manners are about more than just getting a dog to do what we want. The right training can keep Milo safe and make your relationship with him more harmonious."

"Isn't that what we're doing in Dog Kindergarten?" I asked. "I don't get what you mean about learning more than just getting a dog to do what we want. Isn't the point of dog training about teaching the dog to do what we want?"

"In a sense, yes. But the most important thing in a canine–human relationship is that the canine knows who the boss is. I think the Manners class would be beneficial for *you*. You really need to become more comfortable being the alpha in your relationship with Milo. It would be good for you to have the structure and rigor of another class to strengthen the alpha in you."

I thought of telling Mary that there was no alpha in me. I decided there was no need to state the obvious. She knew I had no alpha. That's why she wanted me to sign up for Manners. She hadn't given up on my ability to learn a new behavior any more than she had given up on Milo. We'd managed to get Milo to be quasi-manageable. Now it was time to get me to learn to be the alpha and to be comfortable in that role. If Mary thought it was best for Milo for me to work on my alpha abilities, so be it. I agreed to be there the following day for our first Manners One class.

I managed to make the pretense with Milo that I was number one and he was number six. After he attacked me when I had given him his exercise bone without making him work for it, I didn't make that mistake again. Before I let him in the car, I sometimes made him sit first. I always made him wait until I said, "Okay," when I opened the back door of the station wagon at the dog park or gave him his breakfast and dinner.

Occasionally, Milo reverted to barking incessantly at a dog who didn't want to play with him. He would not stop, no matter how sternly I commanded him. Or he would not come when I called him because he was caught up in some Milo activity, like wading in the creek to capture water creatures, or stalking a squirrel on a tree branch. After all my hard work—after all *our* hard work—it was disheartening for me to be ignored. In such situations, I often found myself forsaking all the training and knowledge I had acquired over the past months. Feeling absolutely fed up with my dog, *I* hurried to *him*.

"Milo, come," I would say when I reached him, channeling all the frustration and annoyance I felt into a sharp tug of his collar. "You are bad! Very bad!" Then I would clip on his leash. Shrieking and yanking, I would lead him to the car.

Milo never resisted my yanking. He didn't take umbrage at my shrieks. He also never seemed upset or remorseful about whatever it was I thought he had done wrong. We both knew who the true alpha was in the relationship. When I made it clear to him that I was angry, he knew to acquiesce. I did not like being mean or angry. I also did not like being ignored and defied by Milo. At times like these when I erupted, I wondered if maybe I did have some small amount of alpha in me. Alpha that had survived my upbringing and the death of Teenie. Alpha that I had never needed to access or use with my two-legged boys or Mattie.

For the most part, any alpha I might have had remained dormant. When we weren't doing Mary's homework, I didn't want to bother impressing upon Milo that I was the alpha. When he didn't follow a command, it was easier for me to do damage control than to revamp our system and make myself Absolute Alpha. It was easier for me to yank him and yell at him as I hurried to the car. I wasn't proud of my tirades or outbursts. But like Milo, I wasn't perfect. Like Milo, I was doing my best.

Thirty-Three

The first day of our Manners One class, I was surprised to see twelve of the fourteen mom–dog couples from our Dog Kindergarten class. I couldn't imagine taking this class unless you were desperate and had no other way to salvage your dog. I could not begin to imagine what kind of perfection these women were striving for with their purebred dogs. Every one of the golden-hued dogs was cute, playful, and obedient.

"We are going to begin Manners One by learning to pair hand commands with the sit, stay, down, and come commands we practiced in Dog Kindergarten," Mary said in her opening remarks to the class.

Hand commands? What good were hand commands going to do me when Milo was across the park?

"You'll be surprised how often you use these hand signals," Mary continued, as if she had read my mind. "You can be on the phone, in the middle of a conversation with someone, and you can give a hand signal without disrupting what you're saying. In any case, it's always good to have a backup means of communication with your dog."

I couldn't imagine who I might be on the phone with that I wouldn't be able to pause if I needed to tell Milo to be quiet. But I knew that it was not about Milo learning sign language. For Milo and me, it was a chance for me to be the controller and for Milo to be the controlled. Still, I had to smile when I pictured myself at the dog park, angry at Milo for not coming when I called and doing a crazy silent mime of reprimands with flamboyant hand signals.

"Okay, let's get started," Mary said, bringing my mind back to the here and now of class. "Anne, could you please hand me Milo's leash?"

"Milo, come," I said.

Milo walked step-in-step with me from our place in the circle of dogs and moms to Mary in the middle.

I handed Mary the leash and stepped aside.

"Sit, Milo," Mary said in a booming voice, holding her palm up at a forty-five-degree angle in front of Milo.

Milo sat.

"Good boy, Milo," Mary said with enough exuberance to lock the gazes of every two- and four-legged creature within earshot. She dropped a treat into Milo's mouth.

She repeated the exercise, using both hand and voice, but this time her voice was softer.

Softer and softer, she did it two more times.

Then, without saying a word, Mary held her palm at a forty-five-degree angle in front of Milo's head. Immediately, Milo locked his body into a perfect Sit in front of Mary.

"Yessss, Milo. Good boy," Mary said, giving him not one treat, but two.

It was like watching a magic show with a master magician.

"I want to see everyone working on this behavior. In the beginning, remember to overexaggerate your hand motion and raise your voice," she said, handing me Milo's leash.

With his tail up and his ears up, Milo trotted beside me back to our place in the circle. He really did love to learn. It occurred to me that Mary could make training videos titled, "Mary and Milo." I did what Mary had done. I began with a loud and overexaggerated voice–hand command. Milo responded perfectly to each one, snapping his butt down without a moment's hesitation. Each time I rewarded him with the treat he deserved.

"Hand signals only," Mary called.

Everyone went silent. The noise in the room hushed. We all began doing only hand movements to a roomful of unresponsive dogs. Except for Milo. I was surprised that he was the only one in the class to catch on so quickly to the hand commands. I was also surprised that even with the surging and receding noise in the room, Milo remained focused on me. I held my palm at a forty-five-degree angle in front of Milo and did not say a word. Down went his butt. My dog was truly amazing. After fifteen minutes, Mary chose a labradoodle named Goldie to be her example dog to show us how to teach the hand signal for Stay.

"Hold the treat between your first two fingers and hold your palm flat out as if you're hitting the wall and say, 'Stay.'"

Mary did as she had said with Goldie. Goldie just stood and looked at the treat between Mary's fingers. Mary and Goldie tried again. And again and again.

"Good girl, Goldie," Mary called, finally. "Good, stay." She dropped Goldie a treat.

"Remember," Mary said as she handed Goldie back to her mom, "these exercises are not only about learning the hand commands. They are also to help you establish a strong bond with your dog. A strong and unique connection. Think of it as spending quality time together. You are building your relationship and making it stronger. This way, in the future, when the need arises, you will be better able to control your dog and keep him safe."

I liked this rationale for teaching Milo hand signals. Nonverbal control of Milo was no more interesting to me than verbal control.

But I liked the idea of having quality time with him. Milo loved learning and practicing the nonverbal commands. He loved the treats. I sensed that he also loved my positive, active focus on him. Teaching him these behaviors wasn't something I would ever do on my own, if it weren't for class or homework. I also liked that doing these exercises and spending quality time with Milo was strengthening our bond. I liked feeling connected to Milo. I liked the idea of his feeling connected to me.

Thirty-Four

As we neared the end of our Manners One class, I was confident we were finally ready to graduate from What A Good Dog. Milo had been with us for four-and-a-half months, and four of those months we had been going to school. With one week left in our Manners One class, I was giddy with anticipation that soon I would be free of dog school. We would go to the dog park and see Anise, and that would be the extent of my out-of-house activities with Milo. But as we were leaving our second-to-last class, Mary stopped me. With a sense of déjà vu, my heart sank.

"Anne, I am putting together a small class of five or six dogs. Some of the dogs are too smart for their own good, and some are not smart enough. We are going to be working outside. I think it would be good for you and Milo to be part of this class."

My shoulders slumped.

"It will be good for you to work with Milo outside. There are more distractions outside. You'll have to work harder to keep him focused. It's also good training for being on your own at the dog park with Milo."

"He seems to do okay at the dog park," I said, hoping to dissuade her. "He's not perfect, but he does okay."

"A dog like Milo really needs to know how important it is to do everything you say. I know you are making an effort to be the alpha in the relationship, but I think you still have a ways to go with this. I cannot stress enough how beneficial it would be for you and Milo to practice your skills and strengthen your bond in the outside class I'm running."

I nodded. "Okay, you're the boss," I said, with a resigned sigh.

"You might find you enjoy it," Mary said, almost smiling.

The outside class turned out to have more of an Independent Study curriculum than our previous classes. There were six pairs of dogs and their owners. In addition to Milo, there were two black Labrador retrievers, a golden retriever, a German shepherd, and a mixed breed about Milo's size. At the beginning of each class, Mary had us mingle our dogs in a controlled manner. Introductory canine sniffing was allowed. But no leash tugging, no jumping, no humping, no playing.

After our introductory mingling, we worked together on individual projects set forth by Mary that played to the behavioral strengths of each breed. The retrievers seemed to be perfecting their retrieving skills, while the German shepherd was learning to jump through a hoop.

"I want you to begin by working with Milo at the pond over there," Mary said, pointing to a perfectly round body of water about fifty yards in diameter. "I want you to begin walking around it with him. Go about halfway. Then stop. Tell him to sit and stay. When he obeys those commands, walk back to the starting point. If at any point you see that he is not waiting while you walk away, you have to take him back to that spot and begin again."

"Can I remind him to stay as I'm walking away?" I asked.

"In the beginning. Also, in the beginning you can walk backward and keep your gaze on him. But eventually, I want you to be able to walk away from him with your back toward him and have him remain in place."

I shook my head without realizing it.

"You can do this," Mary said, responding to my headshake. "It's as much about you being authoritative as it is about Milo performing the behavior. After he's able to do this, you'll work with him on coming to you and stopping. You'll call him. When he begins to come toward you, you'll say, 'Stop.' Eventually, he will. But one thing at a time. Trust me, you've got this."

Each week as I drove to class, I wondered if Milo's good behavior depended on continuous schooling, just as being in good physical shape depends on continuous training. I really hoped that it didn't. I was tired of dog school. I believed that with Mary's coaching and guidance, I might be able to do what she set out for Milo and me. Even though I understood why it was important for Milo and me to learn this, I was dismayed at the thought of doing it. At the thought of having to muck around in the muddy grass of Ardrossan. I just didn't want to do it. If I hadn't trusted Mary so completely, I would never have been circling around the Ardrossan pond week after week.

With some tips from Mary, I managed to teach Milo to stop at a spot near the pond and wait until I called him. I taught him to come when I called him and to stop and sit when I said, "Stop." I might have taken some pleasure in our achievements, except that I had never wanted a trained circus animal. Even less had I wanted to be the circus animal trainer. As the remaining weeks dwindled, I did not allow myself to dream about graduation, nor did I allow myself to dream about freedom. My dreams had been shattered too many times.

Two weeks before the end of our Independent Study, Mary tasked me with a new behavior for Milo, a variation of Hide and Seek. My task was to get him to sit and wait while I walked off into the distance and disappeared behind a fence or a tree. Then I was to call him and wait for him to find his way to me. By the end of our hour-long class, Milo had mastered the game. Mary had even added distractions for Milo to make it more difficult. She stood near him, speaking, but not to him. She had other dogs practicing nearby, anything that might take Milo's focus off his task. Milo did not fall for any of Mary's subterfuge. He seemed to have ears for me and for me only.

At the end of our last Independent Study class, Mary stopped me. "You and Milo really are a good team," she said. "You've trained him to understand that you are his person and that it's his responsibility to do as you say."

I smiled weakly. I knew what was coming after the warm-up compliment. Mary was going to re-up me for another class.

"If you were interested in more classes, Milo would be a natural for agility," Mary said, referring to the dog gymnastics class Jane taught. "He's so smart and athletic, he'd be great at it, and he'd love it."

I winced.

"On the other hand, I understand if you need a break from classes."

I nodded and smiled. Finally! Finally! I was being set free.

"In any case, your work with Milo has just begun," Mary said, her gaze locked onto mine. "Milo is working very hard to do what he needs to do to fit into a civilized society."

She looked at me for a long moment, a long moment during which I did not discern even one muscle in her face or torso ripple or twitch.

"To help him continue to be the dog he needs to be for his safety and the safety of everyone around him, Milo needs time each day just to be Milo. He needs to spend time every day in the woods to run and hunt and chase. It will tire him out, and equally important, it will give him a chance to focus fully on what he wants to do."

"I take him to the dog park at the bottom of our street for a half hour. Now I'm doing it twice a day," I said, bringing my thoughts back to Mary and her latest decree that I begin taking Milo into the woods.

"Are there woods at the dog park where he can go off and run and explore?" Mary asked.

"Not so much. It's about the size of a football field with a path around it and a brook nearby," I said. "There's an athletic French poodle we meet there almost every afternoon who runs and jumps and dances with him. Other than that, he pretty much prances around smelling, and I don't know what else."

"That's fine," Mary said. "I'd say that's okay to do in the afternoon for a half hour. But in the morning, you need to take Milo to the woods and let him romp for an hour or so."

"The woods?" I asked. I had not seen this coming. "For an hour every morning?"

"Milo is a high-strung dog, to say the least. You've worked wonders with him. But once you stop with classes and training, Milo will need another outlet for his energy and aggressiveness. He will need a chance to do what he needs to do. Also, it will give him something to look forward to. It will make him a happier dog."

"The woods?" I said, incredulous.

"There are so many great wooded parks in the area," Mary said. "Try them out and see which ones you like. You could change them up to keep you and Milo from getting bored. Although, I think there's enough change occurring every day in nature that Milo will find something new each time, even if it's always the same woods."

"I'm more of a people person than a nature person," I said. "I don't get anything out of communing with birds and wildlife."

"You won't have a chance to get bored in the woods with Milo.

You'll need to be vigilant all the time, keeping track of him, even when he's out of sight. That's why I had you work on Hide and Seek with Milo. I wanted him to get used to taking commands from you even when you're not looking at him or when he can't see you. I want him to respond to your calling him in the woods, even when he's out of sight."

"So you mean there was a method to your apparent madness," I said, smiling grimly.

"Always," she said, surprising me with a smile. "And the distractions I added with the other dogs and my talking near Milo were to train him to hear you and to respond even when there are interesting things going on around him."

"And all this time I thought you were trying to make us into a circus act," I said, with a smile.

Mary didn't smile.

"You really think it's okay for me to go to the woods and let Milo go loose and out of sight?"

"Not only okay, but necessary. Just don't let him go too long between sightings. You're going to be fine doing this. You'll feel your way at first. But you'll find a sweet spot between letting Milo be Milo and making sure he doesn't run off."

"That's a scary thought," I said. "For Milo and for whomever he finds."

"Milo's a lucky dog," Mary said. "He's lucky you found him."

"You're not usually a sweet-talker," I said. "As much as I hate the woods, the woods it will be."

I said goodbye to Mary and headed back with Milo to the car.

"Well, Milo," I said, as I clicked my seat belt. "The adventure is just beginning. I wouldn't do anything less for you than I would for one of my two-legged boys."

Thirty-Five

As I drove away from Ardrossan after our final class at What A Good Dog, I remembered a time I had pushed myself to do something I didn't want to do because I thought it would be good for one of my two-leggeds.

The previous summer, I was stuck in my seat at the kitchen table one afternoon, unable to motivate myself to move. My depression was making me feel even lower than usual. Which, trust me, is low. I picked up the newspaper, hoping to find something to lift my spirits or at least distract me when Josh, already in his Phillies pajamas, passed through the kitchen. Just as he was about to leave the room, he turned and stepped back until he was across the table from me.

"It's funny. Daddy couldn't get tickets to see the Marlins play the Phillies in Philadelphia this summer. But I was just online, and the seats are wide open in Miami when the Phillies play there in two weeks," he said in a thoughtful, low-key yet wondrous voice. Walking backward out of the kitchen, he shrugged. "In Miami, there are even seats behind home plate. And the Marlins are the World Series champs."

Hearing so many words spill out of my usually silent son, I suddenly felt lifted, buoyed. Josh is an introvert. An introvert's introvert. Trying to get him to say anything, even at the dinner table, was a frustrating endeavor, usually doomed to fail. He wasn't sullen, just silent. "Can I be excused?" he'd ask when he finished eating. That was the extent of his dinnertime chatter.

My mind and heart opened at the sound of Josh's unexpected gush of words. A rush of enthusiasm coursed through me. I went into the den. The television was already on. Josh was sprawled on the couch.

"Josh, why don't we go to Miami?"

"What?"

"You heard me."

"Really?"

"Why not?"

I'm not a fan of baseball. I hate to travel. But I am a big fan of Josh. I suddenly had a chance to do my favorite thing, to encourage and enable a son's passion.

Two weeks later, we were driving down Collins Ave. in Miami. Beside me, in the passenger seat, Josh was tossing a new baseball up and down into his glove, a ball he'd brought hoping to get it signed so he could put it on his bookcase beside his most prized procession, a ball signed by Phillies first baseman Ryan Howard. We were off to a perfect start!

We arrived at the fifteen-story, white stucco Delano Hotel owned by Madonna. A friend had told me it was *the* place to stay in Miami. The white lobby was filled with fit young men in white linen and tiny shorts. After checking in, Josh waited outside the gift shop while I went in to buy a newspaper. As I handed the cashier my money, I saw behind her Penis Gummies, Peppermint Peckers, and Gummy Handcuffs. With a racing heart, I grabbed my paper and steered Josh to our room.

Josh rushed to the safe and locked up our baseball tickets as if they were the Hope Diamond. He picked up the remote, sat down on the bed, and said, "Mommy, can we watch *The Lord of the Rings* now?" I am not a fan of Tolkien, but I am a fan of Josh. All I could surmise after three hours was that a little man finds a ring.

When the movie was over, we headed to Dolphins Stadium, arriving two hours early for batting practice. We found our seats easily in the near-empty stadium, halfway up behind home plate. Josh said, "Wow, these seats are great!" He pulled out his scorecard and pencil and opened his bag of peanuts. I felt the muscles in my body softening. Below us, hanging over the railing, fans reached out for autographs.

"Josh, do you want to try to get your ball signed?"

"No, not today. I just want to sit here and watch."

When the game began, Josh hunched forward, pencil in hand. It was an exciting game. The Phillies were winning, the Phillies were losing, and the Phillies were winning. In the fourth inning, clouds came over the stadium. I am a fan of Josh, but I am not a fan of rain. I left to go inside. I sat on the grimy pebbles of the concourse, hoping Josh was having a good time.

When people started streaming toward the exits, Josh found me and told me there was a rain delay. No Abel has ever left a baseball game before the last out has been played, so I didn't dare suggest it. We sat together on the concourse in silence for ninety minutes. Tarps off the field, I followed Josh back into the now-nearly-empty stadium. We were able to sit directly behind home plate. At one in the morning, two long hours later, the Phillies *lost*. I put my hand on Josh's knee and gave him a squeeze.

"That's okay, Mommy. They play a hundred and sixty-two games a year. They can't win every one. We have two more games. And these seats behind home plate were really cool!" It was two thirty by the time we found our way back to the Delano and went to sleep.

On the way back from breakfast the next morning, I glimpsed

the blue Atlantic Ocean and the glistening white beach. I love beaches, but I love Josh even more, and it was time to watch the second *Lord of the Rings* movie. From what I could tell, the ring the little man had found was still causing him problems.

The second game was almost a repeat of the previous night, except that the Phillies got off to a bad start this time, and when the rain came in the fourth inning, it was a downpour. At ninety minutes, Josh and I were *still* sitting on the concourse.

Over the years, I've tried to learn to be comfortable with Josh's quietness. It's who he is. He seems completely at ease with silence. Sitting across from him, watching him roll his ball around in his glove, I wondered what he was thinking and feeling. I hoped he was having a good time. I hoped he was glad we were here. Josh looked up at me, shrugged, and smiled.

After two-and-a-half hours, the rain delay was over, and we went back into the abandoned stadium. The two-and-a-half-hour rest didn't help the Phillies. At one thirty in the morning, they lost their second game in a row. Josh gathered his things and said, "Maybe they'll win one for us tomorrow."

The following day, we woke up early because our third and final game was a day game. I opened the white venetian blinds and saw nothing but blue sky and sun. There'd be no rain delay today. We jumped in the car and went back to Dolphins Stadium. Josh and I sat down in our seats, and almost immediately, sweat was dripping down us, soaking our clothes and collecting in little puddles around our chairs. It was a hundred degrees and 80 percent humidity. Miami in August, and it was *hot*!

In a quick two innings, the Phillies were down six to nothing. Josh turned to me, sweat dripping into his eyes, and said, "Mommy, can we leave? They aren't even trying."

The trip was already becoming a bad memory. I had dragged

him to Miami in the summer to sit in the rain and then the sun to see his team be crushed.

"Are you sure you want to go?"

He nodded.

I looked at Josh slumped in his seat and saw the ball in the glove on his lap.

"Okay. But just a minute."

I grabbed the ball from his glove and ran down the stairs two at a time toward the bullpen. I climbed up on the railing and clutched the net with both hands, still holding the ball in my right hand.

"Please, sir," I called down to a lone Phillies player standing in the bullpen with his back toward me.

A security guard hurried over. "Ma'am, you've got to get down out of that net."

I turned back to the Phillies player, who was now looking up at me.

"Please, sir, we came all the way from Philadelphia. Will you please sign our ball?"

The player smiled. "Sure, throw it down. Them's good folk up in Philadelphia." He signed the ball and tossed it up to me. Three-by-three, I ran back up the stairs to Josh.

"Who is he? Who is he?" I said, handing him the ball.

"Oh, he's Geoff Geary. He's some relief pitcher they brought up from the minors last night. But thank you."

And we left the stadium.

On his mother's watch, Josh had broken the family tradition of never leaving a baseball game before the last out had been played. At the hotel, I asked Josh if he wanted to watch the last *Lord of the Rings* movie.

"No, I just want to go to sleep."

The next day when we went home, I left my suitcase in the

doorway. I didn't feel like unpacking. I didn't feel like doing anything. I dropped onto the family room couch. Josh headed off toward his room.

Then I heard Josh's voice. "Mommy?"

I looked up. Josh stood in the family room doorway holding the ball I had gotten signed for him in one hand and the case with his favorite ball in the other.

"Would it be okay if I took the Ryan Howard ball out and used the special case for *our* ball instead?" Josh asked with a smile.

My heart lifted. I smiled.

I thought we had struck out. But we had hit a home run.

Driving home from out last class at What A Good Dog, the memory of this trip comforted and reassured me. I hoped that my taking Milo into the woods would be as good for him as the trip to Miami had been for Josh. I hoped it would strengthen our connection. I hoped that doing what I did not want to do and going into the woods every day with Milo would help him be the dog he needed and wanted to be. A dog who could be part of our family.

Thirty-Six

It would be an understatement to say that I did not have the confidence in myself that Mary had in me. Certainly not the confidence she had in my ability to take Milo into the woods and control him while still letting him run free. So it wasn't surprising that the following morning I was worried about heading to the woods with Milo. Worried and scared that I did not have the control over Milo that Mary thought I had. At the dog park at the bottom of our street, he was always visible. If he didn't come when I called him, I could just go get him. But if he didn't respond to my call in the woods, there would be no way for me to retrieve him. It only had to happen once that Milo would take off after a squirrel or a deer or any other creature lurking in the woods, never to be seen again. This wouldn't be good for Milo or me. It certainly wouldn't be good for anyone he encountered. I imagined Little Red Riding Hood with her basket of food crossing paths with Milo. Unlike the fairy-tale wolf who ate the grandmother in order to trick Little Red Riding Hood so he could eat her as well as her basket of food, Milo would take care of things on the spot. One casualty, Little Red Riding Hood or anyone else, would be one too many. I needed a fail-safe plan to fall back on before I could set Milo free in the woods.

I decided I would use the same shock collar for Milo that I had seen someone at the dog park use on their dog. The metal pronged collar delivered a beep or a shock at the press of a remote control. I was well aware that this was the opposite of Mary's positive reinforcement method of dog training. But I was the one ultimately responsible for Milo. I was the one who had to be comfortable taking him into the woods.

There was a wooded park ten minutes from my house. I had driven by it daily for fifteen years. Not once had I been tempted to turn off the main road and see what it was like. I am not a fan of recreational walking on sidewalks or in the woods. After Milo joined our family, what I liked to do had less and less bearing on what I actually did. I had hoped that two thirty-minute walks around the dog park at the bottom of our street would be the last additions to the Milo-Activities-I-Don't-Like-to-Do List. It was not.

On the way to the wooded park, I drove past the dog park at the bottom of our street. I didn't know if I should laugh or cry. Milo recognized the park and stood up, his tail and ears up, in happy anticipation. I always loved seeing Milo happy. On the other hand, it had been burdensome enough for me to go to that park twice a day. Even though I was finally able to take dog school off the list of Milo activities that I didn't like doing, I was now going to spend sixty minutes in the woods ten minutes farther away from home. Milo turned and looked at me when we drove past the dog park without stopping.

"Don't worry, Milo," I said, shaking my head and looking at him in the rearview mirror. "We're going to a different dog park."

When I saw the weathered wood sign, ROLLING HILL, I felt my stomach tighten. I turned off the main road and began driving up the steep driveway.

"Milo, look, we're at a different dog park," I said, hoping that hearing myself speaking in an upbeat voice would lift my own spirits.

Milo stood up and surveyed the trees from the side and back

windows. I was sure he recognized the words "dog park." He also knew this was the time of day we usually went there.

"You didn't think we were going to skip the park today, did you?" I was working really hard to make this new daily activity as painless as possible.

At the top of the driveway, there was an empty gravel parking lot. Extending beyond that was a crabgrass field the size of several football fields. Beyond that on all sides were trees. I got out of the car and opened the back door of the station wagon.

"Sit," I said to Milo.

He sat.

"Good boy," I said, looking into his eyes.

I strapped the shock collar on him. Before we headed into the woods, I needed to train him on it. I needed to reinforce the commands we had learned with Mary. I needed to teach Milo with the shock collar that even if he couldn't see me, even if he couldn't hear me, when he heard the beep or felt the buzz of the shock, it was time to return to me.

"Okay," I said.

Milo jumped out of the car.

"Milo, sit," I said.

"Good boy," I said when he did.

"Stay," I said, as I began to walk away.

My plan was to do the exercises we had done around the pond with Mary as well as Hide and Seek. Even though I had understood why she had us practice the exercises, now that I was in the woods with Milo, it was clear that Mary hadn't been teaching us circus tricks. What she had taught us were survival tools.

"Okay, Milo, come," I said, after walking several steps.

Milo came to me and sat. We continued. Round and round the field we went. He responded to every command perfectly, even though I could see from his roving eyes that he was distracted by the stimulus overload of so much untamed nature. He came to me with his tail and ears up, his feet hitting the ground lightly as if he were skipping. I couldn't help but smile. He was such a beautiful, curious animal.

In order to train Milo on the shock collar, it was crucial that he disregard one of my commands. When he did, I would press the beep button on the remote control to get him to respond. If the beep didn't get his attention, I would dial the shock from one to ten, until he responded. Finally, after two passes around the field, Milo got up before I told him to and began trotting toward the trees.

"Milo," I called.

He ignored me. I pressed the beep. He still ignored me. I pressed shock level one, two, three, four. Finally, Milo stopped and turned around to look at me.

"Come," I said.

He didn't move. I pressed shock level four. He trotted over to me, not looking hurt physically or emotionally.

"Good boy," I said when he reached me.

When I was comfortable he understood that when he felt the shock he was to come to me, I led him toward a path that began at the edge of the field and went into the woods. Immediately, Milo took off and disappeared.

"Milo," I called, right away, wanting to give our system a quick test. "Milo!"

When he didn't come, I dialed the shock to level four, again, and zapped him. Moments later, he was by my side. I was not sure how to balance letting Milo run with making sure he didn't get lost. I decided to let him go off and then call him every two or three minutes. This worked. Soon, he was checking back with me on his own.

"Good boy, Milo," I said each time, rewarding him with a treat.

It was late July. After the previous night's rain, the path was muddy and the air humid and buggy. My hiking boots were immediately caked with mud. They made a thwacking sound as I lifted each one out of the muck. With my hand that wasn't holding the shock remote control, I began swatting flies and mosquitoes away from my face. As much as I didn't want to think about doing this again, I made a mental note to buy insect repellent for the next day. I tried to convince myself how wonderful it was to be able to drive ten minutes and be bushwhacking through the woods. I was surrounded by trees and moss. I really didn't feel lucky to be here. I. Did. Not. Like. Walking. In. The. Woods.

Suddenly, Milo burst out of the trees on my left, soaring through the air. I stopped. I held my breath. He was nothing less than magnificent. He was a marvel. My breathing resumed, and I felt myself soaring with him. He landed on the path in front of me. He looked so happy. So excited. It was spellbinding for me to see Milo being able to be Milo with every ounce of his being.

"Good boy, Milo," I said.

And Milo was off again, across the path and into the woods on the right.

I ambled down the muddy path while Milo crisscrossed me at regular intervals. Seeing Milo in all his beautiful glory, I understood why Mary said he needed a chance to be himself to his fullest in the woods. Each time I saw Milo fly through the air, I felt myself soaring vicariously, energized and happy. Content. Fulfilled. Grateful that I could help Milo be the Milo he was meant to be. Now, more than any time since I'd first gotten him, I felt grateful for Milo. I found myself living for the moments when Milo would fly past me and lift me for a moment. In between these bursts of excitement with Milo, I took solace thinking about how tired he would be when we got home.

At the bottom of the hill there was a creek and a path that went about forty feet to the right and then off to the left. I waited for Milo to join me. Then, wanting to maximize our sojourn for Milo's sake, I led him the forty feet to the right, before turning and backtracking in the other direction. I'd come this far; a little bit more wouldn't kill me.

I found it a bit more pleasant walking along the creek. Even my woods-curmudgeon-self was not impervious to the sound of babbling water. The path had more gravel and was less muddy. When we got to the end of the path, we turned around and began the slip-and-slide climb back up the path. Physically, the trip up the hill was no better or worse for me than going down. Mentally, however, I felt lighter with every step I took toward my car. Milo, meanwhile, showed no signs of tiring as he dashed back and forth in front of me and behind me. I could not believe I had once thought thirty minutes in the dog park near our house was a workout for him. When we reached the top of the path, I noticed a vine hanging from a tree about ten feet off the ground. Nearby was a log.

"Milo," I called. "Look at this vine!"

Milo trotted over, and just as I stepped aside, he began to jump and bark. He wanted that vine, and he wanted it bad. I stepped back to the log on the ground across from the vine and sat down.

"Good vining," I called over and over. "What a good viner you are, Milo."

With each jump, Milo inched higher and higher. At the peak of his jump, his front and rear paws were together in front of him, making him sleek and aerodynamic. I could see the muscles in his hind quarters, perfectly formed. This dog was a natural athlete. A graceful, handsome, natural athlete.

I couldn't imagine what living creature he imagined he was stalking as he sprang upward toward the tip of the vine. It didn't matter. It was luxurious, decadent even, for me to be sitting still watching Milo exert himself. It didn't get better than this. For ten minutes, I sat and watched Milo. Finally, when his barks began sounding hoarse, I stood up.

"Okay, Milo, come," I said, saving him from himself.

He jumped a few more times.

"Milo," I said.

Milo landed. He looked at me.

"Milo, you are the best viner in the world. I am so proud of you," I said, almost singing the words. "You are such a good boy."

His tongue hung from his mouth as he panted and panted. When he heard the familiar words "good boy," his tail swished a sluggish swish. I couldn't believe it. Milo was exhausted.

"Okay, my very good viner. Let's go home."

Happily, tiredly, he followed. I looked at my watch. It had been exactly an hour since we began our descent down the trail. Perfect. When he was settled on his bed in the car, I gave him a treat.

"Good boy, Milo," I said, before closing the door.

As the door clicked shut, I watched him rest his head on his front paws.

I felt a smile spread across my face. Job well done. For both of us. Milo had run, he had jumped, and he had hunted. He had used all of his energy doing what he wanted to do. Now he was content. Seeing Milo this way filled me with unexpected joy.

Thirty-Seven

Our family went on vacation to the Outer Banks of North Carolina in August, eight months after we got Milo. One sunny morning, Andy and the boys went to a beach on Currituck Sound to fly a kite while I took Milo for a walk. As part of our route, I took him onto a dock on the sound about a quarter of a mile from the beach where the rest of the family was launching the kite. I sat on a bench on the deck, happy for the good view and a few minutes of rest. Milo stood on the edge of the dock surveying the rippling water. Suddenly, Milo began barking. I looked up to see that he was barking at a nesting seabird and her chicks on top of an Audubon pole twenty feet from the dock. Before I thought to do anything, Milo jumped from the dock into the water.

"Milo!" I screamed as I jumped up, terrified that he was going to drown. "Milo, come. Now."

Earlier in the summer, I had tried to teach him to swim in our pool. Swimming was both soothing and invigorating for me, and I thought maybe it would have the same effect on Milo. I also thought that if I could get him swimming in the pool, I could tire him out without exerting myself. I had harnessed a dog life preserver to his torso, filled a baggie with chunks of chicken and steak, and lured him down the steps in the shallow end until the water was up to the bottom of his neck.

"Milo, come," I said, standing an arm's length away from him and holding a chunk of steak a foot from his nose. "Milo, come."

As he began to move his body forward, his focus on the steak chunk, I stepped back a few feet.

"Good boy, Milo, good boy," I said.

Thrashing his front paws and bobbing up and down in the water, he finally reached me. I dropped the steak into his mouth.

"What a boy you are, Milo! What a good swimmer you are!"

Bit by bit, I stepped backward, holding onto Milo's collar with one hand as the water got deeper, and dropping the treats into his mouth, one after the other. Thrash, bob, thrash, bob, thrash. Milo continued after me. It was not a pretty sight, but he was doing it. When we got to the deep end, I turned around so my back was toward the shallow end and turned Milo around too. His front legs continued to move clumsily in and out of the water. His swimming stroke didn't resemble anything like the dog paddle I thought dogs instinctively knew how to do. Knowing his life jacket would keep him from drowning, I let go of his collar and began walking backward.

Over and over I called him, always a treat in my outstretched hand. He came to me propelled by nothing but brute force. When we finally got back to the shallow end, I guided him to the stairs and up onto the pavers. After a full-bodied shake that rippled from the tip of his nose to the tip of his tail, pelting me with high-velocity droplets, Milo sat down by my feet. Looking up at me, he opened his mouth like a baby bird awaiting a worm.

"Milo, good trying," I said, pouring treats from the bag into his open mouth. "Just you wait and see. We'll practice and practice and practice. Just like we always do. Just like you always do, you'll succeed."

Practice and practice we did. Every day before dinner, after the dog park, I belted the life preserver around Milo, and down to the pool we went. Day after day for two weeks, we got into the pool where I never stopped chirping, "Good boy, Milo. You are such a good swimmer. A very good swimmer."

After two full weeks of Milo giving it his all, two full weeks of Milo valiantly stepping down into the pool and using sheer, uncoordinated force to get from one end to the other and back, his stroke had no more resemblance to the dog paddle than it had on day one. After two full weeks of extolling what an excellent swimmer he was, I gave up. I retired my title as canine swim instructor. Unlike with children, I reasoned, it was not a matter of safety that he know how to swim. I didn't foresee him being invited to a friend's pool. Or even onto a boat. I was fine with Milo's destiny as a landlubber. Sometimes, the key to success is knowing when to quit.

So the day on the Outer Banks when Milo jumped into the sound, I was terrified he was going to drown. I had not anticipated that any dog who had to be lured into a pool with a steady stream of treats would ever decide to jump feetfirst into a body of water. But of course, Milo was not *any* dog.

"Milo, come!" I shrieked.

"Milo, come!" I screamed.

"Milo, you are so bad! You are very, very bad!"

As I called and yelled, Milo continued away from me. Suddenly, I realized that not only had Milo not come to me, but that he also was not drowning. Not by any means. When I stopped shrieking, when I stopped hyperventilating, I noticed that Milo was swimming, albeit away from me, with the smooth, invisible movements of a swan.

Unlike a swan, however, he released a steady torrent of vicious barks as he glided. The birds didn't move. This really pissed Milo off. He began to swim circles around the Audubon pole, his head up, barking at them. This dog who had been so clumsy and pathetic thrashing across our pool was now the picture of grace with the sound of ugly, disharmonic barking. I was confident that the birds were safe. There was no chance Milo was going to sprout wings and fly up to them. Milo's stamina was matched only by his ability to stay focused. I sat back and watched my dog tire himself out.

A large blue-and-red bird soared through the air. Although I have no interest or knowledge in ornithology, I recognized the species of this colorful creature immediately. It was the kite Joseph, Josh, and Andy were flying from the beach. When I looked back from the kite to Milo, he was now swimming past the Audubon pole, focused on the kite, his barking still piercing and steady.

I made a few more good-faith shouts to him. But it was clear that if Milo had a rearview mirror attached to his head, my image on the dock would be getting smaller and smaller. I ran up the hill to the road. Running as fast as my forty-eight-year-old legs would take me. I ran straight until I got to the turnoff for the small sandy beach where my family was.

"Good boy," Joseph and Josh were calling excitedly to Milo.

Joseph was holding the string of the kite. Andy and Josh were whistling and clapping and otherwise cheering Milo on.

"Mommy, look at him," Josh said, as if I had been in a dark hole all morning and did not know what Milo was up to. "It's amazing he can bark so strongly and swim so effortlessly all at the same time."

The wonder of Milo. His innate athleticism, grace, and focus. I had tried so hard to teach him to swim by dropping grade A cubes of steak and chicken breast down his throat. Clearly, I had not found the right way to motivate him. Why eat days-old meat and poultry when you can find it fresh? For a predator like Milo, the thrill was in the hunt.

As I stood by the edge of the water catching my breath and thinking about the myriad ways Milo might create havoc, even terror, in this frenzied state, my family was enjoying the entertainment as if they were at a backyard party. Joseph and Josh were laughing harder than I could remember seeing in a very long time. Andy stood behind them smiling.

"I'm glad you're all enjoying yourselves," I finally was able to sputter. "But . . ."

The three of them looked at me momentarily. Then they whipped their heads back toward Milo. Joseph had been slowly reeling in the kite as Milo had been swimming. Now both Milo and the kite were directly across from the beach where we stood. Milo in the water, the kite in the sky.

Joseph navigated the kite closer and closer toward us onshore. Beneath it, Milo followed, his barking continuous. I was flabbergasted that he could exert himself like this without pausing for a breath. Joseph caught the kite in his hand just as Milo lumbered out of the water, looking like a lion closing in on his prey. He was an animal on a mission.

"Milo!" I screamed, sounding exactly like the broken record I had become.

Bursting water droplets flowed down his coat. Sand kicked up by his feet stuck in clumps to his legs and belly. With his head down slightly, as if following a scent, he marched right past me. I looked beyond him and saw a family with three school-aged children on a picnic blanket eating lunch.

"Milo!" I screamed, running after him.

I could hear Andy and the boys running up from the water behind me.

Before I could reach him, Milo had reached the picnicking family. A fast-forwarding montage of horror scenes shaded in red, bloody red, raced through my mind. My heart stopped, even as I hurried after Milo. Was this the end? Of the family? Of Milo?

"What a pretty dog," I heard one of the girls on the blanket say.

I shuddered.

"Milo!" I screamed just as I caught up with him. I was about to grab his collar when he moved. I'd lost my chance.

I looked at the picnic blanket covered with sandwiches, drumsticks, cheese, and fruit. The horror scenes continued in my mind, imbued in an even deeper hue of blood red. I threw out my hand, again. This time I succeeded in grabbing hold of my dog. Just as I did, I felt a tug from Milo. I dug my feet more firmly into the sand. Milo planted *his* feet closer together. Before I could counter with another move, he squatted.

"Look, Mommy, the dog is pooping," the little girl squealed.

I felt every bit of tension drain from me as I watched Milo's poop plop onto the sand. I looked up at the family. Every single one of them was grinning.

"I'm so, so sorry," I said, pulling a poop bag out of my pocket with one hand and clutching Milo by the collar with the other. "He's a rescue and we haven't worked out all the kinks."

"Don't be silly," the mother said. "We have a dog at home. The house we're renting doesn't allow dogs, and we miss him. It's nothing we haven't seen before."

"I hope you enjoy the rest of your vacation," I said, turning around.

I took Milo by the collar and guided him away from the picnic. When we were well beyond earshot, I stopped and kneeled beside Milo so we were at eye level.

"Milo, I am so proud of you. You didn't eat those people's lunch. You didn't eat those people. You are such a very good boy."

I gave him some deep rubs behind his ears. As I did, he opened his mouth and licked me on the cheek.

"I love you, too, Milo," I said. "I love you very much."

I stood up and walked toward Andy and the boys.

"Milo, good job," they said, ruffling his coat.

Milo sidled slowly against Joseph's legs. He sidled slowly against Josh's legs. I watched and listened as my family gleefully replayed moments in Milo's most recent escapade. Indeed, it felt like a party. An impromptu Milo beach party. A *fun* party.

Thirty-Eight

Day by day, week by week, month by month, our morning hikes through the woods turned into a year, then two years, then three, four, five, and beyond. There were times when I called Milo, and he did not respond. I would scream and scream until I was hoarse. Then I would start pressing the shock button on my remote control, moving quickly from one to ten. Over and over, I would call and shock, and still no Milo. The shock collar had a range of about a quarter of a mile. I had no way of knowing if Milo had chased some creature out of range, or if he just didn't want to be bothered by me. Milo had a tag with his name and our phone number. He also had a chip in his ear that any vet could read and get our contact information. Sometimes, I would call and shock for five minutes, although it seemed more like an hour. Then Milo would come flying out of the thicket of trees, full of life and looking as happy as could be. I always felt elated when I saw him bounding out of the trees. My elation was heightened when I saw him bounding toward me after he'd been missing. I always tried to picture where he had been and what he'd been doing. I wondered if my shocks had brought him back. Or maybe he just didn't want to lose me any more than I wanted to lose him.

Summer, autumn, winter, spring, we never missed a day. Snow, rain, cold, heat, we never missed a day. I bought waterproof pants and jackets. I bought gaiters to strap over my hiking boots and over the cuffs of my waterproof pants. I also bought crampons to strap onto my hiking boots to keep me from sliding down the icy wooded hills. There was something very satisfying to me about defying the weather and not letting it dictate what I did. After our hikes, I always felt virtuous for having slogged through one more hike in the woods. When I did it in extreme conditions, I felt even more pleased with my accomplishment.

There were summer days when it was ninety-five degrees, 100 percent humidity, and buggy. There were winter days when it was fifteen degrees and icy. There were days of torrential downpours. Nothing stopped me from suiting up and setting out with my four-legged buddy. The hardest part of these extreme weather hikes was the first step. The first rain pelting my green, knee length, hooded raincoat. The first blast of burning fifteen-degree wind through my wool face mask. Once we started down our familiar path, I was always surprised by how quickly I acclimated. Maneuvering down the frozen path, I quickly heated up and pulled off my mask. Sliding down the rain-saturated mud, I soon became one with the layer of brown slop caked on my boots, gaiters, and pants. I took more satisfaction from these extreme weather outings than from our usual walks. I felt adventurous and emboldened about not letting Milo down. Milo, of course, was Milo. If he noticed the weather, he didn't let on. As always, he was happy to be free. Happy to be able to be Milo.

Even though I had moments of elation in the woods with Milo, I never looked forward to it. I dreaded it each morning. I dreaded walking down the hill and walking back up. The bugs, the mud, the cold, the heat. Before Milo, nothing would have lured me into the woods, even on a perfect spring day. Being Milo's person taught me that I could experience joy in the exact place I dreaded being. Seeing Milo being Milo in all his glory made me happier than I could have imagined. It took my breath away every time. In meditation, I had heard about sympathetic joy, but I had never really understood the concept. This was exactly what I was experiencing. Joy in proportion to Milo's joy. Being able to be a good dog mom to Milo was having the desired effect on my depression. When Mattie died, I had hoped that getting Milo would help me cope with my depression. Milo gave me so much more.

The happiness I got from being a good mother to my boys was also a kind of sympathetic joy. My parents' meanness and vindictiveness had always been the more visible part of their abuse. Empathy and sympathetic joy were things my parents were not able to give me.

By being the best mother I could be, I had created happiness for myself. As one by one the boys became adults and left home, I had fewer opportunities to be a good mother. "You're cooked," I said to each one of my boys when they left for college. "I've done for you what I can. I will still be here for you when you need me. But I am now releasing you into the world." Each of the three times I tearily said this, I was reminded that being a good mother had made me redundant. I also realized that without the boys at home, I had lost an important source of sympathetic joy. I had also lost the sense of purpose that had helped me stay afloat for so many years. As sad as I was about my house of empty bedrooms, I was proud that I had sent my boys out into the world with the skills, resilience, and fortitude to find their way. I was proud of them. I was proud of me.

I would never have traded Mattie for Milo. My love for low-maintenance Mattie had been as simple and pure as her love for me. Her needs were minimal. She never frustrated or angered me. Not once did I need to reprimand her. Milo was a different story. He needed not to be a threat to anyone and everyone around him.

For me, the best way to meet Milo's needs was to play to his strengths, to encourage his behaviors that were nonthreatening. Just as my favorite role as a mother was enabling my children to find and pursue their passions, I wanted to do the same for Milo. I wanted to help Milo be the best Milo he could be, even if it meant doing things I did not like to do. I did them ungrudgingly. They helped Milo thrive and have a happy life. He loved learning. He loved exploring the woods. He loved romping at the dog park with Anise. He loved sniffing new dogs. He loved gnawing on his bones while I exercised. He loved being with me.

Knowing that I was helping Milo have as fulfilling a Milo-life as he could have without acting on his aggressive tendencies fulfilled me. Even though I did not enjoy doing the things I did to enable him, I did no less for Milo than I would do for anyone in my family. I never skipped any of the activities that were important for him. Milo was such a large part of every waking hour of every one of my days, physically, mentally, and emotionally, that I found myself feeling increasingly and inextricably tied to him.

I experienced the moments of the day through Milo's eyes. I found a new perspective. His enthusiasm, his joie de vivre lifted me out of myself. Seeing him stand up, his tail high and wagging, his ears up, when we pulled into the parking lot of the woods lightened my dread of the upcoming hour.

Watching Milo being Milo with the exuberance of a creature living his life to the fullest, I often thought back to the dog I had seen curled up in his cage on a bed of rags at Main Line Animal Rescue. While the other dogs barked, their noses sticking through the wires of their cages, Milo lay quietly, his eyes forlorn. Milo was so unwanted by the world, so undesirable that Bill Smith had probably sedated him in order to dupe an unsuspecting family into taking him. The contrast of the dog I had seen in his cage with the dog maximizing every moment with all his vivacious being made my heart soar. The contrast between where Milo had been and where he was now was well worth the work. It made me feel good to be able to make a difference in another creature's life.

I helped Milo, and Milo helped me. It was simple. It was complicated. It was love.

Thirty-Nine

One damp, raw April Monday morning, ten years after I had adopted Milo, we went to the woods as usual. I noticed as we drove up the long, windy driveway that he did not get up and begin pacing back and forth in happy anticipation. I assumed he was focused on something outside his rear window. As much as I dreaded our morning walks in the woods, I always felt myself smiling after I'd parked the car and opened the back of the station wagon. There I would find Milo sitting at attention, head up, ears pointed, back straight, energy and excitement pulsing from his eager body as he waited for my "Okay" command to spring from the car. Each morning when I faced him in the back of the station wagon, all too aware that I had a full hour of woods trudging ahead of me, Milo's enthusiasm as he waited to be set free was contagious, and I felt a shot of happiness go through me. On this morning when I opened the door, Milo just lay in his bed, his head down.

"Come on, Milo. Don't you want to go for a walk?" I asked, rubbing him behind his ears.

He didn't move. I tugged on his collar lightly. He still did not move.

I leaned into the back of the station wagon and wrapped my arms around my dog.

"Milo? Milo?" I said, rubbing my face into his neck.

My stomach tightened. My entire body tightened.

"Milo, don't worry," I said, nuzzling him one last time. "We'll figure this out."

I gently closed the door and called our vet to say we were on our way. When we arrived, I put my arms around Milo's torso and lowered him gently to the ground. Milo followed me slowly into the waiting room.

"Hi, Anne. Hi, Milo," said Kathy, the cheery, fiftyish woman who managed the practice. "I can bring you right into the examining room."

I sat down in a chair in the corner of the examining room and Milo lay down at my feet.

"What's going on with Milo?" said the vet, breezing into the room and closing the door.

"I don't know," I said. "We got to the park, and he wouldn't move. This is not like him at all. I could barely get him out of the car to come in here."

The vet hoisted Milo onto the stainless-steel examining table. I stood next to it, rubbing Milo behind his ears.

"I'm going to take Milo and x-ray him," the vet said after listening to his heart and checking him over. "We'll bring him out to you in the waiting room."

I took a seat in a chair in the waiting room across from Kathy.

A few minutes later, a vet tech came into the waiting room leading Milo slowly behind him. Milo's head hung low, but his tail, even though it was limp, made a weak swish when he saw me. I sprang from my seat and ran across the room, falling to my knees when I reached Milo, and wrapped my arms around his neck.

"The doctor will talk to you after he reviews the X-rays," the vet tech said.

It was noon. The waiting room was empty. Kathy typed, answered the phone, and scrolled through her computer. I sat and watched the clock: 12:10, 12:20, 12:30. The phone rang again. This time instead of rattling off a list of possible appointment times after her cheerful, energetic hello, Kathy gasped, and her face turned ashen. She hung up the phone and bolted out of the waiting room.

I sat with Milo in the silent room. I offered him a treat from the treat jar on Kathy's desk. He didn't want it. I waited. Milo waited.

"Anne, you can come back now with Milo," Kathy said, coming back into the waiting room some minutes later.

I coaxed Milo up and followed Kathy.

As soon as I was seated in the chair in the corner, the vet came in carrying a set of three X-rays. He put one up on the light box and then turned to me.

"Milo has cancer," he said.

"What?" I said, my stomach clenching. "What did you say?"

"Look," the vet said, putting a pen on a spot on the left of the X-ray and moving it along Milo's body toward his head. "From here in his tail all the way to his head, he is filled with cancer."

I don't know how to interpret X-rays. Looking at the lightbox with the vet, my body quivering, I couldn't see the cancer image the vet was outlining. I collapsed into the chair, tears spilling down my cheeks.

"Is there a treatment?" I said, thinking of all the treatable cancers I'd heard about. I had been treated for lymphoma years earlier and had been in remission ever since.

"I am so sorry to have to tell you that there is nothing that can be done to help Milo. He is filled with cancer. I suggest you take him home. When it becomes clear that he is suffering, you will know it is time. I am very sorry. He's a magnificent dog."

I slid onto the floor and nuzzled Milo, my tears saturating his furry head. Monday, Tuesday, Wednesday, and Thursday we watched Milo languish and become more inert each day. It was all

I could do to get him to go into the backyard to pee. I moved in a heavy-footed trance, my stomach queasy. In addition to freelance writing, I was also now teaching English at the Community College of Philadelphia. As difficult as it was for me to leave Milo, I didn't have a choice. On Monday and Wednesday, as always happened when I stepped into the classroom, I forgot about everything except the students who had shown up for class. I was so absorbed by each and every moment that, during class, I actually forgot that Milo was home dying. But at the end of the three-hour sessions on Monday and Wednesday, as I packed up my books and spoke to lingering students, it came to me in unexpected jolts that I was not living Life as Usual.

Milo was dying. The unthinkable, the unimaginable, while still unthinkable and unimaginable, was imminent. I am not known for my optimism. Yet, driving home, I remembered the UPS man standing at the door and telling me he had hit Mattie. Unable to imagine my life without Mattie, I had said, "But she's okay, right?" So, too, on Monday and Wednesday as I drove home from school, I found myself thinking maybe, maybe, maybe somehow Milo would be standing at the door waiting for me. He would be his old self. I would take him back to the vet, and new X-rays would show he was fine. I could not imagine life without Milo. I did not want to imagine life without Milo. Milo was not waiting for me at the door when I got home. He was in his bed exactly where he had been when I left for school.

Friday morning, five days after his cancer diagnosis, Milo would not come into the kitchen for breakfast. I brought his bowl to him in the hall. He lifted his head, looked at me, looked at the bowl, and put down his head.

"I'm going to the supermarket to get him some sirloin," Andy said.

An hour later, Milo was still lying down in the hall. Andy put the steak in front of Milo's nose. Milo didn't move.

I burst into tears.

"It's time, Anne," Andy said.

I nodded, as I sobbed, my body heaving. I got down on the floor and hugged Milo. I kissed Milo. Then I ran to my bed and threw myself down, keening into my pillow. I was grateful that Andy was taking Milo and would be with him in his final moments. I would not let myself imagine the details of the scene.

At one o'clock, I soaked my swollen face with a cold washcloth and then headed to class. I don't remember anything about the thirty-minute ride to school. I was not pulled into the present moment even once by my students. The only thing I remember about the three-hour class was the fifteen-minute quiz during which I could sit down in a void of deep, empty blackness.

After class, I ran to my car and called Andy.

"Oh, Andy," I said, breaking into uncontrollable sobbing when he answered.

"It was very peaceful," Andy said, his voice quivering. "I sat on the floor with him and put his head on my lap. I stroked him behind the ears and rubbed his back the way he always likes. I mean liked. The vet gave him a shot and we waited. His eyes closed and his body twitched. He took what we thought was his last breath. But when the vet checked, his heart was still beating. The vet had to give him another dose to wrench his life away from him. Anne, that boy really wanted to live. He loved his life. He loved the life you gave him. He loved the life you made for him."

"Andy, it's not really surprising that it took an extra shot to end his life," I said, barely able to get out the words. A fast-speed movie showing Milo's unbridled passion for anything and everything ran through my mind. "Milo loved life."

Andy and I stayed on the phone, but neither of us spoke. Apart but together, me sobbing, Andy intermittently emitting a whimper, we shared our mutual grief.

"Andy," I finally was able to sputter. "Not a day has gone by when I haven't pictured Milo in that cage at Main Line Animal Rescue and compared that downtrodden, jailed dog to the one who was able to be the Milo he was meant to be. Whether he was running in the woods or sitting in the car watching people, he was completely engaged in the world around him. Then, when he'd see me approaching the car, he did that swish-swash of his Lion King tail. I loved him. And he loved me."

My sobs overtook me.

"Anne, as I was leaving the vet's, Kathy, the receptionist, followed me outside. She said she would never have believed that even a professional could have transformed Milo from the dog he was when you brought him in for his first visit to the dog you made him into."

"I just helped Milo," I said, swallowing my sobs. "He wanted to be good. No one had ever taken the time to teach him how to fit into a family. He did really well, all things considered, keeping the aggressive part of himself under control. At least he knew enough not to bite anyone other than our family."

I chuckled. Over the ten years we had Milo, he had lost control and bitten either Andy or me about once a year. A week before Milo was diagnosed with cancer, Andy had dropped a plate of chicken on the floor. As he bent down to begin cleaning it up, Milo lunged toward him and bit his wrist.

"It's my fault," Andy said when it happened, shrugging, even smiling. "I should know the rules of the house by now. If it falls on the floor, it's Milo's."

We had both recently updated our tetanus shots, and the

wound on Andy's wrist didn't look like it needed stitches. So we left Milo to finish the chicken and we went upstairs to clean and bandagc Andy's wound.

Sure enough, as always happened when one of us went out with a bandage after being attacked by Milo, friends and colleagues were aghast when they heard what had happened.

"You have to get rid of that animal," people said, each time.

To us, Milo was not "that animal." Milo was a member of our family.

"Milo was not just smart but also savvy," Andy said, bringing my mind back to the present. A present in which we were on the phone trying to cope with the new, sad reality. "He understood that if the aggressive part of him needed to escape, it had to be at home with you or me. He knew we loved him and accepted him."

Andy paused and said, "Anne, come home. I want to hug you. I want to hold you. I want to be with you. What you did with Milo was nothing short of spectacular. You are spectacular."

Tears streamed down my cheeks.

"It's a good thing for me that beauty is in the eyes of the beholder," I said to Andy, repeating my tried-and-true comeback for any compliment he gave me.

"Just know that I love you," he said.

Forty

I hung up with Andy, but I didn't start the car. I sat staring ahead at nothing. Andy's words, "I want to be with you," played in my mind. I thought about how crucial loving and being loved was to my mental health.

Back in our family's dog history, I had not wanted a dog. I had been astounded by the instant love I felt when Mattie bounded into the breeder's kitchen. I had fallen onto the floor and wrapped my arms around her. Before that moment, all I had known about dogs was that they caused heartbreak when they were thrown down the stairs and killed, and that they destroyed houses and required long, boring walks. Before meeting Mattie, I had not thought of a dog as a creature who gave love or took love. I had not thought of a dog as a creature with a unique disposition, with unique likes and dislikes. I had not thought of a dog as a creature with whom I could bond and with whom I could connect. I had not thought of a dog as a creature I would nurture. I had certainly not thought of a dog as a source of happiness.

Yet, that's exactly what Mattie had been from the moment I laid eyes on her. I loved loving Mattie. I adored caring for our undemanding, living, breathing stuffed animal. When she was killed, my goal was to replace her immediately. I wanted another sweet dog to love and be loved by. Despite the immense challenges, it was not *that* long before I found myself in love with Milo. I enjoyed having another unique creature to care for and nurture.

Now that all three boys were out of the house, I had appreciated more and more having Milo to care for. Both Mattie and Milo had taught me that I could love a dog. They also taught me that I *needed* a dog to love. Images of Mattie and Milo were now floating gently in my mind. As I continued to sit in my parked car in the Community College of Philadelphia parking lot, I realized I needed another dog. I needed another dog *now*.

I googled Main Line Animal Rescue. As deceitful as Bill Smith had been about Milo, leading me to believe that he would be a perfect replacement for Mattie, I had never been angry at him. When I realized what he had done, I'd focused on moving forward with Milo. I did not have the emotional and physical energy to cope with Milo and also to be actively angry with Bill Smith. Odd as it may seem, Bill Smith had faded from my mind almost immediately. He wasn't going to be part of the solution to the problem of Milo. Any energy I might have expended thinking about him would have been a waste. I had needed to solve the problem of Milo.

I tapped on the Main Line Animal Rescue number. A woman answered after a few rings.

"Hi, I adopted a dog from Bill Smith ten years ago," I said, my voice quivering. "Today we had to put him to sleep." A steady stream of sobs began gurgling out of me, making it impossible for me to continue speaking.

"I'm so sorry for your loss," the woman said, gently. Even though we were complete strangers, I felt as if she meant what she said.

I had no choice but to let the sobs run their course. I was impatient with myself as much as I was embarrassed that I was not able to control myself.

"Take your time," the woman said, not sounding at all put off that I was taking up her time. I couldn't help but think that she was obviously in the right job.

"I'm sorry," I sputtered. "It all happened so quickly, and I loved him so much."

"I understand. Believe me, I understand."

I took some deep breaths, breathing in deliberately. And slowly breathing out the same way.

"I'd like to come in tomorrow and adopt a dog. I know it won't make me miss my dog Milo less, but I need the distraction to keep me in the moment and help me with my grief. I need someone to love. I need someone to love me back."

When I finished, there was silence.

"Hello?" I said.

"Yes, I'm still here," the woman said. "We book out days, sometimes weeks in advance for appointments with potential adopters. And we would need to have someone come out to your house and check out your backyard. Make sure it's fenced properly. Bill Smith is very strict about this."

"Oh, please," I said, almost whining. "I'm desperate. You can call my vet. You can call What A Good Dog. They will all vouch for me, I'm sure."

"I'm sure they would. But we have protocols. Bill is very strict about following them."

"Could I at least come out and look tomorrow? Then we can figure out the rest. I am desperate. Bill might even remember me and approve of my taking a dog."

"Bill doesn't get involved in routine adoptions anymore. He's far too busy. He's on the road a lot collecting dogs from puppy mills."

This didn't surprise me. Bill Smith had become a hero in the years since I adopted Milo. He was a frequent front-page story in the newspapers. His commitment to helping dogs was so strong that in 2006—five years after he had driven his red Subaru up our driveway and delivered Milo—he had rented a billboard just off the

Kennedy Expressway in Chicago. The billboard read: OPRAH—DO A SHOW ON PUPPY MILLS. THE DOGS NEED YOU. Thousands of drivers, including Oprah Winfrey, had seen the billboard. Bill Smith put up the billboard again in 2007 and in 2008. In March 2008, Oprah's dog died. She decided to have Bill on her show. Before Bill Smith's appearance on the show, Oprah sent an investigative journalist affiliated with her show to spend a week with Bill. Together they went undercover to reveal what goes on in Pennsylvania puppy mills and the pet stores they supplied.

At the beginning of the show, Oprah said, "It is my belief that when you actually see this, America, with your own eyes, you are not going to stand for it." Bill Smith and the reporter then shared their findings. Bill Smith's appearance on *The Oprah Winfrey Show* increased awareness of the puppy mill problem and spurred action on a Pennsylvania House of Representatives bill to tighten regulations and stop inhumane treatment at large dog-breeding facilities.

After his appearance on Oprah, Bill Smith became a celebrity. Money began pouring into Main Line Animal Rescue from all over the country. He purchased a large parcel of land and built a state-of-the-art facility to meet the varied needs of the animals he rescued. He had a series of bright, airy rooms where the healthy dogs were kenneled according to size. There were even heated floors in the kennels. He had separate rooms for the legions of sick dogs he rescued from puppy mills all over the country and the Caribbean Islands. He had acres of woods and paths where volunteers walked and ran with the healthier dogs. In addition to a battalion of volunteers, Main Line Animal Rescue's staff included not only general veterinarians but specialists, as well. So when the woman on the phone told me that Bill Smith no longer got involved in ordinary adoptions, I wasn't surprised.

"Please," I said to the woman. "Can't you squeeze me in tomorrow just to look at the dogs? I don't have to take one home then. It will just help me cope if I find a dog I can at least dream about until I can take him home."

There was another long silence. I girded myself not to cave in and break. Sometimes silence is more powerful than speaking. Once again, I remembered that the only nonnegative word either parent had ever used to describe me was "persevering." I was committed to getting another dog for my own well-being. So persevere I did.

"Well, since you are a past Main Line Animal Rescue adopter, let me talk to my manager and see what we can do. Just hold on. I'll be right back."

I slumped back in my seat in the car and let out a long, deep sigh.

"Okay," the woman said, back on the phone with me in what seemed like a flash. "Our appointments begin at nine on Saturday morning. But a couple of attendants come in at eight to open up and begin feeding the dogs. If you can be here then, I'll leave a note for one of them to show you through the kennels."

"Oh, thank you. Thank you so much," I said, tears resuming, as I felt my rigid body relaxing. "I appreciate it so much. Oh, and if you could please make a note, I am looking for a small lapdog that doesn't shed."

Even in my grieving state I felt my lips turning up into a smile, albeit a bittersweet smile, as I remembered saying these exact words to Bill Smith ten years earlier to describe the kind of dog I wanted. In fact, Milo did *not* shed. Which, as it turned out, had been the most important characteristic I had requested. Walks in the woods, walks at the dog park notwithstanding, once Milo became socialized, he gave me as much physical and emotional succor as any small lapdog. He slept in bed by my feet. He curled up beside me at my desk. He nestled against my legs when I sat on the couch. Sometimes, I slid off the couch, spooning beside him, wrapping one arm around his belly, the other up around his head. As I rubbed his belly and stroked between his ears, I could feel his heartbeat, slow, synchronized with mine, as a sense of shared calmness imbued us. Milo's sixty-five-pound body had the heft to anchor me in a way that a small lapdog never could. And he didn't shed, a trait that no amount of behavior modification could have altered.

"We have dogs of all shapes and sizes here," the Main Line Animal Rescue woman said. "I'd be surprised if you don't find what you're looking for. Again, I am sorry about your dog. I hope that you find a dog here tomorrow that you fall in love with."

I put down my phone. I thought about the woman saying she hoped I would fall in love with a dog tomorrow. Even though I had fallen in love with Mattie instantly, I felt that now I was so in love with Milo that it would be impossible to instantly fall in love with another dog tomorrow. What I was hoping for was that I would find a dog with whom I could connect, a dog with whom the connection would blossom into love. I was hoping to find a dog with potential. That would be enough.

I turned the key in the ignition and began inching out of the Community College of Philadelphia parking garage, headed home to Andy. As much as I wanted to see Andy, I did not want to walk into the house and not see Milo. Even this past week, as he lay languishing, at least he had been there. I had been able to lie down beside him and stroke his belly and neck. He had still been with me. Driving home slowly, I felt a punch in my gut as I pictured the dog, the body that was Milo, now nothing more than a cold, lifeless, soulless carcass. It was difficult for me to imagine that the spunk and zest that was Milo was no more.

It was impossible to imagine a world without Milo.

Andy came into the garage as I pulled in. I opened the car door and hoisted myself to my feet. I had just enough energy left over to let myself fall against Andy's chest and wrap my arms around him. We stood together crying until long after the automatic garage light had flicked off. I could have stood there forever. I did not want to go inside. I did not want to go into a house without my dog, Milo. A house in which my dog, Milo, did not greet me by rubbing his body back and forth against my legs, accepting the myriad pats and terms of endearment I had for him.

"Come on, Anne," Andy said. "You've got to go in sometime."

I let go of Andy and followed him into the kitchen. The first thing I spotted was Milo's red-and-white-checkered bed with I LOVE YOU sewn in red thread across the middle. I had given it to him years earlier on Valentine's Day. Another year I gave him a black leather collar with red hearts. I thought of these things as both ironic and non-ironic items. I truly loved Milo. But they were also daily reminders of the wild and terrifying Milo who had arrived at our house and how very far the two of us had come.

I stood in front of the bed. Except for the "I" at the beginning and the "O-U" at the end, all the I LOVE YOU lettering on the rectangular patch had worn away from years of Milo's nestling body. Even the rectangle was frayed and torn down the middle. I slid down the wall until I was sitting beside it. Often when he was lying there, I had sat in this very spot and patted and rubbed him. Now, looking at the empty, muddy, worn-out bed caused wails of sadness to erupt from me. Still wearing my jacket, I rested my head and torso on the bed and pulled it close to me. It had been a while since I had thrown the dog bed in the wash. I could smell the muddy, mossy dampness that was Milo's essence.

"Oh, I miss him so much!" I wailed to Andy, who had pulled a kitchen chair over to me. "Getting Milo was kind of like having a baby. He required so much work. I felt such a big responsibility to get things right with him, so he wouldn't have to go back to his cage in the rescue. I think that the demands on me to figure out what Milo needed helped me come to love him. I came to respect him too for being the smart, magnificent creature he was. That respect was a big part of my love for him."

I paused and looked up at Andy. Tears were dripping down his face. I sat up, leaning against the wall, and held out my hand. He clasped it and gave me a small, sad smile.

"I don't think I loved Milo more than Mattie," I said. "And it isn't that I didn't respect Mattie. It's more that I was awed by her ability to spread love in our family. She taught us to do Family Hug. Remember how she corralled us into the big front hall and into a circle and conveyed to us that we should put our arms around each other? And then she would dance around us, jumping up and twirling. 'Family hug, family hug,' we called out together, over and over, smiling at each other as we did. Remember?" I asked, looking up at Andy.

He nodded. "And remember," Andy said, "how, finally, when Mattie's twirls became lower and more labored, we all collapsed onto the floor, hugging her and accepting her nuzzles as she went from one to the other of us?"

Now I was the one nodding sadly.

"Anne, I've said it over and over. Other people have said it. But what you did with Milo was nothing short of sensational. Your unconditional commitment to him was inspirational."

I pulled back from Andy and nuzzled my face in Milo's pillow. Oh, if only he were back here, and I could do it all over again.

I sat up. "Andy, I called Main Line Animal Rescue before I came home. We have an eight o'clock appointment tomorrow morning to look at their dogs."

Andy smiled. "Why not? Your system of replacing dogs worked last time. I hope it works as well if *I* die before you do."

"I hope I die first," I said. "But if I don't, I hope my speedy replacement system works for husbands too," I said, smiling.

It was a topic Andy and I were not averse to discussing, including likely candidates from the pool of men we knew, available and not available. Andy and I joked that I would be searching for Husband Number Two before anyone would think it was socially acceptable.

Once, I told a friend about my hope to remarry as quickly as possible.

"Really?" she said, surprising me with her shock. Surprising me that everyone didn't think the way I did.

"Yes," I said. "Wouldn't you want to do the same?"

"Anne, as you know, my husband is ten years older than I am. He'll probably die before I do. And I am not going to remarry. That is for certain. I've put in my time."

I just stared at her, stunned. I believed she loved her husband, a man she had been married to for over three decades. But then I thought about comments she had made over the years, about the many demands he put on her, about his self-centeredness, about his inability to listen to her. His refusal to hear her. Thinking about what she had told me over the years about her husband, I realized it wasn't odd that she would not want to remarry. As heartbroken as I was about Milo, I was thankful that I was on the hunt for his replacement and not Andy's. I was not going to be able to replace Andy with a small lapdog who doesn't shed.

When the UPS driver told me he had killed Mattie, I'd collapsed on the floor sobbing. The first thing I did when I could finally stand up was run through the house gathering Mattie's toys, beds, and bowls to throw them in the trash. I could not bear the thought of seeing Mattie's belongings. But sitting on the kitchen floor beside Milo's dog bed, hours after he died, I did not feel the need to do the same with his things. I found it a bittersweet comfort to be able to smell his pungent presence in the bed. Closing my eyes, I could imagine that he was beside me and feel a moment of relief. Mattie's death had come as a horrible shock to me. She had been alive and healthy one minute and squashed beneath the wheel of the UPS truck minutes later. Although Milo's cancer diagnosis had also been a horrible shock, I'd had five days to live with his looming death. Five sad days to watch him languish as I began to mourn.

Now I knew I could love more than one kind of dog. I knew that, as with my children, I could love a dog for his or her unique qualities. My sons were each very different people, but I loved them equally. After Mattie and Milo, I was confident I could love another dog. I would love this new dog because we would become connected with each other. I would meet the dog's needs. He or she would meet mine. I would rescue a dog and nurture and love that dog. I would give a good life to this homeless creature who had not asked to be born. I would do for this creature what my parents had not been able to do for me.

When I was pregnant, I told Joseph, our four-year-old middle son, "When the baby is born, I will love you just as much as I do now. And that is a whole lot." It was true. I did not love Joseph less after Josh was born. Mattie added an entirely new source of love. A source of incoming love and a source of outgoing love. I did not love Mattie less when I fell in love with Milo. Similarly, another dog would not make me love Milo less. The day Milo died, I was not scared about falling into the abyss of depression as I had been when Mattie was killed. I was more prepared. In the years I had lived with Milo, I had become stronger. I had learned to cope with my depression. I knew that loving and nurturing a dog and being loved in return were important factors in stabilizing my mental health.

Forty-One

"Wow," Andy said as we approached the entrance to Main Line Animal Rescue. "The years have been good to Bill Smith."

The rolling hill property dotted with buildings and fenced-in pens and paths leading into woods was far grander than the nook Bill Smith had been borrowing from the horse farm owner ten years earlier when we met Milo. It was even harder to believe that Bill Smith had founded Main Line Animal Rescue twenty years earlier in the back of his red Subaru wagon. The same Subaru wagon he had used to deliver Milo to our house.

As much as I adored Milo, as much as it helped me to transform him from an out-of-control dog to a mostly in-control dog, I did not want to do it again. I had not wanted to do it with him. Even more, I had not wanted to put the dog with whom I had bonded in the meadow the first time we met back in a cage.

In this new facility, dogs were grouped in rooms according to their size. I planned to insist that I go only to the rooms with small dogs. My heart could not go out to an animal I did not see.

The empty waiting room was large, high-ceilinged, and airy. The sun streamed in past a reception desk in the far corner of the room. Beside the desk was an open door. Beyond that was a long hallway. We heard voices and an echo of barks coming from there. I thought the hallway might lead to a kennel. I asked Andy to go down the hall to find someone to help us. Andy returned a minute later with a woman in her mid-twenties, dressed in khaki pants and a green polo shirt with MLAR and a dog logo below it etched in black.

"Hi," she said, putting out her hand. "I'm Amber. I'm an animal care attendant."

I smiled and shook her hand.

"I spoke to someone late yesterday about coming in to find a dog," I said. "She said the schedule was full but that we could come in at eight and someone would show us around."

"Yes, I know," Amber said. "I got an email probably after she spoke to you, about taking you to see the small dogs. But this morning on my way in I got a call from Bill Smith. I couldn't believe it. I've worked here almost three months and I have never seen him, never mind spoken to him."

My heart sank. My legs suddenly felt that they might not be able to support me. I looked down at the cement floor to see where I was likely to collapse.

"And?" I said, garnering all the strength I could muster to keep myself upright.

"And he said he wants to take you around," Amber said. "He said he'd be here at eight."

We all looked at our watches. It was almost 8:10.

"I've heard Bill Smith is never on time," Amber said.

I immediately thought of the three occasions I knew that he *had* been on time. No doubt he'd arrived on time when he was on *Oprah*. When he introduced us to Milo, we arrived on time and he was already waiting for us. The following day, when he delivered Milo to our house, he was also exactly on time.

"Why don't you just have a seat," Amber said. "His number was blocked when he called me so I can't even try to reach him.

Not that I would. I'm just an animal attendant here, after all."

"Thanks," I said. "I understand. If we have to wait, we'll wait."

"Okay, well, you know where to find me if you need me," Amber said. "I've got to get back to feeding the dogs."

I dropped into one of the hard plastic chairs lining the wall. Andy settled beside me.

"Oh, Andy," I said, resting my head on his shoulder. "I just can't take any more shenanigans from Bill. All's well that ends well. But I really don't want any more surprises from him. I'm done walking in the woods. I'm done spending every waking hour corralling an out-of-control dog. Even if I wanted to, I don't have the time now that I'm teaching."

"Don't get ahead of yourself," Andy said. "Remember the jack story."

I smiled. For years, Andy had been repeating the jack story to the kids and me whenever we became angry at someone before we had all the facts. A man gets a flat tire while driving on a low-volume road. He has a spare tire but no jack. When he sees a car approaching, he puts out his hand to stop it and ask for a jack. The car whizzes by, ignoring him. A second car whizzes by. Then a third, a fourth, and a fifth. The man is fuming. He's cursing. He's stomping his feet. Finally, the sixth car stops.

"Can I help you?" the driver says.

"You can take your jack and shove it!" the man shouts.

The driver shakes his head, gets in his car, and takes off.

"Yeah, I know," I said, lifting my head and looking at Andy. "I will keep my mind open. I will hear what Bill has to say."

At 8:45, Andy stood up to stretch his legs. "Well, the good news is that if Bill were going to try to put one over on you again and dupe you into taking a hard-to-place dog, he'd probably have been on time."

"You're such an optimist," I said.

The door opened. In walked Bill Smith.

"I'm sorry about your loss," he said, locking his gaze onto mine.

A jolt went through me. I felt my eyes fill with tears. I blinked. I blinked again. These were the exact words he had said when he called me the morning after Mattie had been killed. I remembered being relieved that he had called. Relieved that I would not have to chase after him in order to find another dog. After answering the phone when he called, I had leaned against the wall, listening to Bill's sonorous words, hoping he would be my salvation. Hoping he would come to my rescue and fill the void left by Mattie. This was the first time I had seen Bill since he delivered Milo to our house. I remembered Bill wrapping Milo's leash around my wrist. Except for a slightly receding hairline, he looked the same. He had the same intense sense of sincerity and confidence. He had the same aura that had made me feel he was a man I could trust. The ten years since I had seen Bill Smith felt like a lifetime. Sadly, the ten years *had* been a lifetime. They spanned Milo's too-short life. The ten years also spanned the years when all three of our boys had left home. The jolt I had felt when Bill walked in the door moments earlier turned into a sad pang. I missed Milo. I missed my boys.

As Bill and I stood facing each other in the Main Line Animal Rescue waiting room, our gazes tethered, he took a step back from me.

"Let me introduce you to Sam," he said, bringing my attention to a white bichon frise he was cradling waist-level in his arms.

I thought of Scooter, the hyperactive bichon that Bill had let loose on us in the waiting room after we had met Milo. Bill had enlisted Scooter, the blitz of white fur, to seal the deal with Milo.

I looked down at Sam. He seemed completely at ease nestled in Bill's arms, as if he were accustomed to being held and cuddled.

He looked up at me with his big brown eyes. When I had met Milo in the meadow, his steady, soulful eyes had captivated me and connected me to him immediately. Now, looking up at me from Bill's arms, Sam's gaze was every bit as steady as Milo's had been. Instead of soulfulness, Sam's eyes conveyed a sense of openness and trust. And an endearing sweetness. Unlike his fellow rescue dogs, Sam did not look like a survivor with a hardscrabble, traumatic history. He looked like the creature he was bred to be centuries earlier. A cuddly creature who would sit on Her Royal Highness's lap and keep her warm and cozy in a drafty, dimly lit castle.

"Hi, Sam," I said, stepping toward Bill, and stroking Sam behind the base of his ears.

"Let me put him down," Bill said, lowering Sam to the floor and handing me the leash. It was a delicate, black leash, with red hearts all along it. It was about half the width of Milo's leash. I loved it. I suspected it was part of Bill's not-too-subtle sales pitch.

"Sam is a bichon frise, and he's a year old. His owner died a few months ago. I've kept him at home with my mother and me, waiting for the right person to come along. I'd like you to have Sam as a gift for taking Milo."

As soon as I heard Milo's name, my throat clenched. I had been so caught up counting the minutes waiting for Bill that I had forgotten the sad reason we were here. I pulled my eyes from Sam, who was now sitting by my feet staring up at me. I looked at Bill.

"I loved Milo," I said, swallowing the shallow sobs that welled up inside me.

"Of course," Bill said. "As soon as I spoke to you on the phone about your getting a dog, I sensed that you and Milo would make a good pair."

I looked at Andy for a moment. I didn't roll my eyes, visibly. Andy knew what I was thinking. Bill had sensed that Milo and I would make a good pair because probably Jane had told him that I worked from home and had time to devote to taming an out-of-control dog.

"Why don't you two take Sam outside and get to know him. He's yours if you want him," Bill said, motioning to the door.

"Yesterday the woman on the phone told me that even if I found a dog today, I'd have to be vetted before I could take it home. Someone would have to check out our house and our yard."

"Yes, we have strict guidelines for our adopters," Bill said. "But I've seen your house. I know you. As I said, if you want Sam, he can be sitting on your couch with you this afternoon."

It was hard to believe that Bill could remember our house. I also had to laugh to myself about the fence requirement. At the dog park through the years, I had heard many disgruntled dog owners talk about being rejected by Bill Smith because he didn't approve of their yards and fences, even after they installed fences specifically to meet the Main Line Animal Rescue requirements. Bill's assessments of potential adopters were more nuanced than the guidelines detailed in his brochures.

"Okay," I said. "We'll take Sam outside and walk around a bit. How will we find you when we've decided?"

"The receptionist will be here any minute. I'll tell her to call my cell when you come back."

I opened the door and led Sam outside. Andy followed.

"Hi, Sam," I said, crouching down. "You look like such a good boy."

Sam wagged his tail, his gaze tethered to mine. I sat down on the walkway, and Sam immediately walked into my lap, turned around, and rested his head on my hand. My heart opened and I began to cry. I shed tears for Sam, whom I already loved, and for Milo, whom I missed so much. Sam was exactly the dog I had wanted after Mattie was killed. But I was glad I did not get what I had wanted. I would always be grateful for Milo.

I brushed my tears off Sam and gave him a kiss on the top of his head.

"I love him," I said, looking up at Andy. "This is our dog."

"He does look really sweet," Andy said, smiling. "He seems so comfortable with you already."

"Yeah, his owner must have been really kind to him. He's so trusting and at ease with me, even though I'm a stranger."

I turned from Andy to Sam. "Sam, what do you think? Do you want to go home with us?"

It was uncanny. As soon as I said his name, Sam lifted his head from my hand and looked up at me.

"I'll take that as a yes," I said, lifting him from my lap onto the ground and standing myself up.

"Let's go in and find Bill," I said. "I cannot imagine a more perfect dog for us."

A few steps from the door to the reception area, I stopped. When I stopped, Sam automatically stopped, sat down, and looked up at me.

"Good boy, Sam," I said, wishing I had a treat to reward him for his exemplary behavior.

"Andy, there's actually one thing that makes me a little uncomfortable about taking Sam," I said.

"What on earth could that be?" Andy said. "He seems like another Mattie."

"Well, he's so perfect that anyone would want him. Bill could get a gazillion takers for Sam. I feel bad that I'm not taking a dog who might be a little harder to place."

Andy shook his head. "Anne, you were clear you didn't want another Milo."

"Well, there's quite a continuum of dogs between Milo and Sam. Maybe I should try to get one who isn't as happy and as well-adjusted as Sam seems to be. Maybe I could get a small dog because small dogs are easier than big dogs. But a small dog who hasn't had a charmed life like Sam clearly has. A small dog who is a little jittery and needs some TLC. A dog who doesn't present as well as Sam. Maybe a skittish dog who needs consistent, proactive kindness to recondition him. That would be easy for me as long as I don't have to spend hours walking him or months socializing and taming him. I think I would just feel a little better giving a home to a dog who might not be easy to place. It would help me cope with Milo's death just as getting Milo was a way to cope with Mattie's death. By getting Milo I had felt that at least someone was better off after she died. It gave me some consolation that *something* good had resulted from Mattie's being killed."

Standing outside the entrance to Main Line Animal Rescue, I felt my heart sinking. I wanted Sam. I wanted him so much.

"Anne, I think you're being too hard on yourself," Andy said. "You did your good deed with Milo. Now you can think of yourself as making the world a little better by helping your students. *I* can name several you've really made a difference with. And those are just the ones that I've heard of."

I looked down at Sam who was looking up at me as I thought about what Andy said. A sense of ease came over me. Andy had a point. Teaching at Community College of Philadelphia, I loved finding the one or two students in each class who hoped that getting a degree would give them a chance. Teaching was a lot easier on my body than hiking up and down hills in the woods. I bent down and rubbed Sam behind the ears. He wagged his tail and sidled closer to me.

"You're right, Andy," I said, smiling. "Sam is so sweet and

gentle. And he already seems bonded to me. Let's go in and make it official."

A woman in her fifties, wearing the green Main Line Animal Rescue polo shirt, was sitting behind the reception desk.

"Hi, I'm Anne Abel," I said, standing in front of her desk. "We were talking to Bill Smith a few minutes ago . . ."

"Yes, I know who you are," she said with a friendly smile. If Sam hadn't seemed so obviously perfect, I would have been worried that the woman's friendly smile was a cover-up for a shady Bill Smith deal.

"Bill signed the paperwork. Sign your name here at the bottom and Sam is yours," she said sliding a form toward me and handing me a pen.

I couldn't believe it. It was so easy. So straightforward. I signed my name and slid the form back to the woman.

"So we're good to go?" I said, thinking I was stating the obvious.

"Well, yes you are. But Bill asked me to call him on his cell phone before you left," she said, tapping numbers into her phone as she spoke.

I looked at Andy and shook my head.

"It's not over until it's over," I couldn't help saying.

Forty-Two

Andy and I didn't even have time to sit down before Bill appeared in person. In his arms was a small white dog with brown ears, a brown head, and a brown tail. He also had a big brown spot in the shape of a heart at the bottom of his torso.

"I'm so glad you're taking Sam home with you," Bill said.

I nodded. I didn't smile or speak. I waited to hear what he had to say about the elephant in the room. Or rather, the dog in his arms.

"This is Yat," Bill said.

"We're really happy with Sam," I said.

"Yes, yes, of course. And I'm happy that you're happy. I just wanted to introduce you to Yat. He's a Chihuahua–terrier mix, and he's about a year old. We've had him for a couple of weeks. I found him at one of the puppy mills I was raiding. He wasn't part of the operation. I just saw him cowering by the kennels. So I grabbed him and took him with us. I don't know his history, of course. Physically, he's fine. But he was shaky and jittery. He's been staying with one of our animal care attendants at her house. He needs the quiet and individual care to soothe his nerves."

I looked at Yat in Bill's arms. He was shaking perceptibly even as Bill stroked his head. If Milo had soulful eyes and Sam had sweet, trusting eyes, Yat's eyes were absolutely human. Aside from his triangle head and ears, I felt as if I were looking at a ten-pound, miniature person. And this miniature person was looking right back at me. I imagined that with his steady eye contact he was pleading with me to take him home. To take him home and love him. Because he already loved me.

My heart sank. This was exactly the kind of dog I had been telling Andy I wanted minutes earlier. But there was no way I could leave Sam behind and take Yat. Even if it's what I thought I wanted a few minutes earlier, it wasn't what I wanted now.

"Why don't you sit down and hold Yat on your lap," Bill Smith said. "Actually, sit down and I'll put Yat down here on the floor and you can call him."

"How did he get the name Yat?" I asked.

"Someone who had helped us infiltrate the puppy mill saw him in my car and told me his name. We go undercover, you know. We always need to find someone on the inside to help us. Just call him."

I sat down, as instructed, putting Sam on the seat beside me. "Good boy, Sam," I said as he lay down on the seat and curled into a peaceful ball. I could not believe how adaptable and accepting he was. I patted him a few times. Then I looked at Yat who stood between Bill and me. Yat was barrel-chested and top-heavy, but not fat. Just the same, I wondered how his spindly little legs could possibly support all that heft.

"Yat," I said, sliding onto the floor.

Immediately Sam jumped down and sat beside me. I patted him and held out my hand. "Hi, Yat," I said, wishing once again I had a treat to coax and reward him. But I didn't want to startle Yat by changing my focus from him to Bill Smith and asking for some treats.

Yat slowly but steadily moved one skinny leg and then the other and headed toward me. As he neared me, I reached out to pat him, encouragingly. At first he stopped, startled. But he didn't back away, and I didn't stop patting his triangle head.

"Good boy, Yat," I said. "Good boy."

When his front paws were against my legs, which were folded in front of me, I lifted him up and put him in my lap. He was shaking.

"What a good boy you are, Yat," I cooed, rubbing him with one hand.

"You're a good dog, too, Sam," I cooed, rubbing him with the other.

Over and over, I cooed and patted, lulling myself into a trance.

I looked up, startled to see Bill Smith and Andy looking down at me.

"You look like a perfect trio," Bill said, not missing a beat.

I looked down at Yat who was craning his neck and looking at me. I'd heard of prisoners of war who blinked their eyes in Morse code on camera to convey information across enemy lines. Yat wasn't blinking. He wasn't blinking at all. But the message he conveyed with his expressive, human eyes was clear. Very clear. *I like you. Please take me home.*

"I want to take the two dogs outside for a moment," I said, looking back up at Andy and Bill.

They nodded.

I stood Yat up on the floor and then, standing myself up, I said, "Yat, Sam, let's go for a walk."

I gave a tug to Yat's black nylon leash. The puppy mill apparently had not given him a sweet leash like Sam's heart leash. Of course, Yat had his own supersized heart that he carried around on his back. I don't believe in cosmic signs, but I couldn't help but wonder if Yat's big brown heart was a clue about the heart that beat inside him and the love he had to give.

I act on intuition when making decisions—whether choosing a

city to live in, buying a house, or selecting a school for my kids. Sitting with Yat in my lap and Sam nestled beside me, I knew I was going home with two dogs. But I wanted to take the dogs outside to sit with me while the decision settled in my mind. I also wanted to make sure Sam and Yat didn't go after each other.

Sam walked beside me toward the door, looking up at me every few steps to make sure he was following me correctly. It had taken me hours to train Milo to do this. Yat, on the other hand, was pulling on his leash and dragging his feet. I stopped and turned toward him.

"Do you want me to pick you up, Yat?"

He looked up at me, his eyes boring into mine. He began dancing slowly back and forth on his short, sticklike front legs.

"Okay," I said, bending down and looping my hand through Sam's leash. I wrapped my two hands around the middle of Yat's body. "One, two, three, up," I said. I could feel him push off the ground with his feet as I began to lift him. It was uncanny how much he was able to communicate without making a sound.

Outside, I found a bench in the sun. I sat down, putting Yat in my lap, and lifted Sam up to sit beside me. Just as I had done inside, I stroked Sam with one hand and Yat with the other. Sam got as close to me as he could get and then put his head down and closed his eyes. The tremors Yat had exhibited inside seemed to have slowed a bit, but I could feel that he was still shaking a little. He rolled onto his side as if to direct me to rub his belly. I rubbed it slowly and steadily. I could feel the morning sun warming his short-haired coat. After a few rhythmic belly rubs and a few minutes in the soothing sun, Yat closed his eyes. I could feel his heart rate slow and his shaking stop.

I sat on the bench in the sun with the two sleeping dogs. I closed my eyes and felt my own breath slowing. I had not slept much the previous night. Milo's absence from the bottom of the bed where my feet usually rested against him was distressing. It was haunting and overwhelmingly sad. Now, sitting with Yat and Sam, it was impossible to imagine that Milo had not been dead even twenty-four hours. Sadly, however, it was all too possible for me to picture that Milo would not be at home to greet me. To greet us.

"Anne," I heard Andy say. I opened my eyes to find him standing in front of me. "I think you were sleeping."

I shook my head to wake myself up.

"So what do you think?" Andy said. "Do you want both dogs?"

"I have two hands," I said. "Why not two dogs? After all, love is not a pie. The two of them together don't weigh half of what Milo weighed. I wanted a dog who needed a little bit of work, a dog who might not be as easily adoptable as Sam. Yat is exactly that. With a little bit of time and love, I am sure Yat will calm down. How can I not take home a dog who comes with a heart on his back?"

I put Sam and Yat on the ground, and we all walked back into the waiting room where Bill Smith was standing beside the reception desk.

"You're quite a salesman, Bill," I said. "I'm going to take Sam *and* Yat."

"I care about the welfare of animals," he said.

"I believe that's true. I guess that's what makes you so good at what you do," I said, smiling. "You also seem to be able to read people. At least this people," I said pointing at myself. "Coming here, I didn't know that two dogs were what I wanted. Now that I am with them, I can't imagine it any other way."

"Milo was a magnificent dog," Bill said.

"It's nice to hear you say that," I said. "I was very proud of him."

Yat walked around in front of me and looked up at me. I

looked down at him. "Enough with the chitchat? Are you ready to go home, Yat?" I could almost see the word "yes" forming in his unblinking, beseeching eyes.

"I've already filled out the paperwork for Yat, and Andy's already signed it. So you're good to go," Bill said.

Bill and Andy shook hands. My hands were clutching the two leashes.

"Thank you," I said.

Out the door we went, keeping pace with Yat's miniature steps. In the car, Sam squeezed beside me in the front seat, and Yat nestled in my lap.

"There's one thing we have to do immediately," I said to Andy, as he began to back out of the parking spot.

He put his foot on the brake and looked at me, dismay radiating from his face. "What now?"

"Yat is not a name for a dog. I don't know what it's a name for. We need to come up with a new name for him."

"Yeah, that makes—" Andy said.

"I know," I said, interrupting him. "How about Ryan for Ryan Howard?"

Ryan Howard was the six-four, 250-pound superstar first baseman for the Philadelphia Phillies our family loved more than any other player.

"Ryan Howard is so big, and this little chihuahua is so small," I said.

Andy laughed. "I think it's a great idea."

When we got home, I led the two dogs through the garage and into the kitchen. I unhooked their leashes and dropped my coat onto the kitchen table. Then I stepped out of the kitchen toward the hall. Sam walked one-half step in front of me. Ryan's little feet had to take a few steps for every one of mine. When we reached the middle of the front hall—the exact spot where I had collapsed when the UPS man told me he had killed Mattie—Sam turned and walked to the stairs, stopping to wait for us when he got there. It was as if Sam had lived here his entire life. It was as if he knew exactly where we were going. When Ryan and I arrived at the stairs, Ryan leaned back and catapulted his top-heavy body onto the first stair.

"Good boy, Ryan, yes," I said in an energetic, chirpy tone, stepping onto the first step with him. It was a skill I had learned from Mary.

He looked up at me, not recognizing his name yet, of course, but clearly enamored by my voice. It was a start. A good start.

Sam trotted easily up the stairs, and when he got to the top, he turned around and looked at us, ever so patiently, waiting.

From one step to the next, Ryan heaved himself up. When we got to Sam at the top, Sam turned and walked into our room and jumped up on the bed. I had to smile. Ryan, a bit winded from his hike up the steps, waddled beside me to the bed. He stopped and looked up at me.

"Do you want me to pick you up, Ryan?" I asked.

He danced back and forth on his front paws.

I wrapped my hands around his belly. "One, two, three, up," I said, my voice rising on the word "up," his legs rising as I began to lift him.

I got into bed and under the duvet. Sam curled up beside me on my right. Ryan nuzzled his head under the duvet and continued on until his entire body was curled up against me underneath it. I rested my head on my pillow and began stroking Sam on my right and Ryan on my left. I stared out the window in front of me at the branches with their newly sprouting leaves. I missed Milo. I missed him a lot. I missed Mattie. I missed my boys. I imagined them coming to visit, walking in the door and stepping into the kitchen. Mattie would not be there to greet them. Milo would not be there to greet them. Thinking about this made me sad. Then I pictured Sam and Ryan running into the kitchen. I imagined the boys getting down on the floor to tussle them. The sadness we all felt at the death of Mattie and the death of Milo would always be a painful memory. But now, we had two new sources of warmth and love. I stroked Ryan, then Sam. I could hear the steady breathing of each. I matched my breathing to theirs and closed my eyes. Sam and Ryan were going to be okay. I was going to be okay too.

Acknowledgments

But for the idea of Jeanne Griffin that *Mattie, Milo, and Me* was not just a story but a story worth telling, this book would not exist. Thank you, Jeanne.

Thank you to my editors, Nell Casey and Candace Coakley, who encouraged me to dig deeper.

And thank you, Andy. You are my rock. I love you so much.

ABOUT THE AUTHOR

Credit: Eric Michael Pearson

Anne Abel's story about unwittingly rescuing an aggressive dog, Milo, won a Moth StorySlam in New York City. She has won two additional Moth StorySlams in Chicago. Her credentials include an MFA from The New School for Social Research, an MBA from the University of Chicago, and a BS in chemical engineering from Tufts University. She has freelanced *for Lilith; Philadelphia Daily News; The Jewish Exponent; Philadelphia Weekly, Main Line Life* and *Main Line Today*, and formerly wrote a weekly column, "The Homefront," for *Main Line Welcomat*. Anne lives in New York City with her husband, Andy, and their three rescue dogs, Ryan, Megan, and Chase. She grew up outside Boston, MA. For more information, go to anneabelauthor.com.

SELECTED TITLES FROM SHE WRITES PRESS

She Writes Press is an independent publishing company founded to serve women writers everywhere. Visit us at www.shewritespress.com.

Dog as My Doctor, Cat as My Nurse: An Animal Lover's Guide to a Healthy, Happy & Extraordinary Life by Carlyn Montes De Oca. $16.95, 978-1-63152-186-7. A groundbreaking look at how dogs and cats affect, enhance, and remedy human well-being.

Drinking From the Trough: A Veterinarian's Memoir by Mary Carlson, DVM. 978-1-63152-431-8. The story of a suburban Chicago girl who never expected to move "out West" and become a veterinarian, let alone owner and caretaker of cats (many), dogs (two), and horses (some with manners, some without) in Colorado, but did—and, along the way, discovered the challenges, tragedies, and triumphs of lives, both human and animal, well lived.

Not a Perfect Fit: Stories from Jane's World by Jane A. Schmidt. $16.95, 978-1-63152-206-2. Jane Schmidt documents her challenges living off grid, moving from the city to the country, living with a variety of animals as her only companions, dating, family trips, outdoor adventures, and midlife in essays full of honesty and humor.

Being Mean: A Memoir of Sexual Abuse and Survival by Patricia Eagle. $16.95, 978-1-63152-519-3. Patricia is thirteen when her sexual relationship with her father, which began at age four, finally ends. As a young woman she dreams of love but it's not until later in life that she's able to find the strength to see what was before unseeable, rise above her shame and depression, and speak the unspeakable to help herself and others.

Prozac Monologues: A Voice from the Edge by Willa Goodfellow. $16.95, 978-1-63152-731-9. A book within a book—part memoir of misdiagnosis and part self-help guide about life on the bipolar spectrum—that, through edgy and comedic essays, offers information about a mood disorder frequently mistaken for major depression as well as resources for recovery and further study.

Science of Parenthood: Thoroughly Unscientific Explanations for Utterly Baffling Parenting Situations by Norine Dworkin-McDaniel and Jessica Ziegler. $19.95, 978-1-63152-947-4. A satirical take on the early years of parenting that uses faux math, snarky science, and irreverent cartoons to offer hilarious hypotheses for parenting's most perplexing mysteries.